Straight

Straight sex

Rethinking the Politics of Pleasure

Lynne Segal

University of California Press
Berkeley   Los Angeles

University of California Press
Berkeley and Los Angeles, California

This work was first published in the United Kingdom
by Virago Press in 1994.

Library of Congress Cataloging-in-Publication Data

Segal, Lynne.
Straight sex: rethinking the politics of pleasure/Lynne Segal.
p.   cm.
Includes bibliographical references and index.
ISBN 0–520–20000–4 (alk. paper) : $35.00. — ISBN 0–520–20001
(pbk.: alk. paper): $15.00
1. Sex. 2. Heterosexuality—United States. 3. Women—United
States—Sexual behavior.   I. Title.
HQ21.S36   1994
306.76′4—dc20   94–20

Printed in the United Kingdom by
Cox & Wyman Ltd, Reading, Berkshire

9   8   7   6   5   4   3   2   1

····· Contents

Acknowledgements

My love and thanks to all those who have made the writing of this book more pleasurable than it would otherwise have been. Loretta Loach, Sheila Rowbotham, Bob Connell, Alan Sinfield, James Swinson and Judith Newton offered excellent advice or assistance on selected chapters. I am especially grateful for the encouragement and suggestions I received from my editor Ruthie Petrie, and the support of my agent Rachel Calder. Peter Osborne's unflaggingly critical scrutiny of the text in its various versions helped construct whatever lucidity it has. His love gave meaning to its purpose.

I would also like to thank Anvil Press for kind permission to reprint 'Sleeping' from *Mean Time*, by Carol Ann Duffy, Anvil Press Poetry, 1993.

for Peter, again
and to the memory of
my mother, Dr Iza Segal,
1914–1994.

'Psychologists have repeatedly found that heterosexuality is not very good for women,' the opening pages of a recent feminist collection on the topic declares. 'On the rare occasions when heterosexual feminists are challenged about their heterosexuality,' its editors taunt, 'they tend to describe how miserable they are.'[1] Such casual disparagement alongside heterosexual defensiveness has dwelt within feminism too long. This book will show why it is as unproductive as it is foolish, and how reclaiming sexual agency for heterosexual women can help revive a richer and more inspiring feminist culture and politics.

Some lesbian sex radicals have recently urged straight women 'to come out of the closet'. We're still waiting, they complain, for you to discuss your sexuality: 'stop generalizing and get specific'.[2] As usual silence greeted their challenge. It is a silence I have come to expect. For feminists with longer memories, however, and those who have lustily resisted the sound and fury of the last fifteen years, it is a strange phenomenon. How, they might ask, did a movement which came out of and drew its initial strength from the assertive sex radicalism and utopian thinking of the 1960s counter-culture manage to produce so many who would end up so silent on questions of sex and love?

Women's liberation was one of those post-sixties movements which liked to think it would continue as it had begun, welcoming all women to share their experiences about what most concerned and touched them in their day-to-day lives. The fight against sexual hypocrisy and for sexual openness and pleasure provided much of its early inspiration, as women decided that pleasure was as much a social and political as a personal matter. These issues were not only central to the genesis of feminism, they remain central to the majority of women's lives today.

In the early years of the Women's Liberation Movement, women's rights to sexual pleasure and fulfilment, on their own terms, symbolized their rights to autonomy and selfhood. For more than a decade, however, there has been a shift away from such radicalism towards a bleak sexual conservatism. Some of the most forceful and influential writing now claiming to speak for feminism portrays heterosexuality as inevitably incompatible with women's interests – whether coming from Catharine MacKinnon and Andrea Dworkin in the USA, or powerful campaigning and scholarly groups of feminists working in Britain and elsewhere. Autonomy and selfhood have been turned against the idea of sexual pleasure. Sexual discourses and iconography are seen to link dominant conceptions of female sexuality, and hence identity, with submission.

In fact, heterosexual institutions and relations, from marriage and coupledom to adolescent romance, have always been more contradictory than our dominant conception of them in terms of men's power and women's subordination would suggest. Rarely more so than today! (How many of MacKinnon and Dworkin's readers and promoters continue, as they do themselves, to engage intimately with men?) Yet, ironically, it is feminism itself (or strands of it) which is currently reaffirming the ties between heterosexuality and women's subordination. If we really cannot offer a response to much of women's sexual experience, other than to condemn it as part of a repressive social order, we can only dishearten rather than inspire the majority of women.

The Right has always seen the connection between personal life and politics. It has never rested from its labour of mobilizing against women's sexual autonomy, against abortion, against homosexuality, against divorce and sex education, indeed against everything which has helped undermine men's control over women's sexuality. In contemporary Western culture, where we invest so much in sexuality, few things are easier than to displace social anxieties into sexual fears and panics. When as feminists today we abandon our former enthusiasm for pleasure and sexual openness, so often dismissing earlier talk of women's 'sexual liberation' with a wry chuckle or nostalgic sigh (if not actually feeding the rhetoric of denunciation), we participate in the vigorous backlash against the gains which feminists have helped to achieve.

The opening chapters of this book explore the shifts and divisions in feminist thinking and practice around sexuality and desire since the 1960s. It is a complex narrative, best told from many different perspectives. Feminists have made use of, and helped to transform, all the diverse frameworks for understanding human sexuality – from sexology to psychoanalysis, discourse theory to deconstruction. Chapters 3, 4 and 5 examine what they have taken from and contributed to these theoretical exchanges. My goal throughout is to rethink heterosexuality, and in the process all other sexualities as well. Straight feminists may have succumbed, by and large, to the pressure to keep silent about their sexual pursuits and pleasures in the face of impassioned campaigns against men's sexual abuse of women, and the commodification of women's sexuality, but other women along with gay men have had more positive – if contentious – things to say. I discuss the complex legacy of lesbian and gay thought, and its contribution to a rethinking of sexuality in general, in the new 'queer theory', in Chapter 5.

Lesbian and gay studies and writing are blossoming in academic institutions and popular publishing outlets, challenging the 'heterosexual matrix' linking sex and gender. They constitute a rich and exciting new field of cross-disciplinary theoretical work on sexuality. This work comes out of the still confident and campaigning sexual politics of lesbian and gay struggles and self-reflection. Once simply the object of the medical gaze and its scientific systems of classification, lesbian and gay people increasingly set the agenda for a reversal in which 'the interrogators are interrogated', and compulsory heterosexuality, heterosexism and the roping of sexuality to gender themselves become the problem.[3]

However, as Chapter 6 makes clear, decades of campaigning feminism have yet to produce the same kind of confident reversals which will turn around the male gaze and its phallic construction of heterosexuality. Instead, contemporary feminist polemic has been blocked by the negative and reactive language of the anti-pornography campaigns of the 1980s. For all the expert concern of sexologists with female pleasure, both dominant and dissident voices addressing heterosexuality still portray men as the active agents of desire, and women as its passive objects. Such images of female passivity fuelled early feminist moves to assert an active, autonomous sexuality which ended up constructing a notion of 'lesbian' sexual practice as exemplary for feminists.

At the heart of the problem lies the polarity of 'active' and 'passive' which, roped to 'masculinity' and 'femininity' via the existing conception of heterosexuality, must itself be challenged if we are ever to turn around the oppressive cultural hierarchies of gender and sexuality. In contrast with the feminist writing which, in so far as it has 'theorized' heterosexuality at all, has suggested that we can never escape its 'passive' and 'subordinating' meanings for women, there is actually little that is either firmly 'oppositional' or 'hetero' about either sexual difference or the sex act. Conceptually, each side of this binary is inseparable from its opposite, and the two poles of activity and passivity continuously collapse into each other. Psychically, once we choose to look, we find that sexual pleasure – rooted as it is in childhood experiences – is as much about letting go and losing control for men as it is for women. Sexuality is thus a place for male as well as female vulnerability. The merest glimpse of the complexity of women's and men's actual sexual activities suggests that straight sex may be no more affirmative of normative gender positions (and therefore no less 'perverse') than its gay and lesbian alternatives.

Instead of guilt-tripping heterosexual women, feminists would do better to enlist them in the 'queering' of traditional understandings of gender and sexuality. The apparent rigidity of the gendered symbolism of the 'sex' act remains central to the cultural and psychic factors which rob women of a sense of sexual agency. Addressing this problem, we need to question all the ways in which women's bodies have been coded as uniquely 'passive', 'receptive' or 'vulnerable'. But we must also look at *male* heterosexual desire. The two are inextricably intertwined. 'Active' female sexuality is closely tied to the possibility of recognizing the disavowed 'passivity' of male sexuality. A focus on the sexual ambiguities of men's bodies can disrupt dominant cultural idealizations of 'phallic' power. The suggestion that men are motivated solely by sadistic aggression is only a new way of affirming what it pretends to deplore.

xvi ···· straight sex

In my final chapter, however, we see why remaking women's heterosexual experience involves material as well as cultural struggle. There have been great changes in women's lives in Western societies. But their uneven pace inhibits the possibilities for shifting the social context of heterosexual relations, maintaining many of women's existing vulnerabilities and their frequent dependence on men. The instabilities of change trigger women's disillusionment, even as their increasing independence is seen by many men (and some women) as a threat to the old gender regimes of marriage and male privilege. Such fear of change provokes conservative attacks on feminism – seen most clearly in the USA – which in turn fuels political pessimism. Feminist sexual politics is thus inseparable from women's struggle on all fronts.

Personal and social crises and discontents both spring from and are displaced onto sexuality. But unless feminists encourage women to affirm a sense of agency in their sexual activities, we will not be able to claim agency for women at all. If straight sex is ineluctably subordinating for women, lesbianism becomes merely a defensive reaction, not a freely embraced alternative. Exploring the different ways in which the pleasures and pains of sexuality remain public issues can, as I see it, once again motivate a progressive politics in our time. To work out how we might rethink and renew the once passionate hopes of feminists for sexual liberation, a second time around, however, we need to begin where it all began – the sixties.
. . .

1. My generation: sex as subversive

Make love. We must make love
Instead of making money.

Adrian Mitchell[1]

The search for pleasure/orgasm covers every field of
human activity from sex, art and inner space, to
architecture, the abolition of money, outer space and
beyond

Tom McGrath[2]

It is the sex which people are really thinking about when
they talk about the inexpressible decadence of the sixties.
(And it wasn't just heterosex, either; oh, dear, no.)

Angela Carter[3]

However in tune with the times we may try to be, we are all
products of particular historical moments. These are the
moments – and there may be more than one of them – when
we most actively engage and try to make sense of the world.
Political generations matter. The visions of such formative
periods stay with us, influencing our outlook and activities,
even if personal disillusion or reaction overtake them. It is
always worth returning to such periods, reflectively, to
grapple anew with their inspirations and limitations. My
own formation began with the anti-authoritarian agendas
of student life in Sydney in the 1960s. It continued with the
Women's Liberation Movement in London in the 1970s,
and the subsequent debates and conflicts within Anglo-
American feminism and the Left, in the 1980s.

Of course, the ordering of historical memory through decades, however useful, involves quite artificial cut-off points. 'The Sixties' exists today primarily as a powerful metaphor for current ideological contests between progressives and conservatives over economic, political and moral agendas. Yet at the time it was simply the emergence of a wave of Western youth desperate to flee domestic, suburban comfort for inner-city stimulation and squalor: 'We've got to get out of this place, if it's the last thing we ever do.'[4] I was one of them. In 1960 I left home, became a student and hoped never, ever, to find myself in any situation that could remind me of the regret, frustration, bitterness and interminable rowing that suffused my child-hood, as maternal appeasement tried, only to fail and fail again, to soothe paternal impatience and aggression in the family in which I grew up.

Leaving home was leaving behind, as fast and as fully as possible, the bourgeois world of our parents: leaving home, just because they had 'sacrificed most of their lives' for us, just because they had bought us 'everything [their] money could buy', just because they had so much invested in us. For the dissenting children of the professional middle classes, like me, would rather have done anything than end up the way they wanted us to be; would rather have gone anywhere than become like our parents: home-owning, married, and hypocritical about sex.

It was hardly surprising that there was such conflict between these two generations. The parental values of thrift, self-sacrifice and work were the necessary attributes for surviving the anguished years of economic depression and war. Understandably, that pre-war generation had since become acquisitively eager for every new symbol of security and, above all, respectability and status. They lived in a time when order, standardization and uniformity were near universal goals: 'Clothes', as historian Raphael Samuel recalls, 'were worn as an affirmation of social position rather than a display of personal self, and they were regimented to a degree; skirt lengths rose or fell uniformly, above or below the knee, according to the dictates of the season; a man who wore suede shoes was morally suspect . . . for a woman to ladder her stockings was a social disaster, and men hitched their trouser creases for fear of baggy knees.'[5] Now, a newly consumer-driven capitalist market was helping to promote the growing cult of youth – self-emancipation, self-expression and fun – aimed at the 'teenage consumer' with just a little money to spend and scant interest in saving it (wages rose by 72 per cent, and prices by only 45 per cent, between 1951 and 1963).[6]

Yet in Britain it had been working-class youth, whose relative deprivation contrasted most with the cosy assumptions of general affluence in the new 'classless' society, who had first consciously set out to shock and distance themselves from their hard-working and respectable parents. The media of the late fifties had only just recovered from the shock of the arrogant, aggressive Teddy Boy, rocking around the clock to the sounds of Bill Haley or the more sexually provocative Presley, when at the turn of the decade it discovered the full-blooded working-class Rocker: the hot and sulky, Brando-style, leather-clad biker, who was out to mash up his rival Mod, the 'effeminate', super-cool and upwardly mobile lower middle-class, grammar school boy, in to smart clothes, pep pills, soul music, ska and scooters.[7] Only later were these rebellious teenage cultures superceded by the ever widening threat and titillation of large numbers of middle-class youth who, with newly found egalitarian delight, hurried on down into the joys of the generation gap – rejecting middle-class ambition – to dance, get high, and get laid.

Those who made their mark on the sixties were a noisy and vociferous minority, particularly as students, benefitting from the dramatic growth in higher education. This relatively underworked and overprivileged, demographically bulging post-war generation had emerged into an era of unprecedented economic boom with high employment and widespread affluence, only – without fear of lack – to reject them both. Such a rejection was all the more striking and strange when espoused by the young women of the day, because the conservatism of the fifties was so strongly symbolized through women, marriage and family. 'My ambition', recalls Jane Wibberley, expressing so many young people's rebellion, 'was not to have a career and especially not to be a secretary, teacher or nurse and not to get engaged or married.'[8]

Negative, you think? A double negation, as so many saw it then. It was the only way to create something positive for those who had grown up within the tense domesticity and anxious conformity of the fifties, when a seemingly endless and all-embracing conservative consensus held sway throughout almost every Western nation, in both northern and southern hemispheres. It was a consensus rigidly upheld through carefully manipulated paranoia and illusion: a fear of the dangers of communism abroad and an illusion of harmony at home.[9] All the old internal conflicts, whether of class or sex, were thought to have been 'removed' by the expansion of the welfare state. (The subject of race was as yet no more a topic for serious thought or discussion than sexuality, outside marriage advice literature – the scandal of the Kinsey Report notwithstanding.)

This was a time when, in Detroit, *Robin Hood* could be banned from the public library for 'preaching Communist doctrine'.[10] And in Britain in the early 1960s you could still be expelled from school for using the word 'contraceptive'

in an unofficial school magazine.[11] The paradox of that
period of relative affluence, as the British sociologists Bogdanor and Skidelsky were later to summarize it, was that
the first effects of the widening of opportunity had been
to narrow human life to the quest for goods, status and
position: 'The more room at the top there was, the more
energy was expended trying to get there.'[12] In the USA,
G.K. Galbraith had passed much the same judgement on
his society, suggesting that those benefitting from the new
affluence were becoming slaves to the wants 'increasingly
created by the process by which they are satisfied'.[13]

Following the recent interest in the sixties at the close
of the eighties, we now have a rich oral history of those years
to add to contemporary sociological opinion, the best of it
free from both false nostalgia or the now more familiar
dismissal and mockery.

Saying yes to sex

Living a mere two hundred years before the moment of
his greatest glory, it is William Blake who best captures the
spirit of the sixties. It was his 'Proverbs of Hell', celebrating
excess in all its forms, which ended up daubed upon the
corrugated iron concealing empty city buildings or the stone
walls decorating rural communes. The explosive linking
of music, sexuality and, more gradually, politics, in the
youth revolts of that decade meant that love, bursting free
from all pretence of marital constraint, was on the move.
Love, seeking not itself to please, set out to change the
world, through self-emancipation and compassion. Or was
love, seeking only self to please, thoughtlessly nihilistic,
emboldened by newly accessible contraception and relative
affluence? Was there a difference?

The fastest way into an understanding of the new mood of youth in the sixties, especially in its early years, is through its music: a music which took seriously its evangelizing message linking freedom and pleasure. Pop music then had a new purpose, as cultural critic Simon Frith comments nostalgically, 'to make out of pleasure a politics of optimism, to turn passive consumption into an active culture.'[14] The poet Thom Gunn echoes his memory, identifying London in 1964–5 with the Beatles: 'They stood for a great optimism, barriers seemed to be coming down all over . . . there was an openness and high-spiritedness and relaxation of mood.'[15] For Margaret Thatcher, a decade later, a very similar perception of sixties 'permissiveness' and 'sexual freedom' was not something to celebrate, but to incriminate as the source of Britain's cultural decline: 'Instant gratification became the philosophy of the young and the youth cultists.'[16] Subservience to authority and dogged hard work were no longer fashionable, she admonishes, replaced by time wasted in speculation and aggressive verbal hostility.

For women to participate actively in that scene, as so many did, was for them to surrender themselves to the soft seductions of the Beatles – right on cue, in '62; 'Love, Love Me Do' – the group who remained the emblem and toast of the sixties and would write its anthem, 'All you need is love'. It was a time, Richard Neville boasts, 'when all the best girls' got to be fucked by the 'pigeon-chested weaklings', like himself, and John Wayne cantered off into the sunset.[17] Some women, of course, did prefer something tougher, and they tuned in to the harsher lustiness of the Stones, the Animals, the Trogs, the Fugs or any of the many other Beasts of sixties beat. Later, perhaps, they would succumb to the tough-talking political males, Bob Dylan's 'It ain't me, Babe' or Mick Jagger's 'Street Fighting Man'. But whether screaming, swooning and fainting at

Beatles concerts, or lining up to compete with other groupies and score a fuck with the Rolling Stones (and then write about it), it was sexual excitement – primarily hetero-sexual excitement, in some form or another – that so many young women were after. 'The words were subordinate to the rhythm', Sheila Rowbotham remembers, of the time just before she was to help inspire her generation of women into feminism, 'and the music went straight to your cunt and hit the bottom of the spine. They were like a great release after all the super-consolation romantic ballads.'[18]

Marsha Rowe, who was to call together her sisters from the Underground Press in London of the late sixties to co-launch the first feminist magazine, *Spare Rib*, has written of her own teenage time in Sydney, Australia:

> Cut off from a world of touching for so many years, I
> yearned to be loved and caressed. . . . I could see myself
> in how boys reacted to me. We flaunted this desire
> for one another in front of our parents. . . . I slowly
> connected my pleasure in my own body with the pleasure
> of others, but it wasn't a simple matter of doing. This
> part of me where I'd felt most myself, had to be passive.[19]

Yes, the sex was rarely a simple matter, for women, even though the erotic pull of the music, drugs and dancing was simple enough. Here Marsha Rowe's memories of sixties music and women's inchoate sexual agency echo Row-botham's, as she looks back at her young self resonating with the rhythm: 'When the music first changed from rock to rhythm and blues, she danced faster and faster until she was dancing inside the beat, inside the rhythm of her own rhythm . . . her dress clung to her back. She did not hear the words and the music possessed her.'[20]

Having sex with men and flaunting rather than hiding it was the single main way in which young women in the sixties rebelled against parental and middle-class norms. 'As a sixteen-year-old, my parents forbade me to go out with a boy, to ride on the back of a motor scooter, to drink, to go to a pub where the Rolling Stones played,' Elisabeth Tailor recalls about her sex life in London at sixteen, so 'I deliberately broke every one of their norms. . . . It wasn't just adolescent rebellion against being controlled, although that was part of it. There was something keener, fresher in the air. A sense that we were going to do things *our* way, and that there were a lot of us who rejected not just our individual parents but what their values represented socially.'[21]

Rejecting parental values was one thing, but did it actually create a new and better world for women, or just the some-times simultaneous throb of music and clitoris? What it actually did, all the while throwing up new obstacles, hidden traps and lurking monsters, was to encourage more women than ever before to believe that they could, at first all alone and then all together – in harmony and in conflict – embark upon a voyage towards what they saw as such a world.

One reason women could flaunt their sexuality, and virginity could become (in principle as well as in practice) increasingly outmoded was, of course, their easier access to effective birth control, promoted as safe and simple, with the marketing of the high dosage contraceptive pill from 1961. In Britain it was available for married or 'engaged' women from family planning clinics by 1964, and nearly half a million women in Britain were soon taking the pill, available free on NHS prescription from 1967. Many millions of women worldwide used this form of contraception by the close of the decade.[22] And it was the pill which made sex news, which made it possible to talk about it: 'It was the Pill, I think, that made it possible for things to change, for women to find out about fun. . . . I didn't stay on the pill very long

. . . [but] I didn't lose that feeling that the Pill had given me. That I was allowed to have what I liked and didn't have to be frightened of sex because it could trap me into things, I didn't have to be punished.'23

Angela Carter said much the same thing: 'Sexual pleasure was suddenly divorced from not only reproduction but also status, security, all the foul traps men lay for women in order to trap them into permanent relationships. Sex as a medium of pleasure. Perhaps pleasure is the wrong word. More like sex as an expression of is-ness.'24 I agree with them. It is simplistic to buy into the growing consensus of the late 1980s which depicts women as the passive prey of men in the sixties, taking no delight in the affirmation of self which their heterosexual activity was often to bring them. In those years, many women discovered not only that they could set about trying to take their pleasures like a man – almost – but, with whatever uncertainty and confusion in the taking, many decided that they *would* pursue their pleasures, in just that way. 'Throughout the sixties', Sheila Rowbotham explains:

> friends and I struggled together with all the contradictory versions of sex, morality and what being a woman was meant to be about . . . it seemed such an effort to find some alternative to conventions we saw as hypocritical and restrictive . . . I certainly did not want protection. The first part of the sixties were spent outwitting a veritable conspiracy of fathers, teachers, ex-safe breakers, methodist ministers, and university dons, who persisted in trying to prevent me from losing my virginity.25

We need not go so far as to endorse the blithe enthusiasm of Mary Quant proclaiming in 1969:

> Now that there is the pill, women are the sex in charge. They, and they only, can decide to conceive. . . . She's

standing there defiantly with her legs apart saying 'I'm
very sexy, I feel provocative, but you're going to have a
job to get me. You've got to excite me and you've got to
be jolly marvellous to attract me. I can't be bought but
if I want you I'll have you.'[26]

With or without their purchases from Quant's Bazaar in the
Kings Road, heart of Swinging London, women were not
quite so uniformly confident. But Quant is right to suggest
that some women were eager to use the new choices open
to them in new ways: 'Unlike what happened in previous
generations, the modern girl doesn't trade sex for material
gain or marriage.'[27]

Some men would later confess doubts and uncertainties
about embracing the sexual freedoms they, and the women
they knew, so vigorously proclaimed at the time.[28] Quant was
also right to suspect that it was from that time that many men
began to fear, more concretely than ever before, that women
might become the sex in charge. Nowhere was this clearer
than in Norman Mailer's *The Prisoner of Sex*, where he
mourns men's loss of power as women gain control over
reproduction: 'Conceive then the lost gravity of the act, and
the diminishment of man from a creature equally mysterious
to woman (since he could introduce a creation to her that
could yet be her doom) down to a creature who took lessons
on how to satisfy his wife from Masters and Johnson and
bowed out to the vibrations of his superior, a vibrator.'[29]
It was, indeed, overwhelmingly heterosexual women who
gained greater control over their sexuality, and more room
for manoeuvre, from the sexual reforms of the 1960s.
In Britain, not only was contraception now readily available,
but the Abortion Act of 1967 made legal abortions far easier
to obtain for unwanted pregnancies, and it was also to
be women, far more than men, who would take the initiative

in making use of the liberalizing divorce legislation of 1969. Only the Sexual Offences Act of 1967, partially legalizing consenting homosexual activity, would have an equivalent releasing effect on the sex lives of some men – gay men.[30]

What Quant did not seem to see, however, was that when it came to cultural icons, the modern girl had little choice but to switch sex and identify with the roaming, casual and carefree boy, the vagabond apparently even more determined than herself to avoid the ties that bind. As Ellen Willis, in the USA, would later write of her earlier delight in Dylan's rasping braggadocio: 'I understood men's needs to go on the road because I was, spiritually speaking, on the road myself. That at least was my fantasy; the realities of my life were somewhat more ambiguous.'[31] Yet these realities did not lead Willis to avoid the challenge of her new freedom, even if the intensity of the contradictions would, in the end, make the upsurge of feminism as fierce as it was inevitable. The fact that Quant's modern girl might today be scorned as a pitiable fool for forsaking a more acquisitive materialistic exchange for her sexual charms would have cut no ice with that earlier utopian voyager, teasingly demanding the impossible, and refusing to commodify her sexuality.

It would not be until the end of that decade, however, after contact with the blossoming counter-culture and its underground press – and after dipping into Reich, Marcuse or Laing, in the context of anti-Vietnam protest and May '68 – that she might begin to *theorize* rather than simply seem to *feel*, why 'saying yes to sex' was saying no to her bourgeois fate. But by then she was beginning to question it all anew. Meanwhile, the sexual adventuring of some women, we should be clear, was still only that of a significant minority, the *cultural avant garde*. Geoffrey Gorer's sociological survey of the decade found that a now seemingly astonishing 63 per cent of women still did not engage in sex before marriage.[32] There was, as Elizabeth Wilson later reflected, a mainstream cultural pressure on women to be sexual but, in the end, to confine their sexuality to marriage.[33] Although it took another decade for the situation of women as a sex to enter the political agenda, by that time almost everything had been called into question: old certainties – left, right and centre – began to rupture. As Roger Scruton remonstrates today, with only slight exaggeration:

> The left-wing enthusiasm which swept through institutions of learning in the sixties was one of the most efficacious intellectual revolutions in recent history. . . . For a blissful decade, academics and students swooned with fantasies of liberation, jettisoning their traditional disciplines and forging new ties, new institutions and new orthodoxies out of the raw material of knowledge.[34]

Out of apathy, into the counter-culture

It is ironic but revealing that today it should be its triumphant enemies, like Scruton and Thatcher, who at times best capture the mood and significance of the years they wish to obliterate forever – offering us a type of back-handed celebration. It is also the Right, continuing their attacks on 'permissiveness', sex education and the open discussion of sexuality, who remain most aware of the role of ideas of 'sexual liberation' in inspiring the more general political dissidence of those days. As Soviet tanks rolled into Budapest and British and French troops invaded the Suez Canal, within days of each other in 1956, something new began to emerge in the quiescent midst of Cold War politics in Britain: the determination to find a third way between Stalinism and social democracy. From the close of the fifties this New Left was passionately committed to the idea of people taking action for themselves. They supported struggles over neighbourhood and community control and workers' self-management, attempting to build socialism from below, in the here and now, connecting with the diverse experiences and discontents of daily life. 'The task of socialism', as the founding editor of *New Left Review*, Stuart Hall, declared in 1960, 'is to meet people where they *are*, where they are touched, bitten, moved, frustrated, nauseated – to develop discontent and, at the same time, to give the socialist movement some *direct* sense of the times and the ways in which we live.'[35]

This vision inspired a network of New Left clubs committed to independent political activity and debate, searching for new moral meanings and co-operative communities. Rediscovering the humanistic ideas of the young Marx of the *Economic and Political Manuscripts*, who spoke of the 'alienation' of the worker in commodity production, these New Left thinkers saw 'man' under capitalism as alienated from 'his' own labour, and from 'him'-self. The Left clubs, like the Partisan Coffee House in Soho, wanted to reach out to a younger generation then revolting into fashion, impressed by the cynical, anarchic angry young working-class male (Dream-boy), celebrated in the fiction of Alan Sillitoe, John Osborne or Colin MacInnes: 'What I want is a good time: all the rest is propaganda', were the sentiments Sillitoe attributed to his anti-heroes in *New Left Review*.[36] Despite the machismo individualism of such working-class 'heroes', New Left radicalism was deeply passionate about *both* individuality and community. That was its distinctiveness and its appeal.

In encouraging the expansion of people's expectations and capacity for self-expression and creativity this radicalism was to break through many of the barriers between art, the academy, politics and personal life.[37] It was the beginnings of a self-conscious counter-culture, with writers, film-makers and playwrights, like Lindsay Anderson, Ken Loach, Peter Watkins and David Mercer, determined to break out of the Communist Party's cultural isolation of the fifties and entertain a mass audience with themes of youth rebellion, family conflict, suburban angst and repressive government. And they did. A culture of critical opposition to all received wisdom was growing everywhere. The poetry readings and 'happenings' of the early New Left were to prove, Samuel later reflects, a 'nursery of 1960s counter-culture'.[38]

A political identification with those seen as the least powerful, the most oppressed and, just possibly, the most aware and most rebellious of social outcasts, was also being promoted by those influenced by the French philosophers Jean-Paul Sartre and Michel Foucault. In particular, the growing anti-psychiatry movement in Britain, of R.D. Laing, David Cooper and others, suggested that social order, conformity and conceptions of 'normality' were maintained only through the social construction of the 'deviant', through the labelling and mis/'treatment' of the 'mad' and the 'bad'.[39] It was this gang of anti-psychiatrists who would pull off one of the most spectacular conferences of the late sixties, *The Dialectics of Liberation*, addressed by such international luminaries of the day as Herbert Marcuse, Paul Goodman, Black Panther leader Stokeley Carmichael, William Burroughs and Angela Davis, alongside assorted Marxist scholars and 'hippies', like the San Francisco 'Digger' Emmett Grogan from the ambitious Haight Ash-bury co-operative community. The aim was 'to demystify human violence in all its forms' by making links between economic, class and national liberation struggles, on the one hand, and the internalization of authority in the individual psyche, on the other.[40]

However, despite so much concern with culture, everyday life and personal experience, especially the experience of the powerless, most of the British New Left had little to say about issues of sexuality, outside of their personal relationships. They did recommend the writings of Wilhelm Reich (being translated into English by one of their number, Fred Halliday) and support frankness in the portrayal of physical love, particularly in the writings of D.H. Lawrence, but it was the counter-culture, rather than the Left, which would come to equate liberation and the pursuit of sexual pleasure. Meanwhile, most Western cities saw the rise of their own forms of indigenous criticism and protest, many with a more direct focus on the politics of personal life and sexuality.

In the USA, the sixties opened with black and white radicals, for a while, fighting together against the intransigent racism and murderous violence of its Southern states, particularly within the Student Nonviolent Coordinating Committee (SNCC). In a way distinctive to the USA, it was the campaigns of the Civil Rights Movement for the most basic of all democratic rights – for black people to be allowed to vote or attend the same schools and restaurants as white people – which set the tone for radical politics in that country. Its influence was international. Thousands of American students travelled to the South of their country in the early 1960s, registering voters, setting up Freedom Schools and community centres, and learning how to organize in the face of fear and danger. As Ann Popkin recalls, 'Shot at, beaten, yelled at . . . the shared peril, work, and daily life, reinforced by the singing of powerful freedom songs, bound us together.'[41]

In 1963 Martin Luther King headed a march on Washington, addressing an audience of 250,000 with his call for freedom and jobs for black people: 'I have a dream', his historic speech began. But the dream of black radicals turned often to nightmare with 'freedom fighters' assassinated, children murdered and churches fire-bombed, leading Malcolm X, the following year, to denounce the Civil Rights Movement and liberal establishment. With the assassination of Malcolm X and the outburst of black riots in Watts and Los Angeles in 1965 (when over thirty black people were killed by police and national guardsmen) the black movement would became increasingly militant. Meanwhile, the American Civil Rights Movement and black politics had provided the crucible for all the radical protest to come, not least women's liberation. It was, as Bernice Reagon would later assert, the 'borning struggle' for progressive movements everywhere.[42] As early as 1964 Casey Hayden and Mary King, from the SNCC, had produced a declaration which foreshadowed events to come: 'It needs to be made known that many women in the movement are not happy with their status . . . women are the crucial factor that keeps the movement running on a day-to-day basis. Yet they are not given equal say-so when it comes to day-to-day decision making.'[43]

At the same time, New Left thinkers, like the sociologist C. Wright Mills, the anarchist Paul Goodman, the philosopher Herbert Marcuse, and the literary scholar Norman O. Brown, were all – in their radically different ways – writing of the alienation of contemporary man from himself, his fellows and his labour. The American New Left's vision of the liberated society stressed the building of radically egalitarian communities based upon participatory (not representative or parliamentary) democracy. And it had more to say about sex than its British counterpart.

In his most utopian book, *Eros and Civilization*, Marcuse envisaged a society where labour would be transformed into playful gratification and accompanied by generalized sexual release. Historically, Marcuse argued, material scarcity had necessitated libidinal repression to create the body as an instrument of alienated labour, resulting in the desexualization of the body except within the narrow genital area ('genital tyranny') and a radical reduction of humanity's potential for pleasure: 'The normal progress to genitality has been organized in such a way that the partial impulses and their "zones" were all but desexualized in order to conform to the requirements of a specific social organization of existence.'[44] However, he went on to argue, Western technological advance and material abundance no longer necessitated such alienated labour, and men and women could therefore dream of eliminating the 'surplus repression' now unnecessarily demanded by contemporary capitalism, resexualizing their bodies by returning to what they really unconsciously desired – a state of 'polymorphous perversity': 'The perversions . . . express rebellion against the subjugation of sexuality under the control of procreation, and against the institutions which guarantee this order.'[45] Like Marcuse, Norman O. Brown in *Life Against Death* also wrote of the urgent need to 'resurrect the body' in order to transcend a society unconsciously bent on self-destruction because of the burdens of sexual repression and uncontrolled aggression: 'The resurrection of the body is a social project facing mankind as a whole, and it will become a practical political problem when the statesmen of the world are called upon to deliver happiness instead of power, when the political economy becomes a science of use-values instead of exchange-values – a science of enjoyment instead of a science of accumulation.'[46]

As we have already seen, a widespread cultural shift and

a revolution in popular music was soon accompanying the different strands of radical rhetoric. And by the mid-sixties, the intoxicating cocktail of sex and politics, drugs and music, was being poured into the underground presses which, with the developments in cheap offset-litho, had grown rapidly across most of the Western world: 'Three groups of people are bringing about the great evolution of the new age that we are going through now', ex-Harvard professor and self-appointed spokesman of the 'underground' Timothy Leary pronounced, 'the dope dealers, the rock musicians, and the underground artists and writers'. The collages, comics, cartoons, and psychedelic layout of underground artists like R. Crumb, Gilbert Shelton, and Martin Sharpe were as important in underground papers and magazines as their textual content: art, sex and politics kept them going.

Designed to shock, satirize and agitate against hypocrisy, state repression, police harassment, wars and weapons, these publications also celebrated the joys of sex, drugs, music and creativity, reaching for 'the stuff of dreams'. Papers like *IT* and magazines like *Oz*, in London, espoused a type of anarchistic, libertarian pacifism, in line with Tom McGrath's description of the underground in 1967, shortly after *IT* was raided by the police: 'The new movement is essentially optimistic. . . . It is slowly, carelessly, constructing an alternative society. It is international, inter-racial, equisexual with ease.'[47] Hedonism without consumerism was the message.

In London, Release was formed in 1966, to give advice and legal aid to drug users, and more ambitiously, BIT, a 24-hour information and co-ordinating service, encouraged the alternative society 'to act as a society with responsibility for each other'.[48] The first Arts Lab was opened in 1967 in Drury Lane, and by 1969 there were 150 such alternative culture centres. Free pop concerts, 'legalize pot' campaigns and psychedelic shops on the one hand, urban and rural communes, squatting campaigns and claimants' unions on the other, all became part of the newly emerging alternative culture by the late sixties, carrying on into the seventies. The counter-culture was to be a refuge against families, against work, against careers, conventional status and achievement and, increasingly, against state repression. As if to hammer home the need for revolt against obtuse and vindictive officialdom, police raids and arrests in search of dope, obscenity or in response to any number of other completely harmless provocations, were routine experiences in those years. A *papier maché* hamburger, in which a crushed body bled tomato sauce, was seized by the police in one anti-Vietnam demonstration. Police would raid *IT* again for conspiring to debauch and corrupt public morals over carrying gay small ads. They would be defended by their lawyer, Leon Brittan. Later police would arrest and jail the editors of *Oz* for obscenity involving Rupert Bear.

Hedonism and politics came together for so many then because commitment to radical change was not just seen as an intellectual matter, but an emotional one as well – whether opposing the escalating Vietnam war and supporting anti-imperialist struggles in the Third World, or opening up democratic and collective spaces for any number of community projects and pursuing richer personal lives at home. Revolutionaries must begin by feeling in their guts the need for liberation, declared the modish French Situationists and the far-flung urban guerillas, from Dutch Provos to American Motherfuckers, who practised passionate acts of subversion against the boredom of daily life and the pettiness of officialdom. It was not sufficient, the Marcuseans argued, to accept with the intellect alone the message that 'this society is irrational as a whole, its productivity destructive of the free development of human needs and faculties, its peace maintained by the constant threat of war.'[49] Hedonistic 'hippies' and Left politicos alike agreed with Marcuse: 'I think that any radical who rejects Marcuse's work is a moron and not a radical,' the young Paul Breines declared at the 1969 Socialist Scholars Conference in the USA.[50] At the same conference, Ron Aronson, seeing political struggle as inseparable from personal liberation, would insist that 'revolutionary thought must engage the whole person: his feeling, his imagination, his sense of being lost. Not only tracing the structure of capitalism, but also blowing people's minds. Disrupting, shattering, springing people loose: we need to be personal, poetic, disturbing.'[51] In Britain, Laing and his disciples were saying exactly the same thing. 'If I could turn you on, if I could drive you out of your wretched mind', then, and only then, Laing believed, he could make us all realize that 'we are as deeply afraid to live and to love as we are to die'.[52]

The point is that themes of politics and sexuality were being constantly interwoven. Sexual politics was necessary, it seemed then, to understand the impossible longings aroused and left unsatisfied by the manipulations of the market. To really change people, people living in a culture so mesmerized by the spectacle of consumption and the prevailing pressures to conform, you had to break through or break down the polished veneer, to reach the innermost parts of the mind and the body. And one way of doing this, sixties gurus and their followers agreed, was through sexual liberation. 'What satisfaction is now possible for the young?' Allen Ginsberg asked. 'Only the satisfaction of their Desire – love, the body, and orgy . . . the satisfactions of encouraged self-awareness, and the satiety and cessation of desire, anger, grasping, craving.'[53] Aronson put it this way: 'Sensuousness, sensuality, beauty mean first of all freeing the body from

being a tool . . . to end repression means eroticizing all
activities, from working to friendships to cooking.'[54] 'Mad
love: totally subversive, the absolute enemy of bourgeois
culture', was how the American anarchists saw politics. 'The
Underground', Richard Neville, a founding editor of *Oz*
mused, more languidly, 'is turning sex back into play.'[55]
'MAKING LOVE IS GOOD IN ITSELF AND THE
MORE IT HAPPENS IN ANY WAY POSSIBLE
OR CONCEIVABLE BETWEEN AS MANY PEOPLE
AS POSSIBLE MORE AND MORE OF THE TIME,
SO MUCH THE BETTER,' David Cooper promised,
wildly.[56] 'Emancipation is now a reality', Margaret Drabble
decided, in 1969, with reference to the pill, and women
are 'free now, as never before'. By the end of the sixties,
politicos, pranksters, werewolves and mainstream liberals
were all coming to agree that sexual pleasure was a
progressive force capable of transforming human relations,
however divergently they saw such progress.

More and more institutions and values were examined
and found wanting. The institution of the family had long
been the object of particular criticism as conservative,
inward-looking and repressive. But now sexuality itself, seen
throughout the decade as naturally disruptive of authority
and materialistic values, came under closer scrutiny.

Saying no to sexism

It is easy to see the sixties as a quintessentially male decade.
Janis Joplin, its most raunchy and aggressive female star,
tapping into the pain and anger of women's sexual frustration while blatantly defying all bourgeois convention as
she consumed sex, drugs and men, died with the decade,
in 1970: 'Love is draggin' me down/ Just like a ball and

chain.' The New Left, despite its many women members, had largely failed to publish or promote women's voices, even when Doris Lessing, then one of their number, won widespread acclaim for *The Golden Notebook*. The underground's portrayal of sexual liberation was most often arrogantly male: women were 'chicks' to be plastered on every page, the younger and 'softer' the better. Although many women felt uncomfortable with the standard pornographic fare, however psychedelically tinted, they weren't yet quite sure why. It seemed to promise a life-style, sexual freedom and ease which they also wanted. It was the association of women as 'mother' with all the old fifties values which made it so complicated for women. And the best-sellers of the decade made it even harder, for they were either silent, or more often negative, about women's lives and struggles.

Men's battles with authority, as in Ken Kesey's hugely popular *One Flew Over the Cuckoo's Nest*, identified the sexless and fanatical agent of repression as female. Portnoy's problem, in Phillip Roth's best-seller *Portnoy's Complaint*, was his archetypically possessive Jewish mother. Norman Mailer's obsession with manhood meant that in each new novel his hero must conquer anew 'the Great Bitch' woman, and even then would remain forever on his guard in case 'he may be on the way to becoming less masculine'. J.P. Donleavy's *Ginger Man* equated freedom with fucking women and leaving them pregnant. Women as wives and women as mothers were targets for contempt and ridicule, unless romanticized as Earth Mothers, needing no support from their man.[57] 'Lucky Jim', Kingsley Amis's ubiquitous hero of the sixties – rude, crude and cynical – was mockingly critical of what he saw as phoney, pretentious conformity, which all boiled down to a bullying contempt for women and male 'effeminacy'.[58]

These same brash males also made out in Hollywood, where *Easy Rider* was an unexpected box office hit. Every type of male outlaw, madman, or just plain loser unwilling to adjust to the urban jungle (like Morgan in the British film *A Suitable Case for Treatment*) won the hearts of their audiences, male and female. The woman's role, when they got one, was usually to wash, cook and provide sexual comfort, and never, ever, to complain; certainly never to age, if they were to avoid the contempt of Hollywood.[59] In Britain, when the new wave of working-class realist films of the early 1960s, focussed on the male rebel, was replaced by the more frivolous 'swinging London' film, there was still little space for the sexually independent woman who could win admiration and respect. Julie Christie has commented upon the popularity of her own role as the sexually adventurous star of *Darling*, who was allowed to display her independence in resisting marriage and pursuing her own pleasures, but 'of course at the time . . . [she] had to be punished for it'.[60]

These books and films were created by men, but the few commercially successful women writers of the period were also trapped within men's attitudes to women. Edna O'Brien, for example, explained to Nell Dunn that women expect too much when they seek commitment from men, because women age faster than men: 'It's this fleetingness of girlhood that's one of the saddest things in life. It's sad for girls, it's sad for men.'[61] Margaret Drabble described women's lot as bored and dull housewives as inevitable in her fiction of that decade: 'I felt all women were doomed . . . born to defend and depend instead of to attack.'[62] Even Doris Lessing, who seemed to write so powerfully of women's frustration, especially as mothers, and their disappointment in men, felt that men were not to blame: 'If I were a man I'd be the same.' Indeed, fearing the

decline of real manhood, she was contemptuous of homosexual men, affirming that 'the truth is, women have this
deep instinctive need to build a man up as a man. . . .
I suppose this is because real men become fewer and fewer,
and we are frightened trying to create men.'[63]

With women and men, radical voices and conservative
ones, all apparently believing that women had already
achieved as much equality as was possible for them in
the post-war welfare state, it may seem strange to suggest
that everything that happened in the sixties was paving the
way for feminism, and making it easier for women, at last,
to see themselves as social, political and, above all, sexual
agents. But so it was. The New Left may have been gender
blind, but it did contribute, crucially, to the widening of
the definition of politics to include personal life, culture
and the critique of everyday life. The people who emerged
as the student leaders – the Americans refusing to fight
in Vietnam and boasting 'girls say yes to boys who say no' –
may have been men, but women were always most present
and most active when the action was most unexpected and
spontaneous, overturning the old political traditions, rules,
routines and structures. Thus in May '68 in France, as
so many women would later tell Ronald Fraser, people who
had never found a voice before now spoke and acted in ways
formerly quite inconceivable. In Lyons, for example, two
16-year-old girls brought their high school out on strike.[64]
It was a time when many women students felt as engaged
and active as the men. The women may have been doing the
cooking and preparing the banners and caring for the
wounded, but Fraser heard: 'We felt – and I still think – that
by taking care of these material aspects we were being fully
political. The men were making the speeches but we made
sure everything worked. At times like that it's worth being a
woman, you know.'[65]

Alix Kates Shulman, from the USA, has also written of the effects of that time in her fiction, when suddenly women found themselves happier than they ever dreamed they could be, full of energy, confidence and plans:

> But for us [women], who could so easily have spent the rest of our lives letting the men speak for us, the 60s were anything but chaotic. Not that we lived serenely in those years, but we took our first steps on our own. We learned organization, discipline, caring . . . how to be civilized. We stood up for each other, made community, tried to provide sympathy and support and something lasting for all of us and our children. . . . The 60s were over, yes, but some of us were still fighting our holding actions, keeping in precious touch.[66]

Describing her arrival in Britain as a young Asian woman in 1972, Yasmin Alibhai met and made friends with such women, the idealistic white children of the sixties:

> And the woman in me, as a child of the sixties, grew too. It became the free spirit that none of the women in my family had had a chance to be. . . . It happened because during that decade granite turned to water, the impossible became the perfectly do-able. Certainty vanished and with the ensuing dislocation came new beliefs that nothing should be as sacrosanct. And the principle of fluidity, not rigidity, became the moving force of my life.[67]

It may seem odd, but it was from within the apparently irredeemably male fantasies behind the sexist language and iconography of the underground press (where a feature on 'The Sexual Revolution' in *IT* could exhort women to 'learn to give yourselves a bit more . . . even if you don't enjoy it at first'[68]) that women found the strength to go into battle for themselves. That battle was around women's sexuality, its meanings and representation. In January 1970 women on the staff of New York's leading radical paper *RAT* seized control of the paper, following the appearance of a 'sex and porn' issue, and published Robin Morgan's unforgettable warcry: 'Goodbye to All That':

> Goodbye, goodbye, forever, counterfeit Left, counterleft, male-dominated cracked-glass-mirror of the Amerikan nightmare. Women are the real left. We are rising powerful in our unclean bodies; bright glowing mad in our inferior brains; wild hair flying, wild eyes staring, wild voices keening; undaunted by blood we who haemorrhage every twenty-eight days; laughing at our own beauty we have lost our sense of humour, mourning for all each precious one of us might have been in this one living time-place had she not been born a woman.[69]

The aggressive language and style, and even the content, centred upon the daily life and experience of women, are unmistakably sixties radicalism, although later Morgan would be one of many, especially in the USA, to deny its roots. But now it was coming from new voices, with new goals.

In Britain at this time, Germaine Greer was busy at work on what many (and especially the media) would see as a, if not the, seminal feminist text, *The Female Eunuch*. But true to her roots in the anti-authoritarian individualism of Aus-tralian anarchism, and her branches in the sexual liberation rhetoric of the international underground, she was unimpressed by the growing mood of women's collective criticism of a 'sexual liberation' packaged for men's eyes only. She preferred to assert herself, instead, as even more ballsy than the boys, disdainful of lesbian and clitoral-centred sexuality. Writing 'A Groupie's Vision' for *Oz* in 1969, 'Dr G' not only boasts of the pop stars she has 'pulled', or would – or wouldn't – like to pull, and why, but reflects on her desire for group sex:

> I found out I *really* liked being able to hear other people balling close to me while I was, and I was very pleased; you see the group fuck is the highest ritual of our faith, but it must happen as a sort of special grace. Contrived it could be really terrible, like a dirty weekend with the Monkees![70]

Greer joined the editorial board of *Suck*, from 1969 to 1972, which she saw as attempting to create a new kind of pornography in which nothing would be hidden, and all sexual hang-ups blown away. She was also to write for *Oz*'s special issue on 'Pussy Power', iconoclastically marking the first Women's Liberation Conference in Ruskin College in March 1970, and in a later issue on 'Cuntpower', she wrote: 'It's time to dig *cunt*, and women must dig it first.'[71] This was a type of feminism *Oz* could handle ('Everyone digs the ideas of the new female militancy, so long as all it does is demand things from men').[72] It seemed only to encourage the complacent sexism infusing Richard Neville's 'happy, hippie, playful sex' without commitment in *Play Power*, also being written at that time: 'While women may indeed be in the throes of freeing themselves from the vestiges of male dominance, there are as yet no widespread signs of boycott. Not at least, on the girls' part.'[73] Just you wait, Mr Neville; just you wait.

Greer retained her Reichian belief in the revolutionary power of genital sexuality ('What is certain . . . is that the patriarchal state could never survive the reconquest by women of their own sexuality') until the time when she would give up on sexual freedom altogether over a decade later, shifting her exuberant energies to celebrating the importance of Third World female bonding, motherhood and, finally, the joys of celibacy.[74] But other women were becoming feminists precisely because they wanted a new type of sexual liberation, where freedoms for men were not gained at women's expense. In Britain the mood of this new feminism was somewhere between Morgan's militant radical feminist denunciation of men and the Left, and Greer's continuing endorsement of 'free love' and fucking. Sheila Rowbotham had declared 1969 the Year of the Militant Woman in *Black Dwarf*. She went on to reflect that, having been seen as men's belongings and denied control over their bodies for so long, women had recently tried to 'prove that we have control, that we are liberated simply by fucking'. The problem was, she continued, 'we could be expressing in our sex life the very essence of our secondariness and the destructive contradictions in our consciousness, through the inability to meet and communicate and love with a man on every level.'[75] Yet, true to the decade, she was optimistic about change. Women had to discover their own 'dignity' and 'freedom', to 'decolonize themselves'. 'Men', she affirmed, here encapsulating almost all the issues, references and rhetoric of the passing decade – while gently mocking male hopes and fears – 'have nothing to lose but their chains':

You will no longer have anyone to creep away and peep at with their knickers down, no one to flaunt as the emblem of your virility, status, self-importance, no one who will trap you overwhelm you, no etherialised cloudy being floating unattainably in a plastic blue sky, no great mopping up handkerchief comforters to crawl into from your competitive, ego strutting alienation, who will wrap

you up and SMOTHER you. . . . There will only be
thousands of millions of women people to discover, touch
and become one with, who will say with a Vietnamese
girl, 'Let us now emulate each other' who will understand
you when you say we must make a new world in which
we do not meet each other as exploiters and used objects.
Where we love one another and into which a new kind
of human being can be born.[76]

This seems to me to sum up much of the mood in those first
Women's Liberation groups which began meeting in Britain
in 1969. Women wanted to talk about sexuality (conceived
overwhelmingly in terms of heterosexuality), but in all the
ways missing from men's talk: the pain and anxiety
surrounding abortion, particularly before the Abortion
Reform Act of 1967, women's dislike of the objectifying
female pin-ups saturating the alternative press, men's fear of
women's independence (particularly any signs of sexual
autonomy), questions of mothering and problems of childcare. This was certainly the mood which produced, almost
by accident, the first commercially successful British feminist magazine, *Spare Rib*, in 1972, out of the meetings which
had been held over the previous year by the underground
press women's group. 'It was a product of the counter-
culture and a reaction against it,' Marsha Rowe would write
a decade later, its editorial content covering 'ecology, sexuality, communal living, drugs, music, Third World
politics, food, health, mysticism, and psychology.'[77]
   A few men were allowed to write letters and publish
articles in the early issues of *Spare Rib*, especially if speaking
openly about their sexuality. One issue carried an exchange
between Laura Mulvey and the painter Allen Jones, accused
by Mulvey of depicting, not women at all, but male fears
of the 'castrated' female: 'The time has come', she wrote,

'for us to take over the show and exhibit our own fears and desires.'[78] With Anna Raeburn as their resident sex counsellor, regular columns like *Tooth & Nail* ridiculing sexism and the commercial use of women's bodies, articles on body politics, vaginal politics, masturbation and 'the liberated orgasm', *Spare Rib* set out to reclaim sex for women and help liberate women in the process: 'Amongst all the issues raised by the women's movement', *Spare Rib* would announce in 1975, 'the feminist approach to female sexuality is one which has, for many women, completely transformed our feelings about ourselves and our lives . . . giving women a new sense of autonomy and power.'[79]

Saying yes to sex, at least in some form, was now a way of women gaining power; but it had to be a feminist or 'liberated' type of sexuality – with, or without, a man. Women of my generation moved on from seeing sex as liberation, to seeking liberated sex.

2. The liberated orgasm? feminists fall out

Women have a capacity for sexuality far in excess of men. But thousands of years of patriarchal conditioning has robbed us of our sexual potential and deceived us about the nature of our sexuality.

Angela Hamblin[1]

Sexual liberation in the liberal sense frees male sexual aggression in the feminist sense. What looks like love and romance in the liberal view looks a lot like hatred and torture in the feminist view. Pleasure and eroticism become violation.

Catharine MacKinnon[2]

I do not believe that feminism is a matter, first or last, of sexuality.

June Jordan[3]

Whatever the hopes or the fears surrounding women's experience of sex in the 1960s, it was clear that women's emancipation was going to have to mean something more than 'the freedom to get laid'. As male radicals joined vanguardist Left groups or else returned to mainstream careers and conventional comforts, many women surviving that era would make their mark on the seventies in more permanently transformative ways. They began by returning to the early sixties emphasis on 'the politics of self': the need for individual self-discovery, the articulation of personal oppression and discontent. This would lead women into a radical rethinking of the whole area of sexuality and sexual politics.

Women's liberation emerged as a self-conscious movement by objecting to the male dominance and chauvinism
of the Civil Rights Movement and student politics. First
heard in the USA from around 1967, feminists were
popping up in Britain and Europe within a year or so. 'The
Movement is supposed to be for human liberation, how
come the position of women in it is no better than outside?',
Marge Piercy had demanded.[4] 'Liberate the socialist
eminences from their bourgeois pricks!', the Women's
Action Committee of the German student movement
taunted their comrades in November 1968.[5] In Britain, the
clenched fist inside the women's sign, symbolizing women's
liberation, was testimony to its birth within the militant
Left. Its concern with direct participatory democracy and
the creation of alternative institutions, although now taking
the form of nurseries, play-groups, women's self-help and
resource centres, alongside new women's publications, was
also a continuation of New Left strategies and perspectives.
A rhetoric of revolution thus accompanied the birth of
women's liberation. Its goals, as drawn up in a manifesto
for the first national Women's Liberation Conference at
Ruskin College in Oxford in March 1970, were to enable
women to come together 'to further our part in the struggle
for social change and the transformation of society', and to
provide solidarity with women's struggles for a better life,
everywhere, to enable women to be 'in charge of our own
lives'. Social transformation was to accompany women's
search for personal growth and happiness.

One thing which was new, however, was the emphasis
of women's liberation on small groups for 'consciousness
raising', to gain a shared understanding of the subjective
nature of women's subordination, and to work out collectively how to change it (rather than following suggestions
from 'leaders', seen as the practice of the 'male Left').

Another thing which was new, and startling, was its comprehensive questioning of the sexual divisions of labour (both in the workplace and the home). The third and final novel emphasis was the focus on female sexuality, now analysed as something hitherto controlled, and defined, by men. A redefinition of sexuality stressing women's sexual autonomy and right to control their own bodies was thus fundamental to the idea of women's liberation. It sought to assert a positive sexuality for women in a society at best ambivalent, and more often antagonistic, towards any such notion.

Most feminists in these early years held on to the utopian vision of the sixties Left that through our own 'long march', building alternative institutions to replace existing ones, we would help to socialize the economy and revolutionize personal life – at the same time transforming the Left. It was this vision which accounted for the extraordinary joy experienced by many women then. Its force is forever encapsulated for me in memories of women dancing together to the all-women's bands beating out 'The Women's Army is Marching' at the ecstatic socials held during early national Women's Liberation Conferences. For this was the first time women of my generation felt certain that we were making history – for ourselves. It is hard today to do justice to the strength of those passionate beginnings, or to capture, as US historian Rosalyn Baxandall reflects, 'the dynamism, fun, vision, or power we wielded for a brief shining moment, or how the earth occasionally moved under our feet as our theory became practice'.[6] It felt like a great love affair with women everywhere, as Janet Rée reflects, from London:

> You had this feeling of being high, and somehow
> corporate, part of something large, public and significant.
> It was wonderful. The best kind of relationship I've ever

had. The feeling was like you have when you're in love.
The world was re-made in the image of whatever you
were in love with. . . . It was such a turbulent change.[7]

The clitoral truth

Sixties radicals thought sexual repression (produced,
according to Reich, within authoritarian, patriarchal
families) and political repression (evident in militarism and
authoritarian state institutions) were connected. Sexual
repression created isolation and alienation, distancing
people from their 'true' selves: 'Freedom is the consciousness of our desires', declared one slogan from May '68.
Women's liberation thought similarly, but more specifically,
that *women*'s sexuality and desires were repressed and
denied in the interests of men and of 'patriarchy': 'Women
are forbidden to own and use their sexuality *for themselves*,
as a means of personal self-expression. . . . Patriarchal
society deliberately destroys women's contact with her own
inner core of sexuality.'[8] This meant that it was important
for women to 'get in touch with their bodies' and rediscover
their true sexuality. It was important, and not really
so difficult, or so it seemed – for just a few years. It was not
so difficult because 'sexuality' at this stage was thought
of in terms of some type of inner essence available for
self-expression, something separate from what you do when
you have sex (usually seen in terms of an act with others).
This meant that women's sexuality – often unthinkingly
presumed heterosexual – could be thought of in the
singular, and that distinctions between heterosexuality and
lesbianism did not at first come to the fore.

The way to a woman's sexuality was through her clitoris,
as Anne Koedt had declared in her influential essay, 'The

Myth of the Vaginal Orgasm', distributed at the very first national Women's Liberation Conference in the USA, in 1968:

> We must demand that if certain sexual positions now defined as standard are not mutually conducive to orgasm they no longer be defined as standard. New techniques must be used or devised which transform this particular aspect of our current sexual exploitation.[9]

In Koedt's memorable workshop at that conference, Rosalyn Baxandall recalls, women began exchanging 'wonderful, detailed stories about sex', discussing long into the night their sexual lives and fantasies – although some became unsettled by their occasional sado-masochistic and lesbian content. At another workshop, 'Cruising: Or the Rationalization of the Pursuit of Men', Naomi Weisstein and Marlene Dixon, less successfully, proposed that single, heterosexual women should form syndicates, like the one Weisstein had helped to organize in Chicago, to 'add dignity and control' to women's hitherto private struggle 'waiting to be chosen' when wanting to get a man. From the beginning, however, as Alice Echols later recorded, the attempt to overcome old prescriptions would sometimes engender new ones. At that same founding conference in the USA, one woman had felt the need to apologize after having been 'exposed' as claiming to have vaginal orgasms.[10]

The first goal, it seemed, was to expose and to reject the ruling myths of female sexual dependency and sexual availability. One way of doing this was already close to hand, being prominent in mainstream sexology since the 1950s. This was to assert, in a no-nonsense, neutral and 'scientific' discourse, the essential similarity between male and female desire:

Now, after the toing and froing of the last 50 years, we
can safely say that there is no biological difference
between the sexuality of the human female and the
human male. The clitoris and the penis respectively are
the 'seat' of genital release, the orgasm. This release can
be brought about by masturbation with or without
mechanical stimulators; sexual intercourse of many kinds
with one or more partners of either or the same sex;
by sexual fantasy, or imagery, and by dreams. . . .
And that seems to be all there is to say about genital
sexual activity.[11]

'Think clitoris', was how Alix Kates Shulman summed up
much of this early feminist thinking on women's sexuality
from the USA, assuming, as she later recalled, that *if* we
could 'change the way we *think* we could change the way
we live'.[12]

If women's sexuality was essentially the same as that of
men, then it was only the myths and lies about female
genital anatomy which declared that women were the
passive sex. Such myths and lies emerged out of the long
historical repression of female sexuality in the interests of
men's control over women's reproductive capacities, a
control currently organized according to the needs of the
capitalist state for 'the happy labour-dividing family
producing tomorrow's hairdressers and bank clerks':[13]
'Women in Labour Keep Capital in Power', as feminists
had spray painted on the walls of Ruskin College (to the
fury of their sisters who had to scrub it off!). The clitoris
provided the clue to, and the means to undo, the suppression of female sexuality for reproductive ends. In New York
in these early years, radical feminists had organized a
Whistle-In in Wall Street – making sexual passes at men in
the street – protested at the National Bridal Fair in the name
of WITCH (Women's International Terrorist Conspiracy

from Hell), and occupied the *Ladies Home Journal* until they were given twenty pages to promote feminism, including what was seen as a particularly scandalous piece on sex – mentioning lesbianism.[14]

If women's and men's sexuality were now thought to be fundamentally the same, however, both feminists and sexologists were nevertheless only too aware that it was women who were not getting their fair share of satisfaction. Sexologists had their therapeutic regimes of physical stimulation for couples seeking help with sexual problems (mostly aimed at reforming male sexual technique to provide more adequate, clitorally focussed 'foreplay'). Feminists, however, favoured collective self-help, so women could learn to love their own bodies and discover how to give pleasure to themselves, thereby, it was hoped, undoing the damage society had done to women's true sexual potential. While a few feminists would later write of 'frightening American feminists who proposed masturbation in groups',[15] many women did begin, with mirror, speculum, and the writings of Betty Dodson, Barbara Seaman, Lonnie Barbach and Shere Hite, to devote themselves to exploring the anatomy and physiology of female pleasure.

In 1972, Barbara Seaman, an editor with the US magazine *Family Circle*, published her sex manual *Free and Female: The Sex Life of the Contemporary Woman*, which was adapted for the British women's liberation magazine *Spare Rib* the following year. Drawing heavily upon the research of Masters and Johnson, it was the first of several articles which would appear in that magazine over the next three years, instructing women on the importance of taking charge of their sexuality and learning how to obtain orgasmic satisfaction, without shame or inhibition. Seaman both warned women of the health risks of sexual frustration (which 'can even give a woman cramps and headache'), while telling men that 'instead of following sex manuals or trusting the locker-room sexpertise of their fellows, [they] must learn to seek and receive signals from the women they love.'[16] Subsequent articles, no longer offensively assuming that women are heterosexual and coupled, were written more sensitively and thoughtfully by Eleanor Stephens.

Outlining a 'feminist approach to female orgasm' she too suggests: 'if we could demystify sexuality and think of the orgasm response as a skill then we could begin to help women to learn it'. The surest method, she continued, is through masturbation:

> every woman with a clitoris can become orgasmic given the right kind and amount of stimulation. Anyone who can learn to ride a bicycle, and this too can be a slow and fearful process especially as an adult, can learn to have an orgasm.[17]

Physiological response, moreover, is seen in this feminist understanding of the early 1970s as linked directly to full emotional satisfaction, as the way to undo all the negative sexual conditioning women have received: for women to learn to give themselves orgasms is for them 'literally to learn to love themselves'.[18] Orgasm is not something done to us (passive), but something we do (active). Women need to have the confidence to share such knowledge with their partners, if they have them, so they can explore each other's sexuality together.

In the past, I have angered feminists like Stephens, by writing of the limitations of their adaptation of behaviouristic understandings and techniques of contemporary sexology to the sexual empowerment of women.[19] Unlike Masters and Johnson, feminist writing and self-help groups aimed not simply to strengthen the heterosexual couple, but to increase the confidence of all women 'to define their sexuality for themselves'. And there is no doubt, I am sure, that their work was very important in giving some women the confidence to communicate more openly with their lovers, as well as influencing some men to think more carefully about their sexual practices. (A popular feminist novel of 1970s refers playfully to one woman's three 'non-negotiable' conditions for sex with men: 'plenty of dope, three hours minimum, and cunnilingus'.[20]) Stephens herself emphasizes the importance of not exchanging new dogmas for old, and stresses the diversity of women's sexual pleasures, including the fact that 'many women do find that the vagina is an erogenous area and that penetration feels good'.[21] There was, to be sure, little enough room for diversity in traditional conceptions of the old 'sex act', penis in vagina thrusting. Some of what could be the rich creative side of all this talk and thinking about orgasm is expressed by Alison Fell at the close of the 1970s, in a poem she wrote for her women's writer's group, 'in confidence':

> – An orgasm is like an anchovy,
> she says,
> little, long, and very salty.

> – No, its a caterpillar,
> undulating, fat and sweet.

> – A sunburst, says the third,
> an exploding watermelon:
> I had one at Christmas,

> – Your body betrays, she says,
> one way or another.
> Rash and wriggling, it comes
> and comes, while your mind
> says lie low, or go.

– Or else it snarls and shrinks
to the corner of its cage
while your mind, consenting,
whips in and out,
out in the open
and *so* free.

– As for me,
says the last,
if I have them brazen
with birthday candles,
with water faucets
or the handle of Toby jugs,
I don't care who knows it.
But how few I have –
keep *that* in the dark.[22]

Yet more often there was a false optimism, oddly combining with a rather cheerless, unsexy seriousness, in the early feminist writing integrating sexual pleasure and women's liberation. (Mildly mocking its tone, Elizabeth Wilson in a letter to *Spare Rib* in 1975, puzzled over why she just couldn't learn to ride a bicycle, when she'd never had any trouble having orgasms!) Not only did these texts suggest that 'most men are only too relieved when the woman plucks up courage to share what she knows about her sexuality', they further suggested that such communication could in itself both create more egalitarian personal relationships and empower women publicly to change those 'other areas of our lives where women also have inferior status and play a passive role'.[23] Personal pleasure, actively pursued, paved the way to public power.

Unfortunately, many women would soon come to feel cheated by the promise of 'the moon within [their] reach', either in their personal relations, their public lives, or both at once. Tracking down all the reasons is premature and a significant part of the wider project of this book. For a start, there is the problem of the theoretical inadequacy of the scientifically respectable but nevertheless reductive model of sexuality in use in these early feminist writings, based upon the idea of drives and their repression or release. Its limitations would serve to confuse feminist thinking on sexuality – highlighting conflicts so intractable that, before too long, some feminists would retreat into a thorough-going condemnation of sex itself, at least in its heterosexual versions. Less obviously, in ways I elaborate in later chapters, the 'feminist approach to female orgasm' might itself be said to express certain familiar, male-centred notions of sexuality. It rejected and condemned sexual 'passivity' or 'receptivity' as demeaning, promoting instead a notion of self-assertion through sexual 'activity' – the traditionally masculine way of roping sex to power. The difficulties of overturning phallocentric ways of thinking about sex are so pervasive that it is not really surprising that in attempting to avoid them we often, unwittingly, seem to add to their legitimacy. It is also necessary to raise here, as it will be again, the question of whether sexual desire is not, at least partly, about *losing* control. If women who like sex are at least sometimes seeking the autonomy to be in control of the time they can be out of control, it will be far from straightforward how we relate feminist struggles against male domination to actual sexual experience and behaviour.

Autonomy and control

The guiding principles of autonomy and control, regulating feminist attempts to reclaim women's sexuality and treat it as distinct from their child-bearing capacity, were politically useful. Sexuality is a complex terrain, and such principles worked well for asserting women's interests, against those of the medical profession or the state, in the regulation of the more public aspects of women's health, fertility and sexuality. For example, feminists sought and obtained as much information as possible on contraception and abortion, methods of improving childbirth, and combatting the frequently insensitive and inept, if not abusive, medical practices in meeting women's specific health needs. This knowledge fed immediately into campaigns for free contraception and abortion, and the creation of women's self-help groups, all raising a multitude of accompanying issues around public resources, professional expertise, subjective experience and personal relationships.

Women's bodies, previously known and administered through predominantly male professional scrutiny and expertise, still shrouded by popular embarrassment or else distorted by pornographic display, were now at the clamorous centre of the new feminist politics of self-emancipation: *Our Bodies Ourselves*, as the Boston Women's Health Collective put it.[24] And slowly but surely all this noise and action would bring permanent change to the social institutions regulating women's bodies. In many countries women have transformed the conditions under which they obtain contraception, give birth, seek abortion or generally obtain help for gynaecological problems.

My own brief experience of hell on earth is not one which is likely to be repeated today. I gave birth to my son at Sydney's leading obstetric hospital, in Australia in 1969, alone and unaided, my wordless howling punctuated only by phantom voices ordering me to 'be quiet', amidst a background of fiendish screams. This torment continued until my expensive gynaecologist arrived to administer a general anaesthetic. My sole way of consoling myself throughout was the thought that nothing could ever be so terrible again. And it never was. Today, 'a woman's right to choose' what happens to her body is an acceptable professional slogan, not merely the wild wish of feminism it was only twenty-five years ago. It is important to acknowledge this change, however much feminists now rightly complain that Western medicine remains dominated by male authorities, with their frequently invasive, high-technology priorities.

But women's sexuality is no unitary thing (even once we separate off our experiences of physical pleasure or discomfort from the institutions and discourses which regulate disease, fertility, pregnancy and childbirth). The anatomical and physiological explorations which contributed to the feminist approach to female orgasm were useful, and not just in helping women, too ignorant or fearful to do so, to masturbate (the levels of ignorance assumed to surround autoerotic possibilities were always somewhat puzzling). More importantly, I suspect, such feminist discourse around sex gave women the confidence to complain about men's frequently self-centred, or inept, sexual behaviour. When women were warned of the 'dangers' of 'faking orgasm', for example, the real message was surely not so much its potential physiological consequences as the dangers of encouraging or tolerating men's selfishness. (Oddly, feminists then and now have rarely assumed that men might fake orgasms, to give satisfaction to women, although I have found it is not so hard to get them to admit it, if you ask.) But the early feminist approach to orgasm, which involved learning through masturbation, left untouched many other issues which we now see as central to sex.

One of these is the exploration of sexual fantasy, and its bizarre and perverse nature. Another is the whole question of desire, and why we might wish to have, or to avoid having,

orgasms with particular types of people. Yet another, the
sad truth at first so firmly disavowed by feminists adapting
sexological discourses, that having orgasms – however
plentiful – does not mean that we have learned to love ourselves, does not give us power over our partners, does not
give us power in the world. Indeed, it has little to do with
either love or power. Orgasms are the one thing, perhaps
the only thing, that even the most fearful, the most alienated,
the most distressed, desolate, enslaved and wretched person
(or beast), may manage to obtain. Orgasms were never going
to be enough, however autonomously we might control
them. A few writers, like Beatrix Campbell, had always
warned of the dangers of simply pitting the clitoris against
the vagina, and stressed that the 'revolutionary potential' of
the feminist approach to sexuality was 'in taking sex beyond
the tyranny of orgasm, and the virtually exclusive attraction
of the genital areas at the expense of more generalised
sensuality'.[25] When it comes to what feels like our real sexual
longings, autonomy, control and even orgasms may be as
much the weary problem as the warm solution.

Sex and love

While it was necessary for women to politicize the whole
area of sex and reproduction, to try to disentangle women's
interests from wider social forces of regulation and control,
women's own experiences of sex nevertheless remained
highly problematic. It was easy to see the importance
of insisting that 'the personal is political', when both men
individually, and the state more generally, had habitually
related to women as the servicing, subordinate sex –
defined through her economically dependent status in
the family. But it was hard, unsettling and at times painful

to use the slogan to question everything that you did and felt.

Throughout the 1970s, in a great outpouring of articles, novels and poetry, feminists began to write of battles in their relationships with men. Sometimes they involved problems of ambivalence, tied to dependency: 'I would cling to men, whom on most levels I hated because the alternative, being by myself, was so terrifying.'[26] Other times it was men's unwillingness, their seeming inability, to listen to women:

> He thinks we're really making love. He thinks we're really speaking to each other. But he can't possibly hear my body, he's not even listening. He thinks he recognises me, but he's not even looking. He's touching, but he can't feel a thing. . . . He meant well. That was the trouble. That was it. He cared for her and knew what was best for her. Only he didn't know her at all. What's more he didn't know he didn't know, being blind beyond his own eyes, deaf beyond his own noise and numb beyond his own skin . . . . He was a Victorian missionary stuck up the Amazon.[27]

The issue of power was always present, somewhere, with women feeling that men were still in control, even when supportive of women's liberation.

Women themselves were confused and ambivalent. If sex could at times be self-regulated, following masturbatory models, what was to be done about love? For many feminists love presented a major obstacle to their ideal of relations based upon autonomy and equality, wedded, it seemed, to a romantic ideology which served only to keep women subordinate. Love was invidious, leading inevitably to over-dependence on one person (often a man), with accompanying destructive emotions of jealousy and possessiveness.

'We must destroy love', a North American radical feminist manifesto had brashly exhorted: 'Love promotes vulnerability, dependence, possessiveness, susceptibility to pain, and prevents the full development of woman by directing all her energies outwards in the interests of others.'[28] More cautiously, some years on, a British feminist concludes: 'When we are fighting against the feelings of love which seem capable of debilitating us, we should be constantly vigilant about the way we feel, attempting to understand why we behave as we do, and not accepting love as unfathomable and unchangeable.' Immediately aware of the impossibility of it all, she falters: 'However, the real trial comes when we have to put our ideas into reality, and are forced to fight against feelings in ourselves which we know (in theory) to be unacceptable, but which we find almost impossible to combat in practice.'[29]

The theory (ideas of women's rights to personal autonomy) and the practice (emotional dependence in sexual relationships) would never co-exist smoothly, however vigilant feminists might try to be. Some heterosexual women recall early feminist struggles around sex and relationships with pleasure, others with pain. Despite much writing and analysis on the difficulties of changing men, some feminists look back on those early years as a time when they did feel sexually empowered and free to explore and take risks which they never had before. Anna Davin, then married with young children, recalls: 'I'd learnt that I could hold my own intellectually and politically and sexually. . . . My personal life might have been smoother if I had not been emboldened by feminism, but it would probably not have been happier.'[30] Sue Cooper, later choosing to become a single mother after carefully selecting a suitable father, reports much the same sense of sexual empowerment in those years: 'In my own life non-monogamy was an immediate issue – I expressed my freedom through the right to be involved with young men on my own terms.'[31]

Some women chose to live and raise their children collectively, in search of alternatives to marriage and the nuclear family, where women were by law and by custom defined through their dependence upon and relation to a man:

> When I arrived at Laurieston Hall I was in a couple relationship that had lasted ten years. I soon discovered the delights of independence. I had a room of my own and time to spend with other consenting adults who lived only down the corridor, without baby-sitting problems. During my fifteen years of communal life, I spent six months as a single person, the rest of it shared with four main lovers and a sprinkling of other lasting affairs. Life was complicated and upsetting at times . . . I wavered between the excitement and challenge of new lovers, and the dread of disease and expense of travel.[32]

Other women recalled more the rage and frustration of living with men and trying to find new forms of relating: 'after ten years of "politicizing men"', three feminists wrote in 1980, 'the kind of problems that arise in personal relationships go on the same roundabouts, the same compromises, year after year.'[33] From the USA, Alix Shulman now reported that by the late 1970s, when a number of early women's liberationists met together to talk about the changes which had occurred in their own sex lives since the movement began:

> All agreed that sex had changed for them, but few thought that it had really improved. True, some of them were now able to specify what they wanted their sex partners to do, but in some relations the man resented the

woman's desires. Several women who had changed from nonorgasmic to regularly orgasmic were sorry to find that nevertheless they were unhappy in love.[34]

Later feminists would begin to admit that conflict is intrinsic to the nature of love, but only after abandoning the behaviouristic voluntarism of the early years of women's liberation, with its fierce critique of psychoanalytic perspectives. Such conflict was not simply reducible to the ubiquitous power relations of gender. Existing gender relations, securing men's greater social power and authority as a sex are, of course, tightly entangled with the dynamics of desire (leaving aside for now the issue of the symbolic place of the phallus in defining desire). Typically throwing up façades of manly bravado, alongside the greater likelihood of female fears and timidity, gender relations produce a thick smoke which can only serve to obscure the complexities beneath. A few feminists did try to speak of the contradictions they experienced between their aspirations and desires: 'I'd always felt there was something about what happened to men when they spread their trappings of power – I somehow couldn't perceive them as attractive,' Janet Rée recalls. As a member of a short-lived mixed anti-sexist group at the close of the 1970s, she found the expression of such conflict 'difficult and murky, I could hardly bear to articulate it.'[35]

Beneath the smog, sexual love in both women and men is inevitably tied up with personal histories of infantile idealization, dependency, jealousy, aggressiveness and the dread of abandonment. It was always going to provide the most unsuitable site for enacting any feminist paradigm of mutual autonomy. As we shall see in forthcoming chapters, the emotion of love, with its intense fear of and passionate desire to move beyond the routine boundaries of the self, is distinctive, primarily, as 'a crucible of contradictions and misunderstandings'.[36] Although rooted in pleasure and desire, love can never be reduced to either of them. We may, for instance, want to have a lot of sex for the sake of love, without desire; or we may want to have a lot of sex for the sake of desire, without love. In either case the 'pleasure' we may or may not experience is far from straightforward. But neither the early feminist exploration of the anatomy of female pleasure, nor a sociological focus on the hierarchies of gender, can help us make much sense of this. In the meantime, it was much easier to blame men for the pains of love – if not individual men, at least men as a sex.

Women loving women

Not surprisingly, the tendency simply to blame men, which was soon to overtake the passion to reform them, has always been present in feminist thinking and culture – at least, within the white feminist perspectives which have dominated women's liberation movements in both Britain and the USA. But it gained ground with various theoretical and strategic shifts in feminist understanding of sexuality, personal life and women's oppression in the 1970s. The first public and painful split in the North American women's movement of the 1970s, which would soon reverberate in feminist circles around the globe, was a lesbian/heterosexual confrontation.

In the USA liberal feminism was from the beginning a far stronger force within the movement than it would ever become in Britain. Focus on the disruptive area of sexuality tended to be dismissed by these feminists for the more conventional pursuit of civil rights and legislative reform, like the Equal Rights Amendment (ERA) or women's

'reproductive rights' for contraception and abortion. Indeed
lesbians had faced initial discrimination in the liberal
feminist organization, National Organization of Women
(NOW), orchestrated by its idiosyncratic founder Betty
Friedan (who claimed in the *New York Times* in 1973 that
lesbians had been sent by the CIA to infiltrate the women's
movement and discredit feminism!)[37] They also felt themselves to be largely invisible, or at least marginalized, within
the more radical, but still predominantly heterosexual,
women's liberation groupings. In response, lesbian feminists
organized a series of profoundly effective political speeches,
articles and actions in the early seventies. An influential
paper of 1970, for example, written by a group of New
York 'Radicalesbians' who declared themselves 'women-
identified women', defined lesbianism as the key to women
abandoning their dependence on men and male culture:
'Only women can give each other a new sense of self. . . .
A lesbian is the rage of all women condensed to the point
of explosion.'[38] Soon, the charismatic spokeswoman and
novelist, Rita Mae Brown, was accusing heterosexual
women of collaborating with the enemy: 'To give a man
support and love before giving it to a sister is to support
that culture, that power system.'[39] And significant numbers
of US feminists seemed to agree (or at least to fear it might
be true) that, as Charlotte Bunch declared:

> The lesbian's refusal to support one man undermines
> the personal power that men exercise over women. . . .
> As long as straight women see lesbianism as a
> bedroom issue, they hold back the development of
> politics and strategies that would put an end to male
> supremacy. . . . Lesbianism is the key to liberation and
> only women who cut their ties to male privilege can be
> trusted to remain serious in the struggle against male
> dominance.[40]

This was all to prove an exciting and salutary challenge to the unthinking heterosexism and homophobia (or 'dyke baiting') of mainstream gender assumptions, apparent even in some early feminist texts by Betty Friedan and Germaine Greer. 'It's strange, you know,' Sarah Schulman would later write with understandable glee (and mild exaggeration), 'in the early seventies, one day half the women's movement came out as lesbians.'[41] The woman-identified woman position not only began to shift the balance of power between straight and gay women within the women's movement, but also, up to a point, seemed to strengthen heterosexual women's confidence in negotiating with men: lesbian relations served as a very real alternative for women trying to make changes in their relationships with men.[42] As Amber Hollibaugh would later comment, 'lesbian sex' began to be a model for describing what was 'good sex', rather than what lesbians actually do:

> [It] was a way to reject men fucking for a minute and
> a half and pulling out, a way to talk about non-missionary
> position sexuality, foreplay as all-play. And all women in
> the feminist movement were trying to make love the way
> dykes are supposed to.[43]

Women, like Dutch writer Anja Meulenbelt in her best-seller, *The Shame is Over*, could suddenly re-assess and criticize their former dependence on men:

> When I am in love . . . I live his life. Breathe and
> drink theatre if he is a theatre person. Live politics if he
> is in politics. Am interested only in art if he is a
> sculptor. I don't understand how other women can do
> without, how they can live alone or with a colourless
> husband.[44]

Showing just how much the spirit of an era can influence sexual behaviour, Lillian Faderman observes that there were probably more lesbians in America in the 1970s than at any other time in history, 'because radical feminism had helped redefine lesbianism to make it almost a categorical imperative for all women truly interested in the welfare and progress of other women'. Many formerly heterosexual feminists were only too happy to reach out for a sexual alternative, at least in the first days of feminist euphoria – with women discovering the often neglected and up until then so undervalued pleasures of each other's company: 'It was not that they had generally disliked sex when they were heterosexual, but rather they had come to despise all the personal and political aggravations that heterosexuality brought in its wake.'[45]

Political lesbianism entailed significant theoretical revision in feminist thinking about sexuality, as well as behavioural changes. Whereas earlier feminists had stressed women's potential similarity to men in terms of love and lust, the new feminist homoeroticism was defined in terms of its *difference* from what was felt to be the objectifying, exploitative sexuality of men. Women-loving-women meant gentler, non-possessive, non-competitive, non-violent, nurturing and egalitarian relationships. As the heroine of Alix Kates Shulman's exemplary feminist novel reflects: 'For a while I'd begun to think there was something the matter with me – like being frigid or tone deaf – because I'd never been in love with a woman. But now – I see I'm normal after all. What a relief to find out I'm normal!' When she describes her lesbian encounter with her lover, who is also her 'sister' and friend, we learn:

She took me in her arms. And as our kisses stretched on I forgot about many things. About dominance and submission, winning and losing, concealing and exposing, protecting and sacrificing. . . . sinking myself into the soft yielding pillow that was Faith's lovely body, so perfectly matched to mine, I let myself wallow in equality. [46]

Lesbian culture was women's culture. A blueprint could be found in Jill Johnson's *Lesbian Nation* of 1973. As Adrienne Rich explained at the New York Lesbian Pride Rally of 1977, feminists must build their own women-centred, women-loving culture and identity, rejecting the violent, self-destructive world of men – including gay men (or older lesbians who imitated gay male culture with their 'role stereotypes of "butch" and "femme"').[47]

Ironically, with some feminists advancing lesbianism as a political imperative for feminism, it began to appear unproblematic as a sexuality, something which could be simply taken for granted and left unstudied. This had the unfortunate effect that there was no longer any room for feminists to discuss the realities of lesbian desire or the complexities of lesbian relationships: 'It was assumed that your sexuality was successful,' Helaine Harris recalled.[48] Of course, there was even less room to discuss the realities of heterosexual desire, now defined as 'male identified', or the complexities of heterosexual relationships. Within the USA, some prominent feminist figures, like Robin Morgan, wanted to play down the lesbian-straight split, but they did so by emphasizing 'the vast differences' between male and female sexuality:

Every woman here knows in her gut . . . that the emphasis on genital sexuality, objectification, promiscuity, emotional noninvolvement and coarse invulnerability was the *male style*, and that we, as women, placed greater trust in love, sensuality, humor, tenderness, commitment.[49]

Of course, every woman (lesbian or straight), although often confused about the troubled area of sex, did not know; and there were deep disagreements between feminists on the nature of sexuality. In Britain, an early lesbian chauvinist blast on heterosexual women, as either untrustworthy dupes or collaborators with men, appeared when the notorious CLIT statement (from the USA) was reprinted by the London Women's Liberation Workshop in 1974. By the mid-1970s, many feminists were complaining of the negative atmosphere between lesbians and heterosexuals at national women's conferences, leading Berta Freistadt to hold a workshop on communication between the two at the penultimate National Women's Conference of 1977. The lesbians attending spoke of their sexual orientation as a political decision: 'less to do with who you sleep with than where you show your emotional commitment', while many heterosexual women present, like Freistadt herself, 'felt a great ambivalence towards our sexual state: we too put women first . . . I think some of us felt we had a lesbian potential that may or may not one day be realized.'[50]

The idea that lesbian sexual expression, and only lesbian sexual expression, involves mutuality and equality seemed to have become the consensus feminists increasingly reached. Ironically, at this same conference a group of lesbian socialist feminists, calling themselves Lesbian Left, rejected both the prescriptiveness and the heterosexual guilt evident in that workshop, to stress instead that lesbianism was *not* in itself about retreating from or combatting men. Indeed, from the beginning of these disputes over sexuality, some of the most confident opponents of any idea of specifically 'feminist' sexual practices, or distinctively womanly desires for healthy, sensual, egalitarian relationships, rather than of aggressive, lusty, orgasmic sex, would be lesbians. Elizabeth Wilson complained in 1974 that she knew, from her own experience, that lesbian couples could just as easily develop many of the worst features of heterosexual couples:

> I do not want lesbianism distorted into some ideal in the Woman's Movement or anywhere else. I simply want us all to fight to free ourselves so that we can apprehend our real feelings more fully, whether we are straight or gay.[51]

Sleeping with the enemy

These conflicts over sexuality, exemplifying the always potentially prescriptive side of equating the personal with the political, would not have come to silence feminist explorations of sexuality had they not become entwined with a second, even more troubling problem for feminists. Once feminists started listening to the untold tales of women, there was an increasing awareness of the continual fear and danger some women faced in their daily lives with men. It was this which threatened to snuff out the flame of feminist hopes for changing men, and the world they dominated. Men's violence towards women, combined with society's failure to protect women, continued to enrage feminists.

Not only did women face what they would soon come to define as 'sexual harassment' from men at work, in the streets, and most other public spaces, but even when violently assaulted, they were likely to find that their assailant remained unpunished. 'Women who say no do not always mean no,' Judge Wild reassured rapists in Britain in 1982. Whatever women's physical injuries and mental damage, judges, police and media, in one scandalous case after another throughout the 1970s, tended to blame the victim (she was hitchhiking or drinking or a 'good time girl') and sympathize with the aggressor. He 'lost control', or 'allowed his enthusiasm for sex' to get the better of him, Mr Justice Slynn commiserated with the guardsman he released from prison following a particularly violent rape of a 17-year-old woman in 1977.[52] Police proved similarly reluctant, during these years, to intervene in cases of domestic violence. Male researchers like Jasper Gayford began analysing the characteristics, not of the assailant, but of the type of woman who 'provoked' assault.[53] It was only feminists who campaigned for legal changes to protect women from battery and abuse, and who set up what quickly proved to be desperately needed refuges as safe havens from the early 1970s. Only they would fight to set up, fund and administer the Rape Crisis Centres which were instantly overstretched by the large numbers of women seeking relief from the traumas of rape, incest and the legacy of child sexual abuse.

It is hardly surprising that feminist determination to understand and eliminate rape and violence against women (and soon children, as well) came to take precedence over other matters in debates around sexuality in the second half of the 1970s.[54] Susan Brownmiller's influential book *Against Our Will* serves as a landmark of this shift. Here she analyses the prevalence of rape as the single, over-riding means through which men have always sought and managed to keep women subordinate throughout time and place.[55] More feminists now came to accept an analysis which saw sexuality itself as *the* primary source of men's oppression of women, thus isolating sexuality and men's violence from other structures of women's inequality, whether economic, political or cultural.

Whereas second-wave feminists had once insisted that 'women's liberation has no single over-riding issue or panacea', now it had one.[56] Whereas putting sexuality into the political arena had once meant tackling all existing conceptions of gender, and especially the organization of family life, now it reduced to men's sexual practices. (The adoption of a motion, despite catastrophic disagreement, to make 'the right to define our sexuality' *the* over-riding demand of the women's movement at its last national conference in 1978, heralded the significance of the shift in Britain.) Seeing sexuality as the pivot of women's oppression, feminists were soon to analyse all forms of male sexuality in terms of a continuum of violence; proclaiming, as had Susan Griffin in 1971, that 'the basic elements of rape are involved in all heterosexual relationships'.[57] In this type of analysis, men had a 'sexuality' which was synonymous with the need for power and continuous with the expression of violence. More and more feminists had thus shifted from what they once asserted as the *similarity* between women's and men's sexuality to declare instead that there was a fundamental *difference* between the sexuality of women and men, with women's once again the inverse of men's: gentle, diffuse and, above all, egalitarian.

Feminists who did not agree with the analysis that sexual coercion was the root of men's power over women faced a maddening set of associations, which served to disable us and edge out earlier accounts of the complex interface of social relations constructing and maintaining male dominance. We were, of course, aware of men's frequent resort to violence and abuse against women and children, and had often campaigned against it. We were also equally provoked by the outrageous social and juridical tolerance for such behaviour – so often allowing men's violence, when against women, to go unpunished. Just as disturbingly, we could see the neat fit between the prevalence of rape and dominant cultural mythologies of male and female sexuality in terms of predator and prey, conquest and submission.

Reducing male power to male sexuality, and male sexuality to violence, thus had a symbolic resonance with the dominant language and iconography of sex, already saturated with imagery of male lust as instinctive and uncontrollable, triggered off by any hint of female sexual availability. This was just what women's liberationists had entered the political world to attack, but by the close of the 1970s, when the aggressively interventionist Revolutionary Feminists in Britain were publishing their message that 'giving up fucking for a feminist is about taking your politics seriously',[58] few heterosexual feminists had the spirit left to go into print and disagree.

Many feminists recall an intense pressure to keep quiet about their sexuality, even when, like Judith Newton in the USA, they also experienced 'a totally rebellious sense of resentment and determination to do what I felt like doing, despite it all':

> I felt no shame . . . but I did feel intimidated. I can also remember the first break with this intimidation, which came with the s/m sex radicals who first gave 'permission' to heterosexual feminists to feel OK about their sexuality within the context of the larger feminist community.[59]

Anger and resentment against the new radical feminist denunciation of heterosexuality was expressed by many straight feminists, particularly by socialist feminists. We began to avoid each other, and open feminist gatherings became increasingly stormy and unpleasant places to be. Most heterosexual feminists had no intention of suppressing their desires for sexual encounters and relationships with men, but I think that many of us did feel undermined and confused, if not guilty, by the accusation that we were too 'male-identified' and 'soft on men'. It was as though feminists should be able to eliminate all the contradictions of political struggle for the 'purity' of our cause.

Meanwhile, black feminists, whether lesbian or straight, were emerging as a stronger voice and organizational force in both Britain and the USA from the close of the seventies. They did not tend to join their white radical feminist sisters now distancing themselves so thoroughly from men: 'there *is* a way where you can remain whole and be a bridge, still have a foot in a different camp,' Cherrié Moraga and Gloria Anzaldua asserted.[60] Like Angela Davis, black American feminists were particularly critical of the white feminist blindness to the thousands of black men 'maimed and murdered because of racist manipulation of the rape charge'.[61] Fraudulent rape charges against black men stand out in the history of the USA, they made it clear, not as a way of protecting women (least of all black women, who were always raped with impunity by white men), but rather as one of the most formidable weapons of racism for subordinating, controlling and dehumanizing black men. Throughout the first half of this century, lynch mobs operated in the southern states as a form of political terror against all black people, ensuring the social and economic exploitation of black men through the orchestration of the sexual fears and loathing (never unconnected to longing) of white men and women.[62]

It was not that black feminists were uncritical of men. On the contrary, from very early on in the USA black feminist writers like Toni Cade Bambara had satirized, if with humour and affection, the shortcomings of black men and their tendency to blame black women for their problems, at the same time celebrating the solidarity and nurturing skills of black women.[63] Very soon the popular emergence of many other extraordinary black feminist writers, like Toni Morrison, Ntozake Shange, Gayl Jones, Gloria Naylor and Alice Walker, produced far bleaker stories which were passionately critical of insensitive, cruel and abusive black men, attempting to assert their manhood through brutalizing women.[64] Yet, like the lesbian poet and polemicist Audre Lorde, they were not prepared to give up on men: 'As a people we must certainly work together to end our common oppression. . . . Black male consciousness must be raised so that he realizes that sexism and woman-hating are critically dysfunctional to his liberation as a Black man because they arise out of the same constellation that engenders racism and homophobia, a constellation of intolerance for difference.'[65] Similarly, the black feminist Combahee River Collective summed up their politics as a double struggle: 'we struggle together with black men against racism, while we also struggle with black men against sexism.'[66]

Much the same sentiments were expressed by black feminists in Britain where, as Valerie Amos and Pratibha Parmar point out, sexuality has often played a far less central role for them than for white feminists, since issues of racism and personal survival loom so large for black women. They too accused white feminists of playing into the hands of white racists by remaining silent when racist hysteria is whipped up through media images of black muggers and rapists, and when choosing to stage their protests against violence against women by marching through black areas.[67] More succinctly, Rhonda Cobham declared: 'Black women do not spend their lives putting down men.'[68] In fact, black feminists, like white feminists, did not speak with one voice: Michele Wallace wrote of the 'profound distrust, if not hatred' between black men and women in the USA, in a way which held out little hope for change, while Linda Bellos was one of the most active and militant revolutionary feminists in London.[69] Nevertheless, by the close of the seventies, the heightened antagonisms around men and sexuality tearing apart many feminist gatherings were predominantly a white feminist impasse.

Wars without end

From a heterosexual perspective, matters only got worse in the early 1980s as North American feminists like Robin Morgan, Andrea Dworkin and Catharine MacKinnon began to launch their campaign against pornography. Not only was Dworkin insistently certain that male power 'authentically originates in the penis', but that the penis as 'a symbol of terror' is even more significant than the gun, the knife, the bomb or the fist.[70] In the USA Women Against Pornography groups grew rapidly from 1978, reducing women's oppression to male sexuality and seeing the goals of male sexuality mirrored in the most violent and degraded images of female exploitation. Moreover, campaigners like Dworkin, warning women of 'the ways in which we are complicit in our own degradation', were now suggesting that women's pursuit of their own sexual pleasure could itself be dangerous: 'male sexuality does in fact colonize us, set our limits . . . we in fact are defined by this male sexuality.'[71] Important in this analysis of sexuality is the denial of any significant change in the lives of women: 'I think the situation of women basically is ahistorical,' Dworkin confirms, and MacKinnon agrees: 'Our status as a group relative to men has almost never, if ever, been changed from what it is.'[72] Now that sexuality is seen as the single source of women's oppression, we know just what feminism has achieved: nothing at all!

Ann Snitow and other socialist feminists in the USA soon threw light on this new pessimism, explaining why the near exclusive prioritizing of pornography should have occurred just when it did. It was at the moment when the mood of the women's movement changed – especially in the USA where the feminist anti-pornography campaigns first flourished. Having just witnessed the defeat of women's rights to state-funded abortion, won only four years earlier, the Equal Rights Amendment (ERA) was coming under serious attack from the growing strength of the New Right, soon to sweep Reagan to power and to derail the ERA. (Anti-pornography campaigning was the single feminist issue which the Right had no wish to attack; on the contrary, they welcomed and supported it, since censorship of sexual explicitness had always been central to their own moral agenda.) With poorer women facing greater hardship, welfare services being removed, and the conservative backlash against radical politics in the ascendency everywhere, 'pornography' served for some women as the symbol of women's defeat. From that time on many feminists would become less confidently on the offensive, less able to celebrate women's potential strength, less concerned with wider issues of equality, more concerned with a narrower, defensive politics linking sex and violence. 'Pornography' provided its authorization.

Ironically, however, as some black feminists have pointed out, it was white, middle-class women, rather than the real victims of Reagan's conservative agenda – black and ethnic minority women – who formed and led the anti-pornography movement. Cherrié Moraga and Amber Hollibaugh commented, tellingly: 'working-class and Third World women can be seen actively engaged in sex-related issues that *directly* affect life-and-death concerns of women (abortion, sterilization abuse, health care, welfare, etc.).'[73] They are not, however, very visible in the single-issue, sex-related anti-pornography campaign. Or, as Carla Freccero suggested, it is because white feminists already have most of their basic needs met, that they can afford to highlight their sexual experiences as the most restraining, if not sole, source of women's oppression.[74]

However, the new force of feminist sexual pessimism was both inadequate and strange in other ways, quite apart from its lack of focus on class and race issues. For it was specifically in relation to matters involving women's sexual autonomy and reproductive rights that second-wave feminism had been most influential and successful. Through exposing how double standards and sexist assumptions controlled and constrained women's lives and sexuality, *in the name of* women's sexual liberation, feminists had made it possible to define and object to 'sexual harassment', re-define 'rape' and prioritize the need to eliminate violence against women. At the same time they had been demanding women's control over their own bodies, seeking changes in their relationships with men, and validating women's rights to an autonomous sexuality – with, or without, men. All this happened in ways which had, hitherto, been literally inconceivable. 'Part of my attraction to feminism involved that right to be a sexual person,' Amber Hollibaugh muses in 1981. 'I'm not sure where that history got lost.' 'We didn't win,' Deidre English replied, 'We made great gains, but we had enormous losses. Now we're in a period in which a lot of women are looking only at the losses.'[75]

Despite its prominence, there were always many feminists who strongly opposed what they saw as the troubling simplicities of anti-pornography feminism. Like Carole Vance, they would agree that the 'hallmark of sexuality is its complexity: its multiple meanings sensations and connections.'[76] On this view, any condemnation of sexual practices and imagery as oppressive and exploitative, unless clearly opposed to what was described as the 'male sexual model', serves more to strengthen the rigidity of traditional assumptions cementing sex and gender than to weaken them. These predominantly academic socialist feminists organized the first comprehensive re-assessment of the whole complex edifice of sexuality at the Barnard Conference, 'Towards a Politics of Sexuality' in the USA in 1982. In place of the single focus on the danger from men and the degradation of women in anti-pornography feminism, they aimed to provide a forum for a diversity of feminist views on sexuality. They hoped to address not only the damage caused by men's violence, but the sexual timidity, self-doubt and anxiety which the fear of violence could create in women. Such sexual fears, they believed, were fed by many other intra-psychic, interpersonal, cultural and social factors around intimacy, dependency, aggression and possessiveness, and could be mobilized by conservative campaigns against 'deviance' and 'degeneracy': 'Unarticulated, irrational reactions', Carole Vance, the co-ordinator of the conference, announced in the keynote address, 'wreak havoc on our movement and at the same time are cleverly used against us by the Right.'[77] Outside, havoc was indeed being wreaked.

The conference was picketted by the Coalition for a Feminist Sexuality and Against Sadomasochism (Women Against Violence Against Women, Women Against Pornography and New York Radical Feminists), incensed that they had not been invited to participate and by one workshop promising a 'Speakout on Politically Incorrect Sex'. The conference Diary had already been seized and impounded by the Barnard College authorities for its sexually explicit graphics and text. Participation in the event proved a near disaster for some speakers. Individual women were denounced and condemned, their employers contacted, careers and livelihoods threatened, as their feminist opponents deployed straightforwardly McCarthyite tactics to try to silence them.

Amidst all this sensationalized fuss, Vance's paper outlining the main themes and questions the conference hoped to address, seems a model of open and balanced reflection: 'We see the conference not as providing definitive answers, but as setting up a more useful framework within which feminist thought may proceed, an opportunity for participants to question some of their understandings and consider anew the complexity of the sexual situation.'[78] The paper carefully situated all possible discussion around women's diverse experiences of sexual agency and pleasure, and their continuing need for personal autonomy and choice, within social contexts of gender hierarchy where restriction, controls and dangers, though shifting in nature, have always surrounded expressions of female sexuality: 'To focus only on pleasure and gratification ignores the patriarchal structure in which women act, yet to speak only of sexual violence and oppression ignores women's experience of sexual agency and choice and unwittingly increases the sexual terror and despair in which women live.'[79] Denying the variety and significance of women's pleasure, she would later add, neither empowers women nor makes the world a safer place, it merely denies the fact that sexuality can be a site of affirmation, struggle and power for women – whatever their sexual orientation.

Vance also outlined the need for more sophisticated feminist theory and methodology to grapple with the different types of analysis essential for approaching sexuality. These ranged from recording women's experiences of bodily pleasures and exploring the complexities of individual psychic life to studying the power dynamics of interpersonal relations and the social regulation of sexual behaviour. Her important message was to little avail. Divisions between North American feminists would only deepen. A more innovative and sophisticated theorizing, defending sexual pleasure while condemning the surrounding dangers, might perhaps – on balance – win out in intellectual debates among academic feminists. Some feminist sex radicals, identifying themselves as the Lesbian Sex Mafia, would persist and provoke (in turn feeling shunned by) other feminists with their sponsoring of sexual role-playing and the exploration of consensual lesbian sadomaschism. But a more visible campaigning feminism continued to strengthen its own forward march, directing individual fears, anxiety, guilt, frustration and personal unhappiness back to what it saw as the main agenda: men's abuse of power symbolized in pornography.[80]

No longer one step ahead, but simply *out of step* with many women's dreams and desires, feminists were becoming either more pessimistic or more silent about sexual pleasure – especially if heterosexual – just when the mainstream media and women themselves had adopted their earlier, once confidently radical, enthusiasm for sex. From the close of the 1960s sexual double standards were rapidly declining, women and men alike were coming to see sexual pleasure as both necessary and important, quite apart from marriage, babies or even, at least when young, any permanent commitment. Marital advice books were replaced by popular sex manuals, and women's magazines, like *Cosmopolitan*, always carried at least one feature article on women's sexuality in every issue. In Britain, its agony aunt Irma Kurtz, contrasting sharply with her predecessors in women's magazines who had always extolled women's selflessness ('it's never too late to make *him* happy'), now tirelessly urged women to put their *own* needs and interests before any man's ('don't be afraid of offending him').[81]

Reflecting the new liberal approval of women's sexuality outside marriage (with all its patriarchal legacies), marriage rates in most Western countries were dropping, divorce rates were rapidly climbing, many women were choosing to cohabit, postponing parenting till their careers were established and, overall, having fewer children between the 1960s and the 1980s.[82] Married women, it seemed, were also receiving greater satisfaction from their sexual activity with husbands. Morton Hunt's survey of sexual behaviour in the USA in the early 1970s reported far greater variety and frequency of sexual activity compared with Alfred Kinsey's survey a generation earlier: 90 per cent of wives claimed to be happy with their sex lives, three-quarters content with its frequency, one-quarter wanting more.[83] Blumstein and Schwartz reported almost identical findings from their broad-based survey in the early 1980s, with women and men displaying similar sexual preferences, desiring frequent sexual activity and, whether heterosexual, gay or lesbian, discontented if sex was infrequent. As the 100,000 women polled in the mainstream women's magazine *Redbook* seemed to confirm: 'women are becoming increasingly active sexually and are less likely to accept an unsatisfactory sex life as part of the price to be paid for marriage.' British surveys in the 1980s also showed more married women having affairs, apparently reflecting women's heightened sexual expectations and sense of their own sexual options.[84]

There was thus a dramatic lack of fit between what one very visible group of feminists were saying about women's experience of sexual victimization, and what the overwhelming majority of women were reporting as their experiences of sex, and its importance in their lives. However, as Blumstein and Schwartz themselves admit, while the gap between women and men's sex lives and desires was narrowing and more marriages seemed happier, this was perhaps only because of the very high rates of divorce. One in two marriages in the USA in the 1980s were headed for divorce, the majority initiated by women unhappy with the 'unliberated' behaviour of their husbands – behaviour which most certainly includes significant amounts of violence against women.[85] This is the discontent which Shere Hite could tap into to produce her very different survey *Women and Love* in 1987, where she reports that 98 per cent of women desire fundamental change in their relationships with men, wanting greater intimacy and more emotional support.[86] And when women's frustrations do lead to divorce, women (and children) suffer very real economic problems, indeed some feminists have suggested: 'A woman may be just a divorce away from poverty.' The rise in teenage pregnancy would also leave many young women and their children in dire straits.

The persistence of the power relations of gender certainly affect women's sexual experiences, and – when trapped within violent relationships – may leave women very miserable. But overall, women's vulnerability today most directly reflects their failure to achieve economic emancipation (so many still ghettoized into low paid and irregular 'women's work'). Women may indeed end up feeling betrayed or violated, and many are impoverished in relation to men. But the most chronic and immediate problems women are trying to grapple with today are, as we shall see again in the concluding chapter, the lack of adequate welfare services, almost no public assistance with childcare, and deteriorating job prospects. Even Hite was to learn that the women in her survey valued their social and financial independence above all else: '87 per cent of women who are or have been financially dependent feel unhappy in this situation.' And yet at the same time, 84 per cent of Hite's sample still said that love relationships should come first in life (though only 19 per cent said that they actually did).[87] Until feminists can once again tap into the hopes as well as the fears, the joys as well as the pain, of women's actual desires, they will appear – as they have recently seemed to many young women – the leaders of a new type of puritanism.[88] The collapse of *Spare Rib* in the early nineties was but one sign of this malaise.

While the voices recognized by mainstream culture as 'feminist' remain those busy demonizing male lust and pornography as a metaphor for evil, it will not be possible to find any confident – or even hopeful – popular affirmation of a feminist sexual politics. Erica Jong, having made her name and fortune writing the adventurous woman's fantasy of a 'zipless fuck' with a stranger, is now welcoming AIDS for having made sex 'a little more mysterious and precious again', heading us back to a time when 'many women were glad for an excuse to turn away from it'.[89] Germaine Greer, having once urged all women to fuck more freely, is now advising us to welcome the menopause for finally unlocking the 'leg-irons' which hobble us: the shackles of our sexuality.[90] She has moved from exhorting her women readers to 'embrace the penis', to embracing – and promoting – celibacy, while writing paeans to motherhood, nature and gardening. The circle is complete – erotomania to erotophobia – from the media's favourite feminist.

3. The coital imperative: sexology and sex research

Sexology is the science of sex. It is impartial, empirical, and, in the manner of all science, nonjudgmental.

John Money[1]

Perhaps one day . . . people will be surprised at the eagerness with which we went about pretending to rouse from its slumber a sexuality which everything – our discourses, our customs, our institutions, our regulation, our knowledge – was busy producing in the light of day and broadcasting to noisy accompaniment.

Michel Foucault[2]

History repeats itself as men appear to have appropriated the 'scientific' study of sexuality, while women have concentrated upon its social implications.

Martha Vicinus[3]

Those of us who watched in anguish as the women's movement tore itself apart over sexuality at the close of the 1970s, increasingly came to think that part of the problem was the difficulty of conceptualizing sexuality. 'It is impossible to overemphasize just how basic the problem of sexuality *is* for women,' Ruby Rich reflected in her overview of feminism and sexuality in the USA in the 1980s. Yet feminists 'have failed to develop an active feminist theory of sexuality.'[4]

In fact, a decade earlier, a few feminists like Juliet Mitchell were already reporting the impasse women quickly reached trying to discuss sexuality. Her Women and Sexuality group faced a problem: 'We've found we just don't know what sexuality is at all, at the moment. A sort of panic starts in your mind, you wonder, what is this subject I'm trying to think about.'[5] She was explaining why she had turned to Freud to take her beyond the crudely biological or physiological framework in which our culture thinks about sexuality. Other feminists would soon be turning, for much the same reasons, to Michel Foucault, the most significant theorist of sexuality since Freud. A critic of Freud, he rejected the type of repression model which feminists had first adopted (combining Reich with Masters and Johnson) in favour of an analysis stressing the multiplicity of the discourses and dynamics of power which construct sexuality.

To comprehend the force and tenacity of feminist conflicts around sex, however, we need to return to the origins of current understandings of sexuality. Only then can we see how the ongoing debates of the present are harnessed to the past, as today's intensely commercialized interest in sexual matters contends with the equally intensely disputed place of sex in our lives. Recycling old debates and repeating old divisions, feminists have much to learn from looking at the shifting understandings of sex and sexuality over the last hundred years. Digging deeper into the history of sexuality begins to explain why it remains so hard, and yet so necessary, to theorize sexuality *autonomously*, separately from gender – if only to see the possible diversity of their connections. Feminists have battled with each other over sexuality precisely because of the conceptual and practical difficulties of trying to separate sex and gender. Both the most traditional patriarchal thinking, and the most recent forms of radical feminist theory, equate male sexuality with male dominance. The heterosexual genital act, they agree, establishes the truth of the equation. So is the history of heterosexuality the history of male dominance? It's a little more complicated.

Defining nature: sex as energy

It is some decades now since scholars looking at the history of the body suggested that the centrality assigned to sexuality in representing that body is a modern concept. 'Sexuality', as a thing in itself, only makes its appearance in the *Oxford English Dictionary* from 1800, while 'homosexuality' and subsequently 'heterosexuality' were not invented as sexual categories, and used publicly, until the very end of the nineteenth century.[6] Before then, it is suggested, there were references to various types of sex acts and sexualized parts of the body, but not the idea of sexuality as an inner force or essence.[7]

Western approaches to sexual matters fall into three dominant paradigms, each of which continues to exert its influence even as it is replaced by the next. In pre-industrial European societies the regulation of sexual behaviour, like moral behaviour generally, was primarily a religious or spiritual issue. Christian teaching explains the purpose of sex – for procreation – and the place for sex – in holy matrimony. With the birth of the scientific study of 'sexuality' in mid-nineteenth century Europe, however, doctors and scientists would gradually usurp the role of the Church in teaching courts and communities the nature and causes of sexual normality and sexual deviance. The authoritative voice on sexual matters moved away from the spiritual arena to talk of 'nature' and the imperatives of biology: the sexual became synonymous with the biological. This second paradigm has been seriously challenged – although not overturned – in recent decades. Perceptions of 'nature' and 'biology' are now themselves explored as 'social constructions'; the old binaries biological/social, nature/nurture, sex/gender have been undermined. On this view, our experiences of the body and its desires are produced externally through the range of social discourses and institutions which describe and manipulate them.

Although spiritual, biological and social 'imperatives' have all been used to explain and regulate sexual matters, it is the biological which has had the longest and most tenacious grip on conceptions of sexuality in modern times. The reason is simple: the 'biological', once appropriately atomized and quantified, achieves the privileged authority and legitimation reserved for 'science' in modern cultures. It is always important, Paul Abramson reminded sexologists at the beginning of the 1990s, 'to reaffirm the necessity of a rigorous sexual science' and not to leave sexuality 'relegated to poetry and fiction'.[8]

The dictates of biology or nature have thus proved tenacious, yet also malleable for social and political uses. Oscar Wilde understood: 'The only thing one really knows about human nature is that it changes. Change is the one quality we can predicate of it.'[9] Catching up with Wilde a century later, the historian Thomas Laqueur elegantly documents these shifting constructions of the nature of sex. For thousands of years he argues, in *Making Sex*, Western medical texts and popular thinking had adopted and depicted a homologous or one-sex model of primary sexual characteristics – except that women's genitals were seen as turned inward rather than growing outside the body.[10] 'Turn outward the woman's, turn inward, so to speak, and fold double the man's, and you will find the same in both in every respect,' Galen explained in the second century AD.[11] As doggerel still around in the nineteenth century, at a time when scientific opinion was decisively inverting its former conceptions, summed it up: 'Women are but men turned inside out.' Although male and female genitals and their functioning were seen as fundamentally the same up until the seventeenth century (the vagina being portrayed as an inturned version of the penis and women's orgasm and ejaculation from the ovaries thought necessary for conception to occur), women's anatomical equipment was nevertheless judged less perfect, an inferior version of that of men. Ideas of sexual sameness thus served, throughout these centuries, to support notions of women's inferiority rather than of women's equivalence to men.

Only from the late eighteenth century, Laqueur argues, was sex 'as we know it' invented.[12] By 1800 the idea of male and female bodies and passions as essentially similar began to come 'under devastating attack'. Genital and reproductive organs were no longer depicted as similar, but rather as different: 'different in every conceivable respect of body and soul, in every physical and moral aspect.'[13] By this time it had been discovered that female orgasm was no longer necessary for procreation, and women's sexual passions, it was soon being extensively asserted, were the opposite of those of men. Laqueur's main thesis, however, is that these shifts in interpretations of the female and male body bore little relation to actual empirical 'discoveries'.

Indeed, far from fresh evidence of intrinsic sexual opposition being observed in the nineteenth century – when the idea of sexual incommensurability reached its height – this was a time when the evidence for a morphologically androgynous embryo was first discovered. Support for certain sorts of sexual homologies was thus actually stronger than ever before. Rather, Laqueur illustrates, political, economic and cultural transformations of the late eighteenth century, not scientific advances, created the context where sexual differences needed to be articulated to bolster shifting gender arrangements: 'no one was very interested in looking at the anatomical and concrete physiological differences between the sexes until such differences became *politically* important.'[14] It was in response to the developing democratic ideals of 'citizenship', women's participation and interest in the French Revolution of 1789, the rise of women's suffrage movements in Britain in the 1870s and women's assertions of democratic rights in the USA, that the thoughts of male philosophers like Rousseau would be used to articulate the separate spheres of men and women. Mary Poovey, Mary Jacobus, Emily Martin and many other feminist scholars have shown how scientific accounts of sexual difference shift in accordance with economic changes and men's contests for power.[15]

Woman, unlike man (the model citizen), was now depicted as shackled to an essentially destructive and demanding reproductive biology, disqualifying her from higher education, most professions and public life more generally. In these Victorian discourses of the female body, women were always at the mercy of their wombs and their debilitating menstrual flow. Knowledge of women's spontaneous ovulation, and conception without orgasm, were used to construct women's nature as reproductive and nurturing, not sexual and passionate. Women were never free from the pressures of their sex, always in danger of provoking male sexual arousal, although essentially self-sacrificing and passive. They were *the* sex, and yet in most Victorian thinking, curiously, themselves asexual.[16]

Such were the physiological thoughts and metaphors accompanying the birth of sexology, with its attempts to observe and classify what it saw as the overpowering instinctive force of human sexuality – overpowering, at least, in the male of the species. In 1886 Richard von Krafft-Ebing, professor of psychiatry at the University of

Vienna, published the first edition of one of its founding texts, *Psychopathia Sexualis*. By the time of its 12th edition, in 1903, he had meticulously recorded 238 case histories detailing the different forms of sexual 'degeneracy' and 'abnormality' afflicting the sexual offenders coming to the attention of the Austrian courts. His elaborate classificatory system aimed to separate off natural sexuality, directed towards procreative ends, from its unnatural or perverse forms – homosexuality, sadism, rape and lust murder. Just over a decade later the first volume of Havelock Ellis's influential seven-volume *Studies in the Psychology of Sex*, on 'sexual inversion', would appear in Britain, and face prosecution as 'lewd and obscene'. Both writers saw sexual behaviour, with all its destructive potential (stressed by Krafft-Ebing), or multiple variations (stressed by Ellis), as the biological core of human character, and the most powerful force in human society.[17]

These pioneers of sex research equated sex and gender, and saw male and female sexuality as fundamentally opposed: the one aggressive and forceful, the other responsive and maternal. A sexual and social reformer, Ellis upheld the possibility and importance of female genital sexual pleasure. He criticized the strand of Victorian doctors who, like William Acton, had pathologized sexual pleasure in women as 'unnatural' – the cause of a variety of physical and mental diseases from epilepsy to hysteria. Yet the biological metaphors of his day meant that Ellis too saw women as creatures weakened by their reproductive biology, since the 'worm' of menstruation 'gnaws periodically at the roots of life'.[18]

The rigidly gendered sexual polarities of late nineteenth-century thought contained no space for any notion of women's sexuality as independent from men's. Insisting upon the reproductive purpose of sexual activity, the only female pleasure which could be recognized was one responsive to male initiative: the maiden 'must be kissed into a woman', Ellis explained.[19] Lesbian sexual pleasures would suggest a different narrative. But her active sexuality was, by definition now, a type of gender inversion. It had, as Krafft-Ebing put it, 'the stamp of masculine character', always to be suspected in women with short hair, who engaged in male sports or pastimes, and in opera singers.[20] She would be the type, Ellis agreed, more sympathetically, who was congenitally boyish, deep-voiced, capable of whistling, tending towards a heightened artistic and moral development. This 'mannish lesbian' would be celebrated and displayed to the world by Ellis's friend and supporter, Radclyffe Hall, in *The Well of Loneliness* (1928). Her semi-autobiographical heroine, 'Stephen Gordon', had the body of the newly identified female invert, 'with its muscular shoulders, its small compact breasts and its slender flanks of an athlete'.[21] Lesbianism was also seen by these writers, and in contemporary thinking and iconography more generally, as linked to feminism.

Ellis promoted the scientific study of sexuality in Britain from the 1890s both to stress its pivotal place in human life and society, and to rescue sexual behaviour from the general horror and denunciation with which it was customarily associated in his day. (Magnus Hirschfeld had embarked upon a similar mission, in a similar context, in Germany. He would come to fulfil his own ambitions, for a while, when he finally set up the Institute for Sex Science in Berlin, in 1919.) Concern with the regulation of sexual behaviour, tied in with what would soon be overwhelming scientific support for eugenics and the breeding of the fittest and best, had grown rapidly following the acceptance of Darwin's account of 'sexual selection' for evolutionary advantage in his *Descent of Man*, published in 1874. Sexual and social fears and panics intermeshed and heightened in the closing decades of the nineteenth century. The struggle to prevent imperial decline as Western nations competed for world dominance in the late nineteenth century tied in with a multitude of new social anxieties and moral panics. These accompanied the apparently inexorable spread of poverty and violence in metropolitan life, the growth of large-scale workers' movements alongside the emergence of the women's suffrage movement, all at a time when syphilis continued to destroy the minds and bodies of many men, women and children, and Jack the Ripper stalked the streets of late Victorian London.[22]

One response to these various upheavals was the growth of sexual purity crusades, especially in Britain, Germany and the United States. These campaigns sought to stamp out sexual immorality and prostitution as responsible for the spread of venereal disease, and condemned masturbation as the cause of physical, mental and moral decline. Victorian doctors almost all warned of the dangers of masturbation, or 'self-abuse', as destroying men's strength and vitality and as a possible pathway to homosexuality.[23] Such alarming discourses of sexuality, in both popular and medical writing, not only fed deeply misogynist fears of female temptresses, especially in the form of servants or prostitutes, but generated a host of psychically crippling anxieties in men around strength and manhood.

Havelock Ellis and the other social reformers who supported his British Society for the Study of Sex Psychology or its affiliated World League for Sexual Reform hoped to weaken some of the burden of fear then accompanying masturbation and sexuality more generally. But assumptions of the potentially dangerous and deleterious effects of men's failure to control what was seen as their uniquely powerful sexual drive would continue as a dominant theme right up to the mid-twentieth century, despite the growth of opposing discourses and practices.

Early battles between the sexes

The pioneers of sexology played their role in re-affirming male domination as biological inevitability, portraying 'the sex act', understood as heterosexual genital engagement, as its exemplary moment. A woman's sexuality, although given a more autonomous existence, still required a man to initiate and release it. In the bedroom, as in life, women remained subordinated to the needs and desires of men. With women's sexuality seen as passive, diffuse and pre-eminently maternal, the use of a certain level of aggression in male courtship was necessary, Ellis wrote, to overcome 'normal feminine modesty' – though he criticized male selfishness and brutality in the sex act: 'The sexual impulse in woman is fettered by an inhibition which has to be conquered . . . her wooer in every act of courtship has the enjoyment of conquering afresh an oft-won woman.'[24]

However, men's definitions of biology and the female body were not entirely determining of women's own experiences, nor entirely uncontested, even at a time when there was so very little social space, or discursive possibility, for women to live out or imagine any alternative. In her richly detailed and stimulating research on the freethinkers who participated in a mixed discussion group on the topic of sexuality in London between 1885 and 1889 (the Men and Women's Club), Judith Walkowitz shows the women at times disputing the views of the men on questions of sexual difference and heterosexuality. Karl Pearson, the Club's founder, insisted upon a fully 'scientific' approach for understanding individual behaviour and sexual relations which was at the time synonymous with the ideology of Darwinism. What this entailed, as elaborated in his paper 'The Woman Question', was the need to assess the natural role and capacities of women for improving their race: 'Race-evolution had implanted in women a desire for children, as it has implanted in men a desire for women.'[25] Darwin himself had seen men as more evolved than women, since they were the sex more actively engaged in the struggle for sexual selection. All the women who discussed his paper agreed with Pearson on the fundamental difference between male and female sexuality. The women were also well aware of the dangers of men's coercive sexuality, a sentiment expressed most powerfully by the Fabian Emma Brooke in a private note to Pearson: 'The truth is, you men have murdered love. . . . You have killed the inspiration in women's hearts by abuses of all kind.'[26]

A minority of women, however, like the feminist Olive Schreiner – who chided Pearson for probing the position of women while ignoring the investigation of men – as well as Brooke, felt that he had exaggerated the maternal instinct in women and neglected women's sexual passions. Schreiner, like her socialist friend Eleanor Marx, stressed the importance of female sexuality, and dreamed of a utopian world of 'perfect mental and physical' union and equality between the sexes, insisting that men too were alienated from the potential of their own human and sexual development.[27] (Both Schreiner and Marx, however, were to suffer deeply as they tried to live out their lives as sexually emancipated women who loved men.) Other women in the group, like the journalist Henrietta Muller, were more in line with the views held by most educated women of the day. They fully agreed that men were biologically hypersexual, but argued that women's natural self-restraint and passionlessness provided them with the type of 'moral strength' which society now needed. Advancing a theme soon to be widely circulated by suffragettes like Christabel Pankhurst, Muller believed that it was time for women to replace men as the dominant sex in society.

As we saw in the last chapter, these disagreements between radical freethinkers over attitudes to sexuality would become part of a recurrent debate between women, and especially between feminists, which continues as fiercely as ever over a century later. The dominant view of women at that time, however, was to stress sexual purity and female moral superiority. Prostitution was the ubiquitous metaphor for social disease and decay, the wretched fate of female victims of male lust and an abomination which should be eliminated. On the eve of the First World War, Christabel Pankhurst was busy writing her series of essays *The Great Scourge and How to End It*, denouncing male sexual behaviour for spreading venereal disease, and insisting upon the need to control it and eliminate the spread of prostitution: 'Self control for men who can exert it! Medical aid for those who cannot!'[28] She claimed that most men had gonorrhoea and many had syphilis, for which she neither saw, nor ever wished to see, any cure – other than 'the way of purity'. The only natural solution to sexual disease, Pankhurst announced, was 'Votes for Women and Chastity for Men', the former being seen as the precondition for the latter.

In the early decades of the twentieth century many first-wave feminists were inclined to agree with Christabel Pankhurst's conclusions: 'There can be no mating between the spiritually developed woman of this new day and men who in thought and conduct with regard to sex matters are their inferiors.'[29] Other feminists, like Francis Swiney, also stressed that men's sexual relationships with women were inevitably demeaning and destructive, and urged women to raise 'sex relations from the physical to the spiritual plane'.[30] Not only did social purity feminists support the arrest and punishment of prostitutes, but some were to join in the policing of working-class morals. A few former suffragettes enlisted with Damer Dawson's Women's Police Volunteers (later 'Service') and the Women's Patrols, both operating from 1914, harassing prostitutes and courting couples alike, arresting anyone they could find indulging in sexual activity in public – whether for money or for free.[31]

Yet then, as now, other feminists – although a minority – always resisted such condemnation of sex. The young Rebecca West and the women like her who wrote for the feminist journal *The Freewoman* between 1911 and 1913 passionately rejected what they saw as the obsession with sexual puritanism and the vote, arguing instead in favour of sexual freedom, communal living, and any cultural or political projects for advancing the position of women. *The Freewoman*, West reflected many years later, performed an immense service for women by trying to shatter the romantic pretence that they existed 'in a bland state of desireless contentment'.[32] 'If this romantic conception had been true,' she continued, 'there would have have been no need for the emancipation of women.'[33] In the United States the anarchist writer Emma Goldman was also urging women to fight for sexual freedom, and to refuse to become subservient to husband, church or state, just as Victoria Woodhull and Elizabeth Cady Stanton, before her, had asserted the importance of women's sexual pleasures and desires.[34]

At a time when there was little access to reliable contraception and women were still barred from most professions on the grounds of their sex, prospects for economic independence from men were extremely limited, and it was to prove a near impossibility for most women, either at the close of the nineteenth or in the opening years of the twentieth century, to hold on to the belief that they could be both sexually liberated and equal in their relationships with men. More realistic, it might seem, was the position of the French socialist feminist Madame Pelletier, who wrote in 1908 that she intended to remain celibate 'because under present conditions sexual relations are a source of debasement for the married woman and of scorn for the unmarried.'[35]

Yet as feminist historians Linda Gordon and Ellen DuBois have suggested, although the majority of first-wave feminists were realistically concerned with protecting women from the various dangers of male sexuality – disgrace, disease, forced sex and unwanted pregnancy – what is more surprising is the number of women who resisted the sexually repressive culture of the time: the young sexual 'delinquents' who flaunted their sexuality, the women who passed as men to take female lovers and even the 'respectable, middle-class, married women who had orgasms more than they were supposed to'.[36] And while many nineteenth-century feminists had rejected any talk of birth control in favour of 'voluntary motherhood' – to make it easier for a woman to reject her husband's unwanted sexual demands and restrict his carefree indulgence in extra-marital sex – a new generation of feminists, though never large in numbers, would soon distance themselves completely from such views in the relatively affluent and more permissive decade of the 1920s. This new permissiveness, especially amongst groups of middle-class women, as they gained the vote (in Britain in 1918) and the right to enter professions hitherto barred to them (in Britain in 1919), was partly a response to growing awareness of the work of sexologists and contact with Freudian ideas.

Political activists, like Stella Browne and Dora Russell in Britain, Margaret Sanger, Crystal Eastman, Elizabeth Gurley Flynn and many more in the USA, were to embrace birth control as a central plank of their feminist aspirations for women's rights to control their bodies and their lives. Birth control was taken up, although never without considerable dissent and embarrassment, by some socialist and feminist organizations from the 1920s. Abortion, however, would remain a taboo area right up until the 1960s, with Stella Browne almost a lone voice prepared to argue for its importance, and refer to her own experience of it.[37] More feminists were, however, vigorously asserting women's rights to sexual pleasure and fulfilment in the immediate inter-war years, at least until they were interrupted by the depression of the 1930s. Relying on contemporary ideas of the 'natural' basis of sex and engaged in battles against the social purity attitudes of older feminists and the denial of women's sexual autonomy more generally, they would do so, predominantly, from an intensely heterosexual perspective. Illustrating this new rhetoric of sexual emancipation for women, Crystal Eastman wrote in the *Birth Control Review* of 1918:

> Feminists are not nuns. . . . We want to love and be loved, and most of us want children, one or two at least. But we want our love to be joyous and free – not clouded with ignorance and fear. . . . We want this precious sex knowledge not just for ourselves, the conscious feminists . . . we want it for all women.[38]

In fighting for the significance of women's heterosexual pleasure, these sex radicals became increasingly uncritical of men, except in terms of attacking the male dominance of the labour force and the political arena – especially as the first wave of feminism began to fragment in the 1920s. Although in principle they asserted, like Stella Browne, 'the variety and variability of the sexual impulse among women', in practice birth control feminists used arguments which tended to belittle the celibacy and 'artificial or substitute homosexuality' they believed older feminists encouraged.[39] Older feminists had mostly chosen to ignore or deny the issue of women's sexual desire altogether, but their immediate followers were not yet able to create a language to assert women's full sexual potential, separately from male-defined and reproductive ends. It would never prove easy.

From difference to sameness

Whether feminists demanded or decried the expression of women's active desire for sex with men, metaphors of male conquest and female submission have remained, to this day, tied in with conceptions of heterosexuality. And yet twentieth-century sexology would increasingly challenge assumptions of sexual difference, provoking conservative reaction, even as it sought ways of securing existing gender patterns through the institution of marriage and the promotion of the pleasures of heterosexuality.

A move away from an emphasis on the spiritual companionship of marriage to the sexualization of love was characteristic of Western societies in the early twentieth century. Inadvertently accompanying this was the steady erosion of emphasis on sexual difference, the emergence of complex relationships between new and proliferating sexual identities, and an ever more consumer-oriented society.[40] True, those doctors, psychologists and sex therapists who first made use of the new sexual science wanted to stress the enormous difference between male and female sexualities. They were eager to teach men the skills necessary to *initiate* women into sexual responsiveness within marriage. The most successful at the enterprise was the Dutch gynaecologist, Theodor Van de Velde, credited with inventing the modern sex advice manual, who would sell over a million copies of his *Ideal Marriage*, first published in English in 1928, and remaining popular for the next half century. In it Van de Velde, while acknowledging the importance of the clitoris and women's multi-orgasmic capacity, displays the full measure of paternalistic prescriptiveness which was to characterize most marriage manuals: 'The wife *must* be taught, not only how to behave in coitus, but, above all, how and what to feel in this unique act!'[41] In sexual activity, Van de Velde agrees with Ellis, both men and women expect and desire male dominance. And while Van de Velde thought it up to the man to 'woo' his wife into sexual responsiveness, urging men on to ever greater virtuousity and resourcefulness in manipulating women to 'concert pitch' in pre-coital 'preliminaries', other marriage manuals of the 1920s were complaining more bitterly of female 'frigidity', and blaming 'sexual apathy and coldness in women' on their 'resistance' to being sexually aroused.[42]

Marriage advice manuals were also written by women for women, as well as for men. Indeed, Britain's birth control pioneer and sex reformer, Marie Stopes, published *Married Love* in 1918, and quickly sold over 400,000 copies before its rival *Ideal Marriage* appeared. Stopes was committed to ideas of women's sexual autonomy and condemned any sexual coercion from husbands, urging them to adapt to their wives' sexual needs and rhythms, while stressing the importance of female orgasm. Like her male colleagues, however, she too saw men as the sexual initiators, wrote of the need for simultaneous orgasm and, rather eccentrically, emphasized the beneficial effects of the absorption of vital sexual secretions, especially semen, in the 'post-coital embrace'.[43]

Helena Wright, publishing her sex advice manuals in the 1930s and 40s, would pay more attention to the role of the clitoris in female orgasm. But heterosexual coitus remained the central act of sexual significance in all the sex and marriage literature. And by the mid-century women were increasingly the ones to blame for any sexual failures in marriage – accused by female and male experts alike. The pressure was now on women to ensure that both they and their partners were enjoying coital sex. As Maxine Davis instructed wives in her best-selling *The Sexual Responsibility of Women* in 1957: 'A man's sexual nature is so dissimilar from her own that a wife has to give it full attention for a long time in order to understand it with her reflexes as well as her brains.' Nor should the dutiful wife expect a similar 'adaptation' from her husband, who at best may try 'to meet her half-way'.[44]

Although most sex advice literature was undoubtedly aimed at securing the woman's sexual interest in and responsibility for maintaining marriage and family life, while leaving her satisfaction strictly subordinate to and dependent upon that of her husband, the sexological literature it drew upon could prove a double-edged sword. This is apparent from the work and influence of Alfred Kinsey, who is seen as having revolutionized the scientific study of sex with his detailed interviews and statistical analysis of the sexual behaviour of over 12,000 white Americans. An entomological biologist in training and outlook, Kinsey fervently believed that all tensions between men and women, indeed conflict and prejudice generally, could be resolved through the acceptance of scientific data – which he saw as synonymous with biological truths.

There was, and is, nothing unusual in Kinsey's biological reductionism, nor in his over-riding faith that it held the key to resolving all human conflict and every social problem. But Kinsey's resolute rejection of any social, cultural, moral or political explanation in favour of biological accounts of the 'sexual outlets' he so meticulously documented did serve a particular cultural and political end: one, at that time, still at odds with the sexual conservatism of many around him. And although an overnight best-seller and immensely influential on subsequent research and thinking, the immediate response of professional and popular bodies to Kinsey's two publications, on men in 1949, and on women in 1953, was mainly that of outrage. In 1954 the American Medical Association would publicly condemn Kinsey for helping to create a 'wave of sex hysteria', and the Rockefeller Foundation terminated its funding for his Institute of Sex Research after learning that it was under congressional investigation for its support. Two years later Kinsey died of a heart attack.[45]

Meanwhile, when biology was interpreted in support of new social ends, it once again obligingly changed its nature. As Kinsey separated out the anatomical and physiological facts of 'our mammalian ancestry' from what he saw as the artificial impositions of social conditioning, he confirmed and extended the trend of twentieth-century sexology to see sex as a straightforward biological function 'which is acceptable in whatever form it is manifested'.[46] Once we know that bears do it, bats do it, and especially when we know the higher mammals do it, we know that it is 'natural', and hence that it is healthy. As he ponders the problem of distinguishing marital and premarital sex down among the animals where 'there is no institution of marriage', Kinsey concludes that the issue cannot be of any significance since 'physically and physiologically they are one and the same thing in man, just as they are in lower mammals'.[47] Such comprehensive approval of sex was all quite at odds with the multiple perils envisaged by his nineteenth-century predecessors, or the more ambivalent attitudes of Freud and the psychoanalytic tradition for whom sex was still enmeshed with perversion, neurosis, conflict, fears and danger.

Kinsey did his research at the height of the conservative Cold War and McCarthyite years of the late forties and fifties, in a climate of moral panic around any form of sexual (or political) 'deviance'. It was a time when his dogged determination to disclose the variability and fluidity of sexual behaviour provided an important weapon for sexual minorities who, like Kinsey himself, wanted to abolish the distinction between 'normal' and 'abnormal' sexuality and insist that sexual conventions should encompass sexual realities. For example, he reported that at least 37 per cent of the thousands of American males he interviewed had had some homosexual experience: 'more than one male in three of the persons that one might meet as he passes along a city street', he noted with the grammatical infelicity characteristic of sexology.[48]

It was also, above all, a time of renewed gender tension and heightened marital conflict as men in uniform left behind the male bonding of military life to settle down with newly domesticated women in aprons in the ubiquitous consumer-oriented celebration of family life, fanning the flames of post-war reconstruction. Sharing the general anxiety over the increased divorce rate of his day, Kinsey thought that it was not moral or religious denunciation of 'immorality' but scientific enlightenment which could teach men and women to be 'more effective marital partners'.[49] He believed, a decade ahead of the more widespread acceptance of such views, that a liberal rather than a repressive attitude to sexual expression was best suited to a more prosperous world in which men and women were no longer seen as occupying separate spheres, but encouraged to believe that they had become 'equal partners' – equal consumers – in the intellectual and social life of Western cultures.

Towards this end, and in a way he hoped would promote better understanding between the sexes and increase wives' orgasmic satisfaction (attributing much marital conflict to its absence), Kinsey emphasized the similarities between women and men: 'in spite of the widespread and oft-repeated emphasis on the supposed differences between female and male sexuality, we fail to find any anatomic or physiologic basis for such differences.'[50] The rhythmic muscular movements which Kinsey considered the central feature of sexual arousal and climax operated in identical ways in women and men, he stressed. And yet, using quantities of orgasms as his unit of measurement, and tracing their achievement to six possible sources (masturbation, nocturnal emission, heterosexual petting, heterosexual intercourse, homosexual relations and intercourse with animals), what he actually collected was massive evidence of sexual *dissimilarity*. Before marriage, Kinsey's average male had experienced 1,523 orgasms compared to the average woman's 223 orgasms. (They usually derived from only three sources, which thereby achieved an equal prominence in Kinsey's writing: masturbation, homosexual relations or heterosexual intercourse.) After marriage, almost all husbands achieved orgasm in almost all acts of intercourse, whereas at first only only 39 per cent of wives experienced orgasm always or almost always, and after twenty years only around 50 per cent almost always experienced orgasm in coital sex, while 15 per cent never had. (Women found greater orgasmic satisfaction in marriage if they had been enjoying pre-marital orgasms, masturbation being particularly relevant.)[51]

What is more, true to his biological leanings, Kinsey attributed these sexual differences not to cultural factors or power inequalities, but to some neurological factor creating a lower psychological 'conditionability' in women – evident in their lesser interest in pornography, voyeurism and cross-dressing. Women's supposed lesser conditionability to psychological stimuli, Kinsey further argued, could explain their more characteristic sexual passivity and men's greater interest in sexual variety and, at that time, much higher rates of extramarital activity. Kinsey went on to point out the different patterns of sexual ageing in men and women, making them seem, as Paul Robinson would later comment, more 'like ships passing in the night' than sexually compatible creatures.[52] (His survey revealed men reaching their peak sexual performance 'somewhere around 16 or 17 years of age', and in decline from their late teens; women, however, only reached their maximum level of sexual activity in their early thirties and retained it into their fifties and sixties.[53]) Kinsey's sexual similarity was, therefore, always similarity with a difference.

Despite his commitment to creating marital harmony, Kinsey's findings downgraded the significance of 'the sex act' in conventional heterosexual and marital practices. He reported that the clitoris was the main site of sexual response in women, and emphasized the physiological irrelevance of vaginal penetration by the penis to a woman's orgasmic achievement – although accepting that she may gain some peculiar psychological satisfaction from it. (He attacked what was described as the Freudian notion of the 'vaginal orgasm' as 'a biological impossibility'.[54]) Moreover, at a time when masturbation was still disparaged as an immature if not dangerous sexual practice, Kinsey raised it to a place of central importance, and declared it the most effective and certainly the most efficient route to female orgasm: women who masturbated reported achieving orgasm in 95 per cent of attempts – some 45 per cent in between one and three minutes.

The contradictory legacy of Kinsey's work for women was that, while completely ignoring issues like pregnancy and disease, and consistently downplaying the significance of sexual coercion by men of women and children, he was as determined a debunker of the penis and of the significance of 'the sex act' for female pleasure as his followers, Masters and Johnson, would prove to be, in a world of feminist revival a little less hostile to their message. His emphasis on the multiplicity of individual sexual outlets would come to serve the interests of those women, two decades on, eager to reject male sexual practices and marriage. His attempts to describe and explain human sexual activity as though its cultural significance and social meanings were essentially irrelevant, however, were comically blind to all its most troubling ingredients. Yet such biological reductionism remains an abiding ingredient of both sexological and popular discourses on sexuality to this day. Indeed, the search for scientific respectability through an emphasis on biomedical methods and theories has escalated rather than abated in recent years, reinforced by the greater funding available for medicalized projects.[55]

Sex therapy regimes

An even narrower focus on the minutiae of physiological response to explain 'the fundamentals of human sexual behavior' would appear in the next landmark of Western sexology, *Human Sexual Response*, published by Masters and Johnson in 1966 (and this time enthusiastically endorsed by the medical profession). They comprehensively recorded the bodily contractions, secretions, pulse rates and tissue colour changes occurring during more than 10,000 male and female orgasms, produced in the laboratory by 694 white, middle-class heterosexual men and women, building upon Kinsey's surveys to provide a new paradigm for Western studies of sexuality.

The first 'discovery' to be stressed by Masters and Johnson was their description of the 'entire sexual response cycle' in terms of four successive phases of sexual arousal: excitement, plateau, orgasm and resolution. Linked to this description was their ever firmer emphasis on sexual sameness: 'again and again attention will be drawn to direct parallels in human sexual response that exist to a degree never previously appreciated.'[56] Despite the scientific authority still accorded their four-phase description, however, subsequent researchers have found no reliable indicators of any such clearly separated sequences of arousal. It is, as Paul Robinson indicates, a model particularly irrelevant to male arousal patterns, designed merely to create 'the impression of precision where none exists'.[57] More significantly, as Janice Irvine argues in *Disorders of Desire*, although Masters and Johnson stress over and over again 'the *similarities, not the differences*, in the anatomy and physiology of the human sexual response', they do so only by interpreting their data selectively.[58] They in fact recorded so many physiological differences between men and women that their decision to emphasize similarities was clearly ideological.

Masters and Johnson choose to downplay the physiological differences between the sexual responses of men and women they measure so precisely (like the 'great variation in both intensity and duration of female orgasmic experience' compared to the more 'standard patterns of [male] ejaculatory reaction with less individual variation'), in order to construct largely meaningless 'neorophysiologic parallels' (penile erection, for example, is presented as 'the same' as vaginal lubrication!). They even conclude from their diverse physiological monitoring that not only physically, but also emotionally, 'men and women are incredibly and constantly similar'.[59] Yet the link between pulse rates, the speed of muscular contractions, colour changes in the labia minora in the immediate preorgasmic phase, and so forth, with people's emotional experiences, male or female, is never even vaguely sketched out: no attempt is made to supplement their physiological measurements with any type of psychological data. This does not, however, diminish their enthusiasm for solving any and all psychological problems men and women may encounter in relation to sexual experience. On the contrary, it is Masters and Johnson who provided the classic formulas for the contemporary explosion of sex therapy, in their next book, *Human Sexual Inadequacy*.[60]

Masters and Johnson are so eager to stress gender similarity because they can only conceive of equality in terms of similarity; indeed, the two concepts are for them synonymous. Only equality – meaning similarity – in the bedroom, they believe, creates good sex, which in turn is pivotal to good marital relations. Far more consistently than Kinsey, Masters and Johnson present marriage maintenance as the single, over-riding motivation for their work (and funding). The 'greatest single cause' of divorce in the USA, they insist in the opening of their very first publication (though with no evidence to back the claim), 'is a fundamental sexual inadequacy within the marital unit'.[61]

Moreover, they have stated repeatedly – again, despite their relentless commitment to empiricism, using figures plucked vaguely from undocumented sources – at least 50 per cent of marriages suffer from sexual problems. Evangelistically, they warn that the 'only hope' of preventing continuing marital disaster is the creation of 'a major postgraduate training program to develop seminar leaders for therapy training centers throughout the country'.[62] (Other studies have failed to support their claim that marital discontent correlates significantly with sexual dysfunction.[63])

Again, more dramatically than Kinsey, there is a wild irony in Masters and Johnson's research and writing, giving it a bizarre relation to women's search for sexual autonomy and fulfilment. Almost exclusively addressing and working with the marital couple in their early work, unbending in their commitment to maintaining monogamous marriage – even when faced with hostility or homosexual preferences in husband or wife – Masters and Johnson's most memorable finding is the *irrelevance* of 'the coital partner' to sexual pleasure or desire:

> Understandably, the maximum physiologic intensity of orgasmic response subjectively reported or objectively recorded has been achieved by self-regulated mechanical or automanipulative techniques. The next highest level of erotic intensity has resulted from partner manipulation, again with established or self-regulated methods, and the lowest intensity of target-organ response was achieved during coition.[64]

With orgasm defined as the single, universal goal of what they call the human sexual response, masturbation wins out every time as the most effective means for reaching it! Masters and Johnson, accordingly, warn us of the 'psychic distractions of a coital partner', and describe the pleasures of the penis which is 'unencumbered by vaginal containment'.[65] (Indeed, they offer treatment, successfully, for a group of women with 'masturbatory orgasmic inadequacy' who, though able to orgasm during sexual intercourse, had never managed to achieve 'orgasmic release by partner or self manipulation'.[66]) When it comes to pursuing sexual pleasure, the last thing most of us need, it would seem, is a husband or wife. And the very first thing to do, should we find ourselves saddled with one, is to teach him how we masturbate, so he can assist us – with a minimum of interference – in the process. Here we have the essence of Masters and Johnson sex therapy for female orgasmic problems, always completed in two hard-working, seven-day weeks, almost invariably, so they claim, effective. Even when closely following masturbatory techniques, however, coital intercourse *still* proves to be an inferior, less intense, form of sexual release.[67]

Contradictions only deepen as we read the thoroughgoing critique of centuries of 'phallic fallacy' provided by Masters and Johnson, with their insistence that sexual encounters should be geared to women's sexual gratification, that is, to the direct or – usually preferably – more indirect, stimulation of the clitoris. They not only discard the idea that women are less sexual than men, but affirm women's sexual capacity as greater and more varied than that of men: 'her physiological capacity for sexual response *infinitely* surpasses that of man.'[68] Women have welcomed Masters and Johnson's rejection of myths of male sexual potency and superiority, and their therapeutic regime of 'sensate focussing' geared to female pleasure rather than simply to male pleasure. And historians of sex research, like Paul Robinson, have insisted that 'women have no better friends' than Masters and Johnson, who 'have done more to advance the cause of women's sexual rights than anything else written in the last quarter century'.[69] But there are many reasons why feminists may well wonder whether these are not friends women could do without.

Women are not just allowed but commanded by Masters and Johnson to take more sexual initiative and responsibility for ensuring mutually orgasmic heterosexual satisfaction. Moreover, as recent feminist critics have noted, Masters and Johnson ignore the prevalence of women's social subordination to men, and their frequent experience of violence from men, to assert that in heterosexual relations the worst feature of gender inequality is the unequal sexual burden shouldered by men:

> The most unfortunate misconception our culture has assigned to sexual functioning is the assumption, by both men and women, that men by divine guidance and infallible instinct are able to discern exactly what a woman wants sexually and when she wants it. . . .
> The second most frequently encountered sexual fallacy . . . is the assumption that sexual expertise is the man's responsibility.[70]

Determined to eliminate such cultural misconception, they assign women the major responsibility for overcoming any sexual problems of the 'marital couple', a serious business when in their opinion 'the ultimate level in marital-unit communication is sexual intercourse'. In most of Masters and Johnson's therapeutic procedures the woman is put in charge of the man's movements, whether manual or genital, following 'prescriptions' from the sex therapist (or, as Masters and Johnson recommend, pair of sex therapists – a man and a woman). All this may seem promising for women gaining control of a sexual situation, but it looks a little less auspicious when we realize that Masters and Johnson discourage any lengthy discussion of women's personal histories or experience of sex and relationships in favour of immediate instructions on how she should get on with the serious 'work' of learning more effective sexual response patterns. They also insist that women worried about sexual problems must seek advice only from medical professionals: 'Your best friend or your partner may be your worst therapist.'[71]

An apparently pro-woman, strictly egalitarian rhetoric somehow keeps turning itself around into a new set of instructions and reprimands for women. It is they who are held responsible for their own orgasmic satisfaction *and* for eliminating male fears of failure. On the one hand, men and women 'must' learn that 'the most effective sex is not something a man does to a woman but something a man and woman do together *as equals*'.[72] On the other hand, it is mysteriously the sexual activity itself (and a very reductive account of what that is, in terms of women's equal participation and orgasmic satisfaction), rather than any positioning within structures of power, which creates women's 'equality'. Finally, it seems to be always *women* who are to blame for any state of 'inequality' in sexual activity:

> In too many marriages the wife may never say no but never really say yes. . . . But even saying yes – and meaning it – is not the answer. Active participation does not mean merely initiating matters which the man is then expected to complete. The woman who wholeheartedly commits herself *as an equal* in the sexual union is involved in continuous response to her husband's changing needs and desires, as he is involved in hers.[73]

With equality now defined in terms of sexual performance, and sexual performance sounding indistinguishable from a further set of duties for women, the new egalitarian rhetoric seems to be serving a very old conservative agenda: women servicing their men – their activity stripped out of any deeper personal, social or political context which might highlight conflict, confusion or any number of other troubling incongruities of experience.

Masters and Johnson, like sexologists before and since, are wilfully blind to social and linguistic contexts of gender and power (in and out of the bedroom), where men typically have, or expect to have, more power than women, and where male sexual activity has come to symbolize that power. Extraordinarily, even when discussing sexual assault (a topic Masters and Johnson, like their colleagues, generally avoid), Masters sticks to his gender-neutral analysis which passes for theory, to conclude from his sample of 11 men raped by women that its nature is 'identical' for women and for men – as though the grotesque disparity in vulnerability were irrelevant (and as though one rape was the same as any other).[74]

Overall, Masters and Johnson's exhortatory psychologizing consists of a disarmingly crude behaviouristic voluntarism, quite detached from any theorizing of the dynamics of sexuality. It is simply assumed to function in some instinctively healthy way within its proper place – marriage – when not distorted by 'false beliefs'. Theorizing neither gender nor sexuality, they assert that it is 'the double standard' and sexually repressive upbringing which causes whatever problems women may have with sex, as well as men's performance anxieties. What women and men are each most in need of is, therefore, the progressive enlightenment of sexologists. Once couples are given knowledge of their 'biological nature' – of women's orgasmic potential, and of men's erectile capacities – their fears and anxieties fall away:

when they can have their rationales for sexual failure and their prejudices, misconceptions, and misunderstandings of natural sexual functioning exposed with nonjudgmental objectivity and explained in understandable terms with subjective comfort, a firm basis for mutual security in sexual expression is established.[75]

Masters and Johnson provide no evidence to back their psychological certainties that it is ignorance and misconception which lie behind their clients' sexual miseries, so we have only their claims of quite extraordinary therapeutic success rates (around 98 per cent for many sexual disorders) to support their beliefs. Were they, however, as successful as they claimed?

It took ten years for anyone to dare to challenge the remarkable therapeutic achievements of Masters and Johnson, but when criticism came it again exposed the void at the centre of the scientific rigour and hi-tech methods of their empirical research. No criteria for success were ever provided by Masters and Johnson, and few other sexologists have produced the success rates reported by them, leading Bernie Zilbergeld and Michael Evans to conclude in 1980:

Masters and Johnson's research is so flawed by methodological errors and slipshod reporting that it fails to meet customary standards – and their own – for evaluation research. . . . Because of this the effectiveness of sex therapy – widely assumed to be high since the advent of Masters and Johnson – is thrown into question.[76]

By the 1980s, with sex therapy clinics proliferating in the USA and spreading to other Western countries, some sex researchers and therapists were already wanting to supplement Masters and Johnson's behaviour modification therapy and stimulus-reponse framework (attentive only to the concrete and visible response patterns of the present moment, and how to play around with them) with something new. It was to certain popularizations of psychoanalysis that they turned, adding the problem of childhood traumas to that of inept and untutored sexual handling. Helen Singer Kaplan is representative of such amalgamation, a highly influential North American sexologist, who has retained the biological emphasis of Masters and Johnson and their interest in technique, but added a 'desire' phase to sexual activity. This allows her to bring in individual psychopathology to help explain the rapidly growing 'disorders of desire', despite the post-sexological enlightenment of mainstream culture. A disorder of desire might thus be attributed by Kaplan not just to 'ignorance', but to 'unconscious hostility', but would still be dealt with if, and only if, it distracted from successful sexual functioning: 'The patient [seen as hostile to women] was advised not to think about his wife during this experience [the wife's stimulation of her husband's penis], . . . but to focus his thoughts exclusively on his genital sensations as he experienced mounting excitement and impending orgasm.'[77] Once again, the sex therapist separates off sexual functioning as *the* essential ingredient for satisfaction and communication between couples – irrespective of hostility, power struggles or analysis of the wider social significance of interpersonal conflicts which, for sex therapists, are almost always the gender conflicts of the heterosexual couple.

Such characteristic disregard for broader issues of gender has led Leonore Tiefer, one of the few feminists working critically in the field, to suggest that although sexology has had a significant influence on feminism, and many of its proponents think that it is feminist, feminism has had surprisingly little impact on sexology.[78]

Feminist sex research

Feminists, as we saw in the last chapter, at first enthusiastically endorsed sexological research and thinking, in particular that of Masters and Johnson. Their emphasis on sexual similarity was used by feminists as a way of attacking double standards around sexuality. Their cheery optimism was very much in tune with the early high hopes and aspirations of feminists that by changing their ideas about women's potential for and entitlement to sexual pleasure, they could change their lives, change their world. Without doubt sexologists saw themselves as, and seemed to be, allies of feminism in combatting ignorance and sexism.[79] Moreover, although feminists today often argue that sexology has always only provided a means for men to define and dictate women's sexuality,[80] many women became prominent in sexology in the 1970s – especially in the USA – where Mary Jane Sherfey, Helen Kaplan Singer, Mary Calderone, Lonnie Barbach and Shere Hite (as well as Virginia Johnson) were to enter the field as experts on women's sexuality.

Women were joining men to provide a model of female sexuality which dismissed the 'harmful' view that women were more sexually passive than men, and went further to assert women's complete sexual autonomy. One study of sex manuals in the USA between 1950 and 1980 shows this development of a sexological sexual autonomy model becoming the dominant one from the mid-1970s, for the first time moving beyond the 'marital unit' to focus on women's individual experience and depict them as independent sexual agents, self-sufficient and in control of their own sexuality.[81] Over and over, women were being told by one expert after another 'it is *your* choice', '*your* body, '*your* responsibility': 'Your focus must be solely on *your sexual stimuli* and whatever increases it': 'Nowadays women like to think that they have something to do with their own orgasms and that they are not dependent on a man for sexual fulfilment'; 'He can give you his penis to enjoy, but the extent to which you enjoy it is *your responsibility.*'[82] These women experts were also confident that women's sexual independence and fulfilment, seen as a type of learned competence, would 'spread to other areas of a woman's life'.[83]

Here, quite at odds with all traditional discourses of marriage and sexuality, and yet evolving out of Masters and Johnson's emphasis on the egalitarian heterosexual couple, women's sexuality is seen as both separate from men's, and as active and initiating rather than passive and responsive. This challenge to traditional images and discourses is obviously important in affirming the idea of a woman's right to be sexually active when, and only when, she chooses. Although still confronted by multiple competing discourses of the randy male and his passive female prey, pervading popular culture and professional practices, the availability of this model of female sexual autonomy in Western cultures can, and almost certainly has, served to strengthen at least some women to make more demands on men in heterosexual encounters or relationships. But in its emphasis on success, performance and efficiency, all delivered in the optimistic tones of pragmatic expediency, this sexual autonomy model still suffers from the limitations of the behaviourist mind at work. 'If you can have orgasms with one partner, you can probably have them with another,' Barbach assures her readers. Women can always 'recondition themselves to respond positively to erotic stimuli.'[84]

What is disowned in such casual cheeriness is all interest in a woman's complex emotional life, here reduced instead to her cognitive awareness of what is seen as her biological potential for orgasms, and her right to have them. There is no hint or whisper of the often troubling, irrational or 'perverse' nature of sexual desire and fantasy, which may bear little relation to our conscious ideals and commitments as autonomous agents in the world. At the very least we might expect some mention of the frequency with which sexual desire does not restrict itself to the most suitable person, in the most suitable place; and its not unfamiliar habit of forsaking us when we do find that person, whatever the presence or absence of technical virtuosity on offer. What arouses desire, as almost any women's fiction can illustrate, rarely obeys the dictate of conscious feminist pursuit, but as often includes inappropriately submissive, aggressive, hostile, or in other ways 'deviant' impulses. Yet in sexology, feminist or otherwise, all experience is seen as manipulable, from the outside in, and the possibility of desire arising from and expressing contradictory, conflicting or quite literally impossible impulses cannot even be expressed, let alone explained, from within this framework.

Nor, given the ease with which change is presumed possible, do we find in this literature any genuine analysis of the shifting political and social regulation of gender relations and sexuality. This would have to include what we know of many women's – not to mention men's – enormous investment in such regulation. The existing patterns of gender hierarchy which maintain male dominance in political, cultural and economic life, though contested, have helped to shape our individual histories of desire and identification. These histories include the most passionate attachment (however ambivalent) to ideas of the nurturing female and the powerful, authoritative male. They are not so easily transformed into egalitarian sexual interactions through awareness of the equal, or potentially 'superior', orgasmic capacity of women.

And even if women's individual sexual performance and its rewards change from being male-focussed to being self-focussed, dominant sexual language, representations and beliefs (like that of male 'potency' and female 'surrender') remain in place to confuse and trouble us. Women may learn how to make their partners submit to their every desire, and the earth quiver and move between the sheets, and still find wider patterns of exploitation and abuse of women by men all too solidly erect and stable. But such gloomy thoughts are absent from these texts, where good sex can still conquer all: 'consistently orgasmic women tend to describe themselves as contented, good-natured, insightful, self-confident, independent, realistic, strong, capable and understanding.'[85]

That it is the poverty of its conceptual framework, rather than any absence of commitment to women's sexual rights and gender equality, which confounds the feminist inclinations of some sexologists is best exemplified by Shere Hite's twenty years of sex research. It may seem ungenerous or unjust to assess Hite's legacy critically when some of her work was the target of an orchestrated anti-feminist attack in the US media in the late 1980s as 'flawed, murky and muddled' for its supposedly 'preconceived feminist' notions.[86] (Hite's third Report, published in 1987, was the object of particular ridicule for suggesting that most women are unhappy and frustrated in their love relationships with men, who habitually refuse to treat them as equals or to listen to their grievances.) But some sexologists fully endorse Hite's work – despite doubts about her methodology, which certainly lacks the appearance of the 'scientific rigour' most of them strive for – and she received an award for distinguished service from the American Association of Sex Educators, Counselors and Therapists in 1985. Her work is mainly important, however, because it has been so very influential in feminist research and scholarship – which has cut its cloth from the same pattern. Many feminists today would support Dale Spender's recent assessment that Hite has presented us with 'a new perspective of female sexuality', one which has 'stood prevailing theory on its head'.[87]

My assessment of Hite's research and writing is almost exactly the reverse. Her work is a problem because it replicates the limitations of prevailing theory. Hite leaves sexological reflection exactly as she found it: addicted to self-righteous voluntarism, biological reductionism and exhaustive quantification drained of theoretical elaboration. For my purposes, therefore, Hite's work provides a very useful reckoning on the promise and the limitations of the sexological imagination, at its most feminist, for over-turning centuries of male dominance and sexism through changing how we think about and experience sex and love.

Hite's main claim is that 'most women do not orgasm as a result of intercourse'; her second – antithetical – claim is that we need to redefine sex so that 'it's not specifically just *orgasms* we are talking about'.[88] The bizarre irony here is that in *The Hite Report on Female Sexuality* 'almost all' women say they like penetrative sex, but it is Hite who seems obsessed with orgasms.[89] Hite's basic finding 'that 70 per cent of women do not have orgasms from intercourse, but *do* have them from more direct clitoral stimulation', adds little to the focus or findings of either Kinsey or Masters and Johnson. Like Masters and Johnson, Hite discusses how women may learn to increase clitoral stimulation during intercourse to increase the likelihood of orgasm. Yet this discussion sits oddly alongside Hite's criticism of sex researchers as too focussed on orgasms.[90] It also downplays what should be the very real strengths of Hite's research, women's own reports of their experience of sex.

Although Hite and others have used women's frequent nonorgasmic experiences of intercourse to suggest its irrelevance to women's sexual pleasure, her subjects were reporting something rather different. Under the pejorative heading 'Sexual Slavery', Hite informs us that 87 per cent of the 3,000 women in her first study *do* enjoy coital sex. Indeed, it is the only sexual engagement about which they write euphorically:

> 'I love it. Feeling your man's penis deep within you is ecstasy.'
> 'During intercourse I feel secure, assured of his love, and wanted – whole, warm, loved, womanly.'
> 'I like penetration because it feels warm and sweet and mutual.'
> 'Yes I like it . . . it's an intimate closeness, one is kind of enfolding the other person.'
> 'I really do like the feeling of a man's penis inside of me, and those moments seem less detached, much less contrived, less like people "operating on" each other than the others.'
> 'It is the ultimate of physical and psychological fulfilment. The act is something only God could have imagined that is so beautiful.'
> 'There is one position with me underneath with my legs over my partner's shoulders that I can come with no arousal. It blows my mind.'
> 'To be filled is a great body pleasure. There are nights when I want just *everything* in me – including in my mouth, my ears, my vagina, my rectum – wow'.[91]

Wow! So what does Hite make of all this penetrative ecstasy, with or without orgasms? She tries very hard to dismiss it: 'Perhaps it could be said that many women might be rather indifferent to intercourse if it were not for feelings towards a particular man.'[92] Perhaps, indeed! And perhaps it could be said women might be rather indifferent to any other type of sexual encounter were it not for the feelings involved. The problem, and it is a crucial one, is that despite her own and others' belief that she offers a new theory and research paradigm for studying sexuality, Hite fully shares traditional sexology's penchant for biological reductionism, and its inability to take seriously either the nature and significance of desire, or the social meanings embedded in bodily experience (unless they correspond to what she sees as physiological imperatives).

Hite sincerely wants to avoid the traditional focus on orgasms, but nevertheless asserts: 'All we really know about our sexuality is that we have a desire for orgasms, and that certain situations stimulate this desire more than others.' Some of her informants contradict her meagre piece of 'knowledge': 'My sexuality has more to do with desire than with satisfaction. I am not interested in "satisfaction".'[93] Hite herself strains at the behaviourist leash which ensnares her, assuring us:

> Intercourse was never *meant* to stimulate women to orgasm. . . . Orgasms during intercourse in this study usually seemed to result from a conscious attempt by the woman to center some kind of clitoral area contact for herself during intercourse . . . [which] could be thought of, then, as basically stimulating yourself while intercourse is in progress.[94]

One could indeed think of intercourse as clitoral masturbation, but it would seem a rather extraordinary way of thinking about it, and not how most of her female informants seem to be thinking. As we will see in Chapter 6,

Hite's all-too-blatant bias has served as a model for almost all subsequent feminist research on heterosexuality, which continues to take for granted women's negative experiences of vaginal penetration. Anja Meulenbelt begins her survey of female sexuality in Holland with the information, citing Hite, 'that many women still don't care too much for this kind of sex [penis-in-vagina contact] has been accepted by a large number of scientists'.[95] A current, ongoing survey of young people's sexual behaviour in London and Manchester in the 1990s similarly concludes that 'sex as penetrative sex is for men's pleasure in which women find fulfilment primarily in the relationship, in giving pleasure, and only secondarily in their own bodily desires.'[96]

The strangeness of this certainty that women derive little 'bodily' pleasure from penetrative sex is heightened by the incongruity that feminist theorists today who recycle Hite also dismiss the possibility of providing any account of bodily experience which is pre-social or pre-discursive. They emphasize, after Foucault, 'that although physical bodies exist, bodies are primarily social constructions', we cannot experience the body *except* through the discourses we wrap around it.[97] Somehow, in ways mysteriously manifest to feminist sensibilities, bodies are known only through discourse, yet known to be misrepresented by discourse. (I will be exploring these tensions of social construction theories of the body more fully in later chapters.)

It is clear, of course, why Hite and other feminists have wanted to downplay the significance of intercourse. It is connected to the desire to separate sex from what was its only traditional legitimation or 'purpose': the goal of reproduction (stressed by moral conservatives to this day). More important in contemporary feminist thinking, however, is the continuing resonance that penetrative sex has as a cultural reality expressing gender-specific images of dominance and submission. But this is just what I think we should question, rather than try to by-pass. In my view, Hite and others handle the problem of gender symbolism, which confers all power to the erect and thrusting penis (or 'phallus'), in exactly the wrong way. She confirms rather than queries the gendering of intercourse, as if it is in fact an enactment of dominance and submission. The best she has to offer heterosexual women is to suggest that 'a passionate desire to be "taken" or "possessed" by some-one during sex is not *automatically* a sign of victimization, as long as it is not the *only* feeling you ever have.'[98] But even if it *were* the only feeling we had, I would say, in contrast, that a desire to be 'taken' or 'possessed' does not in any way lead automatically to 'victimization'.

For feminists to reject and condemn so-called sexual 'passivity' or 'receptivity' as demeaning, promoting instead a notion of self-assertion through sexual 'activity', is for us to adopt the most collusive metaphorical or 'masculine' discourse roping sex to power, when other discourses for describing sexuality are, if less available, at least possible. After all, it is Hite herself who tells us in her *Report on Men and Male Sexuality* of 1981 that many men like receiving penetrative sex:

> Most men, of either heterosexual or homosexual experience, who have tried being penetrated said that they enjoyed it; it brought feelings of deep pleasure and fulfillment. The main characteristic of being penetrated described by men was an extreme feeling of emotional passion – followed by a feeling of peace and satisfaction. Many men said that orgasm, when accompanied by anal stimulation, could be physically exquisite.[99]

Just like a woman, Hite assures us here, men used words like 'feeling "full", "complete", and emotionally satisfied, in describing the pleasures of receiving penetrative sex (with penis, finger, small object, or whatever).' If men are allowed to enjoy penetration without 'victimization' why, one might ask, not women?

Asking 'why, physiologically speaking' men might like being penetrated, Hite points to the the physical stimulation of men's prostate gland just inside the anus. But her male respondents have a few meanings of their own to add to this source of physical stimulation: 'it feels like a delicious pain, an openness, a vulnerability, a focussing of all my energy and desire.'[100] Deeply ironically, it is here and only here, in her writing on *men's* sexuality, that Hite for the first and last time comes close to describing the force and contradictions of sexual passion, so lacking in the many thousands of pages of commentary she has devoted over twenty years to detailing women's experiences of sex and love:

> Most men did not want to be penetrated, either physically or emotionally – and yet *did* want it . . . they want to penetrate the other, to be in charge, in control . . . and yet they long for the opposite, to be out of control, also dominated by the other . . . most men *do* want to be in deeper contact – to feel more – to not only take, but also be penetrated and taken. . . . Passion is one of the most beautiful parts of all sensuality – the desire to possess, to take, to ravish and be ravished, penetrate and be penetrated. . . . What is love? Love is talking and understanding and counting on and being counted on, but love is also the deepest intermingling of bodies. In a way, body memory of a loved one is stronger and lasts longer than all other memories.

Quite. Just for a moment, orgasms are almost forgotten, biological reductionism abandoned. Just for a moment, Hite manages to transcend the metaphor that 'penetration enacts the subjugation of men by women', as some feminists – like Andrea Dworkin – insist upon. It is this insistence, I would argue, which dangerously reinforces rather than combats phallic illusion. It is this insistence, even more insidiously and disablingly, which denies the distinction between coercion and consent in women's experience of penetrative sex with men. But it is, sadly, a level of perceptiveness which disappears in most of Hite's writing, as she scolds some of the women she has interviewed: 'Of course, the thirty percent of women who said they *could* orgasm regularly during intercourse often bragged about it', and elsewhere warns us that some of these women may be lying.[101]

The other very understandable reason Hite and many other feminists in her wake have wanted to dismiss the significance of penetrative sex is to criticize men's frequently driven, unimaginative and selfish sexual routine. So often the single *main event* of sexual contact, Hite's respondents complain that intercourse all too often left them wanting 'more kisses, more time, more tenderness', 'more love and gentleness', 'more emotion and communication', 'more passion'.[102] Many women have been empowered by Hite's scorn for the limitations of men's most typical sexual performance (and her contempt for men pressurizing women into sexual contact they do not want). But women have not been empowered by the creation of a new feminist orthodoxy which suggests that 'anatomically' they are not 'meant' to like penetrative sex even though they say they do.

After all, it was not better sexual technique, or even more orgasms, that Hite's respondents seemed to be wanting when they wrote wistfully of tenderness, communication and passion. True to sexological reflection, though, Hite seems to think that it is, or should be, and she repeatedly puzzles over the problem: 'women *know* very well how to orgasm during masturbation, whenever they want . . . why don't they feel free to use this knowledge during sex with men?' The knowledge, it seems, is simple: 'Female orgasm is *not* particularly mysterious, it happens with the right stimulation, quickly, pleasurably, and reliably. . . . The whole key is adequate stimulation.'[103] It is more mysterious to me. Masturbation is one thing, and love and passion something else. The reasons for having sex with another may not be joint masturbatory homework; indeed, the presence of another's all too solid flesh can transform, twist, release or block the lock to passion, quite irrespective of the multiple keys to orgasm we have acquired, at home, alone.

Hite knows, or partly knows, that the shared application of masturbatory skills cannot by itself produce love or passion. The conspicuous absence in all sexological writing – its inability to theorize desire – weakens the work of its leading feminist writer. Sexology's inability to get to grips with desire, and the uncertainties of masturbatory skills for arousing it, are both bizarrely illustrated by the work of Seymour Sachs at the Center for Sexual Behavior in Chicago. Sachs adapts the very same masturbatory methods which have been used in the service of producing orgasms in nonorgasmic women, but with the opposite goal of *eliminating* unwanted or 'deviant' sexual behaviour. Subjects are instructed to masturbate until satiated and beyond, in order to extinguish rather than arouse desire – or so it is hoped. The ludicrousness of such attempts to modify the manifest behaviour of desire is less than amusingly apparent in the evidence of those undergoing such 'cures', which suggests that masturbatory activities, however skilled at producing orgasms, have little impact on desire – either positive or negative.[104] Such theoretical hollowness may explain why Hite says very little at all about either sexual pleasure or desire (despite 900 pages of commentary!) in her third Report, *Women and Love*, which suggests that most women are dissatisfied in their relationships with men. We are reminded of the significance of her own earlier report on the importance of clitoral stimulation to clear up 'the ideological misunderstanding of female sexuality' and pointed towards 'the most advanced information presented recently' in the form of anatomical drawings 'which show the interior clitoral system in detail'.[105] Otherwise, Hite is here concerned with women's frustrations in their love relations, and sex seems to have very little to do with it.

What the 4,500 women in this report do complain about is the lack of adequate communication and emotional closeness with their male partners (98 per cent want more verbal closeness, 84 per cent are not satisfied emotionally with their relationships). We also learn that 70 per cent of wives are having extra-marital sex (after five years' marriage), 49 per cent with one regular lover, and 15 per cent with more than one regular lover. But 87 per cent of these women believe their husbands are 'faithful' to them, and only 21 per cent suggest poor marital sex is the reason for their adultery. Indeed, 44 per cent of wives say they can count on close physical affection on a regular basis. However, when Hite provides descriptions of women's experiences of love, or hopes of love, we leave behind the language of adequate physical stimulation for the narratives of romantic fiction:

> Love is a longed-for feeling of unity, bliss, fulfillment.
> A strong feeling you have for someone right from the beginning – a feeling of well-being all over. Sexual passion and the desire for a relationship are indistinguishable.[106]

With love, as women supposedly experience it, portrayed as a seamlessly positive, uplifting passion (no infantile anger, fear, dependency, or efforts to manipulate and control to spoil our bliss) it is not so surprising to learn: 'Strangely, hauntingly, most women in this study . . . say they have not yet found the love they are looking for.'[107]

Hite may believe, in my view mistakenly, that there is political mileage in her complacent and sentimental denial of conflict and ambivalence in women's experience of love and passion (except as the product of men's typical refusal to treat them as equals). But we need not doubt many men's determination to hold on to privilege and power, to wonder whether women are quite so all-knowing as Hite affirms. Women are reminded not only that we 'are magnificent, resourceful, strong, brave, creative, sensitive, warm and intelligent', but assured of all that we already know: not just how to orgasm, not just how to love, not just how to get what we want, but we know as well, though men refuse to notice, how to solve the economic and political problems of the world at large – through the dissemination of our 'female knowledge' of love and caring. Women, we learn, have already 'moved into another world, another century, another reality – leaving behind psychological allegience to "the way things used to be", to "male" ways of doing things, the "male" ideology.'[108] Confidently exemplifying what Richard Sennett long ago analysed as 'the reigning myth' of American culture, 'that the evils of society can all be understood as evils of impersonation, alienation and coldness', Hite seems convinced that the only problem with the world today is that men have yet to catch up with women.[109]

Leaving aside Hite's totalizing parody of the complexity and divisions in women's lives and allegiances, and her dismissal of all that feminists have written rejecting notions of universal female experience, I can find no possible psychological insight in her glib disavowal that our sexuality and love relationships (as women or as men) include fear, anxiety, ambivalence and confusion tied in with their potential for joy and pleasure. I can find here, in the end, only echoes of behaviouristic voluntarism stretched out to breaking point. However well intentioned.

One hundred years of sexological theory and research has at times facilitated, but more often merely reflected or tried to contain, women's long struggle for control over their lives and sexuality. It has increasingly called into question traditional contrasts between male and female, 'normal' and 'deviant', sexualities. It has characteristically defended everybody's entitlement to, and more recently stressed their duty and responsibility for, individual sexual satisfaction. But it has repeatedly failed to see that sexuality is more than a physical experience, more than the sum of its parts. It has yet to affirm that sexuality can be as much about fear and anger as love and affection, as much about domination and subjection as mutuality and respect. It cannot agree that sexuality is more than an interpersonal matter, more than a family affair, reflecting quite specific historical and cultural meanings. Such thoughts lie outside its conceptual categories, beyond its explanatory power.

4. Laws of desire: psychoanalytic perspectives and disputes

From the point of view of psycho-analysis the exclusive sexual interest felt by men for women is . . . a problem that needs elucidating. . . .

Sigmund Freud[1]

The tremendous advance accomplished by psychoanalysis over psychophysiology lies in the view that no factor becomes involved in the psychic life without having taken on human significance; it is not the body object described by biologists that actually exists, but the body as lived by the subject.

Simone de Beauvoir[2]

When psychoanalysis produces woman, the woman, as not-all, it falls short, remains locked in a static assignation. It is not the woman who is not-all but psychoanalysis, which is what the latter has been so generally unwilling to grasp.

Stephen Heath[3]

Some of the fiercest criticism of sexology, and especially of its emphasis on sexual sameness, has come from psychoanalytic theory and practice. Sexology ended up suggesting that there are no inherent difficulties preventing anyone from experiencing the full joys of their sexuality, indeed we owe it to ourselves to do so – the most inexhaustible of pleasures being those available to women. Psychoanalysis, in morbid contrast, has always stressed the inherent difficulties of sexuality – the most intractable of problems being those inevitable for women.

Superficially at least, this is curious. Psychoanalysis emerged at much the same time as the modern science of sexology (towards the end of the nineteenth century), was always in dialogue with it, and addressed the same problem: the place of sexuality in human life. Sexology began by explaining human sexual behaviour in terms of instinctive imperatives, and moved on to emphasize the place of learning and the acquisition of skills, but all the while from within a biological perspective. The psycho-analytic account of sexuality was elaborated with concepts describing an altogether different site of sexual reality: psychic life. Oddly, perhaps, this is an area about which academic writing in both psychology and sexology remains suspicious, preferring instead to move between descriptions of internal biology and external stimulation or environ-mental forces. Since 'desire', in whatever form, is first and foremost a psychic reality, it would be foolish even to try to comprehend it without some knowledge of the troubled and troubling legacies of psychoanalysis.

Sexual drives, psychic realities

In his *Three Essays on Sexuality*, written in 1905 and revised repeatedly, Freud set out to overthrow popular conceptions of the sexual drive as a biological instinct, absent in children, and emerging only after puberty. In psychoanalytic thinking sexual drives are present from the beginning, because sexual sensations attach themselves to infants' attempts to satisfy essential biological needs, first of all, that of hunger:

> To begin with, sexual activity attaches itself to one of the
> functions serving the purpose of self-preservation and

does not become independent until later. No one who has seen a baby sinking back satiated from the breast and falling asleep with flushed cheeks and a blissful smile can escape the reflection that this picture persists as a prototype of the expression of sexual satisfaction in later life. The need for repeating the sexual experience now becomes detached from the need for taking nourishment.[4]

As specifically sexual drives appear, they do so inextricably entwined with, or propped upon, non-sexual drives. They emerge as a tension or force which is exerted on the mind for the repetition of the pleasure experienced in particular erogenous zones, first of all the oral, and later the anal, urethral and genital zone. Thus, the image of the mouth in feeding becomes as much a sexual as a nutritional one. Freud went on to suggest that *any* area of the body, or *any* activity, could become erotogenic or the source of a sexual drive: 'precisely as in the case of sucking, any other part of the body can acquire the same susceptibility to stimulation as is possessed by the genitals and can become an erotogenic zone.' The exact character of erotogenicity, or the feeling of pleasure, evoked in different parts of the body was hard to specify, Freud believed, although the 'rhythmic character' of the stimulation seemed to be important.[5]

Sexual drives are thus seen as an offshoot of any bodily area or activity which, because it can sustain a certain level of excitation, can be eroticized and, in fantasy, invested with sexual value. The images or representations of the body which are suffused in this way with fantasy are produced through the stimulating attention and handling the infant has received from its caretaker:

A child's intercourse with anyone responsible for his care affords him an unending source of sexual excitation and satisfaction from his erogenous zones. This is especially so since the person in charge of him, who, after all, is as a rule his mother, herself regards him with feelings that are derived from her own sexual life: she strokes him, kisses him, rocks him and quite clearly treats him as a substitute for a complete sexual object.[6]

The psychical manifestations of sexual life have an object, they are directed at whatever it is which has provided the sexual arousal – at first the breast, and later – when the infant can register the total object or person – usually the mother. From the beginning, however, when removed these objects are immediately internalized as fantasy, stimulating auto-erotic activity: the fantasized breast accompanying the first autoerotic activity of thumb sucking, the maternal imago accompanying the enjoyment of genital masturbation.

By 'enlarging the concept of sexuality', and extending it back into childhood, Freud was rejecting the idea of any pre-given aim or object for the sexual drive or 'libido'. His chief purpose was to emphasize that adult sexuality always grows out of and reflects its infantile origins: 'The finding of an object is in fact a refinding of it.'[7] His chief preoccupation was not so much the nature and origins of the sexual drives as such as their early polymorphous expression and the obstacles or disturbances ('vicissitudes') they encounter, which lead to their repression and thereby to the formation of the unconscious. Adult sexuality is always the result of the repression of the earlier 'poly-morphous perversity' of infancy, and only ever comes under the sway of the reproductive function, if it does, by 'a series of developments, combinations, divisions and suppressions which are scarcely ever achieved with ideal perfection'.[8]

Freud's conception of sexuality is thus completely at odds with any biomedical model, or sexological attempt to impart correct 'knowledge' about sexual anatomy (the psychic significance of the stimulus is always more important than 'the nature of the part of the body concerned').[9] The psychic manifestations of sexual life, understood as the autoerotic repetition of memory traces of bodily pleasure, are a world apart from sexology's unwavering quantification of orgasms. Ironically, given the fraught relations between feminism and psychoanalysis, we might mischievously suggest that we have here a possible answer to Shere Hite's demand that we need to redefine sex, so that 'it's not specifically *orgasms* we are talking about' (though Hite remains fiercely anti-Freudian).[10] Freud himself, despite his reputation as the inventor of the 'vaginal orgasm', never used the phrase. In fact, as Appignanesi and Forrester point out in their exhaustive survey of Freud's writing, he rarely used the word 'orgasm' at all, 'preferring the less physiological phrase "sexual satisfaction"'.[11]

The other startling feature of Freud's early accounts of infantile sexuality, apart from his assertion of its existence, is that there is no gendered dimension to the multiplicity of bodily sites and objects connected with the sexual drives. The sexual life of the little girl and the little boy run along similar pathways: the little girl like the little boy expresses active sexual wishes towards the mother, and passively enjoys her physical ministrations. The girl will also come to enjoy the active pleasures of genital (for her clitoral) masturbation. Moreover, in the girl as in the boy, a sense of self or 'ego' is born through a process of self-love or primary narcissism: the ego is 'first and foremost a bodily ego'.[12] The child comes to love itself through an identificatory investment in the object of the one she/he loves (usually the mother): the child both desires the mother and through internalized identification with her, desires the object of her desire, thus coming to focus its libido on itself.

With such strong emphasis on the mobile psychical reality

of sexual drives, and such firm rejection of their reduction to reproductive genitality, how did Freudian thinking from the 1930s, and for many decades after, come to serve as one of the first bastions of conservative thinking on sexual difference and women's place? The dilemma, which was always 'far from being cleared up' to Freud's own satisfaction, and most certainly to the satisfaction of many of his followers, was just how the bisexual libido separates out into the patterns of 'masculinity'/'femininity' as activity/passivity which provide the foundation of what we have come to know as the 'great antithesis' between male and female. Remarkably, for the first thirty years of his writing, Freud had paid relatively little heed to sexual difference, and he only tried to provide a psychological model for it in the last years of his life. Ironically, the harder he tried to tackle the problem, the more the muddle and the greater the offence – to followers and critics alike.

Family romances and sexual difference

If sexual drives grow out of an original bisexual disposition common to both sexes, if they involve areas other than the genitals and take up a variety of objects, what explains the relentless insistence and apparent inflexibility of sexual identity and heterosexuality in adult life? The first offence, and the source of much of the confusion Freud was to cause, comes from his description of the original nature of sexual drives, or 'libido', as 'masculine': 'the sexuality of the little girl is of a wholly masculine character.'[13] (It would be equally pertinent, if still misleading at this stage, to suggest that the sexuality of the little boy is 'feminine'.) In the beginning there is only one type of sexuality and Freud calls it 'masculine', although the bisexual constitution of libido means that boys will enjoy the pleasures of passivity, 'which we describe as the feminine attitude', while girls will be active or 'masculine' in their erotic pursuits.[14] Sexual difference occurs only through the mediation of the Oedipus Complex, and is always precarious, constantly threatened by the dramas of perverse desire taking place in the unconscious.

The boy's early libidinal attachment to the mother brings him into a threatening rivalry with the father, figure of authority and representative of the external world beyond the home, especially during what Freud comes to call the 'phallic phase' – between three and five – when the boy is narcissistically enjoying the masturbatory pleasures of his own small penis. What becomes so threatening about such sexual rivalry is that this is also the time when children are trying to solve the problems of sexual life. This is when they first take note of what they see as the differences between the sexes, try to figure out where babies come from, and form a strong image of the sex act between the parents as a sadistic act – the father forcibly taking possession of the mother – which Freud believed to be children's perception of what he called 'the primal scene'.[15] At this stage, the possible visual contrasts which can be made between the sexes are registered by little boys and little girls in terms of 'possessing a penis' or 'not possessing one' – that is, being 'castrated'. Access to the mother, as the boy now sees it, is reserved for the father and his penis, and therefore requires a paternal identification. But the boy not only desires but has internalized and identified with the figure of the mother. It is the realization of sexual difference and its importance, alongside awareness of the heterosexual act of penetration, that initiates in the boy a profound castration anxiety, the fantasy of castration as punishment for his primary attachment to the mother. Or so the story goes.

The boy's alternative Oedipal wishes, which involve not rivalry with but passive libidinal attachment to the father, seem equally to threaten the boy with a feminine identification with the mother, and the consequent loss of the penis. The deeply troubling combination of fear and confusion over sexual desire (attaching the boy to the mother) and sexual identity (requiring an attachment of the boy to the father) is only resolved, if it is resolved, through the boy renouncing his desire for the mother for an identification with the position and authority of the father, and the formation of the super-ego:

> If the satisfaction of love in the field of the Oedipus complex is to cost the child his penis, a conflict is bound to arise between his narcissistic interest in that part of his body and the libidinal cathexis of his parental objects. In this conflict the first of these forces normally triumphs: the child turns away from the Oedipus complex.[16]

This means the boy accepting the Oedipal polarity which affirms: 'You cannot be what you desire; you cannot desire what you wish to be.'[17]

It is such sexual renunciation which forms the nucleus of the boy's unconscious in Freud's account, attracting to itself all subsequent experiences reminiscent of earlier desires for the mother. The incestuous origins of sexuality mean sexual desire is always associated with the forbidden, and in boys can tend either towards an overvaluation of the loved object as untouchable, or towards its degradation as debased. Many men, Freud suggests, will never manage to unify the sensual and affectionate currents of their sexuality, accounting for the prevalence of psychical impotence in men and a need to debase their sexual object.[18] Nevertheless, Freud always suggested that the boy's trajectory towards normal masculinity and a heterosexual object choice, though threatened by repressed layers of 'feminine' passivity and homosexual desire, was always more straightforward than the girl's progress towards normal feminine heterosexuality.

The girl's situation in the Oedipal family scenario is different, and was only finally clarified by Freud in his writings from 1923.[19] The problem Freud kept observing, and found so hard to pin down, was that female sexual development and identity seemed to be neither simply the same as that of men (as later sexologists would come to think), nor simply the opposite or complement of that of men's (as Freud's contemporaries believed). How do girls come to abandon their first libidinal tie with the mother, and turn, if they do, towards 'normal' adult heterosexual bonds? It is not rivalry and fear, he finally decided, but envy and desire (of and for the penis) which leads girls to abandon their original attachment to the mother, once they have registered the psychic significance of anatomical difference. Sighting the penis, they 'at once recognize it as the superior counterpart to their own small and inconspicuous organ, and from that time fall a victim to envy of the penis.'[20]

The desire for a penis leads to a double renunciation of sexual object and sexual aim in the girl, Freud argued. She renounces her hitherto intense desire for the mother (who is now not only seen as lacking the penis herself, but held responsible for the girl's similar 'disadvantage') to turn instead towards the father in the hope of gaining the penis or its symbolic substitute, a baby. And she renounces her active 'phallic' or clitoral masturbation for the passive sexual aims of the 'vaginal orifice' and 'normal femininity': 'to receive a baby from her father as a gift – to bear him a child.'[21] However, the girl may react to her realization of her lack of the penis in other ways. First of all, because of her penis envy, she may turn away from sex altogether, wishing for a child instead of the penis. Secondly, she may refuse to accept her lack of the penis, holding on to her 'masculine' libido and pursuing an active homosexual object choice. If and when the girl does accept her own lack of the penis, the two sexes diverge. And it is the woman who will suffer most in the process of double renunciation towards heterosexual womanhood, with her development of the truly feminine attitude where, in the words of Joan Riviere, the woman knows: 'I must not take, I must not even ask, it must be *given* to me.'[22]

No sooner had Freud installed 'penis envy' as central to female sexuality than some of his fellow analysts in the 1920s and 1930s began to object – first and most forcefully, Karen Horney, Melanie Klein and Ernest Jones. They did not dispute its existence. The advantage for the boy of the penis (which he can see, touch and display) elicits disappointment in the girl, whose hidden genitals are less accessible for early erotic gratification and narcissistic pleasure (obliging her to display her whole body, preferably naked, instead). But these early critics contested the significance given to penis envy in adult womanhood. In contrast, they asserted the little girl's awareness of the existence of the internal vagina and her fundamental heterosexual orientation towards the father. For Horney, the girl's wish to be a man is defensive in character, a 'flight from womanhood' and the guilt and fear created by her primary feminine fantasy of being raped by the father. It disguises the girl's 'libidinal wishes and fantasies in connection with the father'.[23] Horney also wrote of male envy and fear of women's role in reproduction leading to their constant 'overcompensation in achievement', while pointing out the cultural determinants of penis envy in a male-dominated society where women are at an actual disadvantage.[24]

Jones too saw the little girl as 'essentially female', with a desire for rather than envy of the penis, while Klein argued that it was the deprivation of the breast, not the lack of a penis, which helped turn the little girl away from the mother and towards the father in line with her natural predispositions. For all three a specific feminine form of sexuality, an awareness of the existence and function of the vagina, and attraction to the opposite sex, were largely innate.[25] Ironically, however, in attempting to eliminate what Jones described as Freud's 'phallocentrism' by a return to 'natural' heterosexuality and a distinctly feminine libido, these early critics let go of what would seem to be Freud's most radical significance: the rejection of any type of innate sexual aims or objects in either sex. It is this unFreudian reinstatement of women's sexuality as naturally attuned to her reproductive destiny which found its fullest expression in the writings of Helene Deutsch, and which came to serve as the new Freudian orthodoxy after the Second World War.

For Deutsch the struggle between the girl's early active clitoral sexuality and the discovery of vaginal sexuality 'through a masochistic submission to the penis' is biologically preordained for the achievement of womanhood. It is Deutsch, too, who most strongly allies female sexuality to passivity and masochism, as the girl's active clitoral aims are turned inwards to allow for her reproductive destiny: 'The mechanism of the turn from active to passive . . . pervades woman's entire instinctual life.'[26] In fact, she suggests, it is only childbirth which provides 'the acme of sexual pleasure' and 'constitutes for women the termination of the sexual act, which was only inaugurated by coitus'.[27] The 'truly passive, feminine attitude of the vagina is based upon the oral, sucking activity' of the infant at the breast, and thus coitus for women can restore to her that original condition of 'perfect unity of being and harmony in which the distinction between subject and object was annulled'.[28] Women's only real problems are around the difficulty they may have throwing off any residual active libido:

> But for the bisexual disposition of the human being, which is so adverse to the woman, but for the clitoris with its masculine strivings, how simple and clear would be her way to an untroubled mastering of existence![29]

'But for', indeed. So is 'feminine' passivity and masochism preordained, or is it not? Deutsch aggressively strives to bury alive female 'masculine' strivings, so she can ordain innate heterosexuality. It was this vein of normative moralizing and prescriptiveness around women's reproductive destiny, so at odds with the emphases and potentialities struggling against it in Freud's own writing, which would, unsurprisingly, be condemned as thoroughly oppressive to women by second-wave feminism two decades later. But then Freud himself could never really solve his own dilemmas around sexual difference. He was continually confronted with the centrality of sexual identity to his explorations of individual subjectivity, although its accompanying tensions, pain and neurosis suggested the worthlessness of contemporary certainties of biological sexual difference.

Until the 1920s Freud tended to regard the sexual life of girls and boys as parallel. Moreover, he warned repeatedly that sexual polarity has no biological or physical basis: making '"active" coincide with "masculine" and "passive" with "feminine"' serves 'no useful purpose and adds nothing to our knowledge'.[30] Nevertheless, in what has been called his 'characteristic double gesture', his 'masculinity' as 'activity' does in the end refer to what is in some fundamental way male, his 'femininity' as 'passivity' to what is in some fundamental way female. Yes, bisexuality is real, yet heterosexuality is normative and naturalized. Yes, sexual polarity is uncertain, yet sexual opposition is inevitable. In his 1920 case study of homosexuality in a woman, we learn that when his 18-year-old patient took a woman as object of her desire 'she changed into a man'. Homosexuality is viewed as merely a mixed-up form of heterosexuality (although in other passages contradictions and inconsistencies once again abound).

At a deeper level, there is something fundamentally incoherent about Freud's whole account of sexual polarity, because he cannot really specify what the 'feminine' side is, other than as something to be 'repudiated'. The most 'feminine' of all wishes the woman can aspire to is the wish for a baby, but the wish for a baby, Freud is quite certain, is the wish for a penis. This leads him into the logical but seemingly extraordinary position that 'perhaps we ought to recognize the wish for a penis as being *par excellence* a feminine one'.[31] What is most distinctively feminine is one and the same thing as the desire to possess what is most distinctively masculine: the penis. The difficulty of using Freudian thinking on sexual difference to move beyond a seemingly sexist affirmation of the 'masculine' and negation of the 'feminine' is, ironically, nowhere clearer than in recent attempts to rescue it from any taint of biological reductionism, by emphasizing instead that it is never anatomy which is at issue but always only the body as represented in the patriarchal symbolic order.

Phallic presciptions, penile practices

The threat of castration and its corollary 'penis envy' sum up the child's experience of sexual difference in orthodox Freudianism. But why? 'The fantasy of castration, so embarrassingly in excess of either biology or biography, an outrage on common sense and provocation to feminist indignation', as John Fletcher comments, nevertheless does seem to capture something about men's uncertainty over ever achieving 'manhood'.[32] It echoes men's intense anxieties: 'Being a man', as one of its champions lives to preach, 'is the continuing battle of one's life.'[33] It also expresses something about women's dissatisfaction, rather than uncertainty, over the destiny of 'womanhood': 'Women? Incompleteness, perpetual dependency', as one woman sums up her feelings, 'they have the role of Vestal Virgins guarding the flame . . . God the Father is a man! . . . I've always held women in contempt.'[34] But what it captures, so obviously irreducible to actual anatomical difference, clearly functions as patriarchal *myth*.

In recent decades some feminists have argued (to the intense irritation of others) that it is the French post-structuralist and psychoanalyst Jacques Lacan who is best equipped theoretically to return us to a Freud freed from any presumption of penile supremacy – however notoriously abstract his theory, however opaque, elliptical and sadistically 'playful' his prose. Indeed, it is the writing of Lacan and his École Freudienne, they suggest, which can place the Freudian legacy beyond all possible taint of prescription, moralism or normativeness regarding the 'natural' state or status of anything at all, in the human sphere.

Although Lacan is most often cited in Britain and North America for his thoughts on sexual difference, their origin lies in his account of the illusory nature of subjectivity. The infant, or what Lacan with characteristic wit labels the 'hommelette' (its polymorphous desires moving off in all directions), is not a human subject. And it will only gradually become one through an alienating or illusory sense of subjective autonomy, created at first through identification with an external image or reflection. The reflection arises in the gaze of the mother, and in the infant's jubilant, but still illusory, sense of unity gained through the appropriation of its reflection in the mirror. However, this is not the beginning of a 'true self', but of an inevitably alienating and constraining ego, a self-for-others, always 'referential to the other' and therefore distanced from the infant's inner drives and desires: 'The core of our being does not coincide with the ego.'[35]

Moreover, this misleading, pre-symbolic sense of infantile wholeness arising from the 'mirror phase' can only evolve into a human subject through the further alienation of its insertion into the 'symbolic order' of language. And it can only position itself within language by taking on a sexed identity, within a system of patriarchal meanings and representations which pre-exist the individual subject, where 'the phallus' is *the* mark of sexual division, and is situated in language as *the* 'privileged signifier'.[36] The 'phallus' is not something men possess, but something hegemonic within a seemingly timeless symbolic order, just as, in classical antiquity, the phallus was both a representation of the erect male organ and a symbol of sovereign power.[37] The phallus is not the penis, but its representation as symbol of the father's power and desire: 'it is in the *name of the father* that we must recognise the support of the symbolic function which, from the dawn of history has identified his person with the figure of the law.'[38] The phallus is not a biological attribute, but a discursive position which constitutes women in terms of lack and men in terms of the threat of a lack. It creates a sense of difference from a power which is *illusory* – the fantasized possession, or lack, of the phallus.

Illusory or not, however, the consequences of Lacan's fascination with language (and a very specific interpretation of language at that)[39] are depressing for understanding women's subjectivity, their place in culture and psychic life. Lacan acknowledges this: 'There is for her something insurmountable, something unacceptable, in the fact of being placed as an object [of the phallus] in a symbolic order to which, at the same time, she is subject just as much as the man.'[40] In this symbolic order, a woman cannot exist except in the shadow of the phallus, which is what makes her sexuality so enigmatic. Lacan does speculate, observing the ecstasy of St Theresa, that perhaps in the safety of her place of 'not-being': 'There is a *jouissance* [extreme pleasure] proper to her of which she herself may know nothing, except that she experiences it – that much she does know.'[41] But the unknowable truth of women's surplus of pleasure cannot, it seems, belong to the human sphere, to the symbolic world of the hegemonic phallus. It cannot, therefore, provide a woman with any way of communicating her existence as an agent of her own desire, but can only engage her in the mystery of women's place as the foreordained object of phallic fantasy: 'there is no limit to the concession which [a woman] makes for a man with her body, her soul, and her possessions', Lacan elaborates.[42] Playfully, of course.

The 'rush to Lacan' in Western cultural – as distinct from clinical – analysis of the late 1970s and early 1980s,[43] did much to reinforce the idea of representation and language as areas of oppression, internalized through women's subjective relations to them. They are oppressive in their seemingly ineluctable phallocentrism, cementing phallic representation to images of activity and power. They are oppressive in their exclusion of any equivalent symbol representing women in terms of power or desire – except for the phallus. In her uniquely influential essay on visual pleasure and cinema, for example, Laura Mulvey applies a Lacanian analysis to Hollywood productions, to take us 'nearer to the roots of our oppression'. Discussing classic films, like those of Hitchcock, she finds *all* their female images to be images of women on display, sexualized and possessed, positioned as the passive objects of the male gaze and the active male protagonist – who is never himself sexually objectified:

> In a world ordered by sexual imbalance, pleasure in
> looking has been split between active/male and
> passive/female. . . . Mainstream film neatly combined
> spectacle and narrative. An active/passive heterosexual
> division of labour has similarly controlled narrative
> structure.[44]

Observing images of masculinity in westerns and epic cinema, Steve Neale agrees with Mulvey that the dominant look is male, and men's bodies cannot be presented as sexualized objects – although repressed homosexual desire is often discernible beneath the surface.[45] Richard Dyer also writes of 'the excessive, even hysterical, quality of so much male imagery', exploring the inaccessible, tough, hard, active attributes necessary to overturn the impression of the male model as object of the gaze, and therefore any possibility of maleness as perhaps passive and feminine.[46]

The main attraction of Lacanian theory for feminists lay in the distinction it draws between the phallus and the penis, with the latter never able to match up to the power of the phallus, and thereby creating a sense of lack ('castration') in men as well as in women. Lacan's emphasis on the invariably perilous and unstable construction of subjectivity and sexual identity at the level of the unconscious has similarly been welcomed by those feminists wanting to assert that 'most women do not painlessly slip into their roles as women, if indeed they do at all'.[47] The main disappointment, however, is that Lacan frees understandings of sexual difference from any biological or sociological reductionism, only to freeze them forever within a universal symbolic order unaffected by either personal biography and bodily encounter, or the specificities of historical and cultural context: 'no sexual revolution will shift these lines of division,' as one of his female followers affirms.[48]

It would seem that Lacanian thinking can provide only impediments to feminist attempts to represent women in terms other than lack and passivity. Lacan's personal mockery of women's 'complaints' is not the least of them: 'they don't know what they are saying, which is all the difference between them and me.'[49] 'The nature of femininity is to be cause of a man's desire and, as corollary, not to be able to be recognized other than by a man is the nature of femininity', another Lacanian woman analyst sums up her master's message.[50] Is Lacanian theory not therefore, as its critics suggest, an obstacle to feminist goals of equality, a theory perpetually seeking only sexual difference, and portraying that difference only as phallic difference? But if Western intellectual discourses and imagery *are* essentially phallocentric, everywhere built upon the ideal of thrusting manhood, how can we ever represent the desiring or assertive female other than as she has been traditionally portrayed, in terms of the 'masculine' or 'phallic'? How can we renounce Lacan, and subvert cultural phallocentrism?

Feminists have used a variety of strategies. Some, like Luce Irigaray and Hélène Cixous, celebrate an oppositional, pre-symbolic, fluid and multiple feminine difference, abandoning the existing realm of symbolic rationality to men.[51] Others have used the neo-Lacanian Jean Laplanche to illustrate the multiplicity of subjective identifications available in fantasy, thus disordering the active/passive, male/female positioning of sexual difference.[52] A growing number have addressed the significance of differences other than those of gender, noting that class, race, ethnicity and sexual orientation, for example, have no place in psychoanalytic formulations of subjectivity.[53] I think the most useful way to acknowledge, while trying to move beyond, cultural phallocentrism is to address the interminable confusions which beset all attempts to specify the relation between the penis and the phallus; indeed, which beset the most rudimentary attempt to specify the meaning of this most significant of signifiers: the 'phallus'.

Most Lacanians will argue that the phallic signifier denotes neither gender nor superiority: no one, male or female, 'can ever be the wholeness that it represents'. In their view, criticisms of Lacan's phallocentrism simply fail to understand the distinction between penis and phallus. Lacan himself suggested that the phallus is 'the signifier for which there is no signified'.[54] Instead, it marks the role of language in the 'advent of desire', and the inevitable alienation of the subject in language.[55] But if there is no penile reference in the phallus, it cannot serve as a theory of sexual difference, nor indeed of desire, at all. And as a number of recent commentators on Lacan, like Kaja Silverman, clarify, the equation between penis and phallus is in fact always sustained, despite its continual denial. The child's learning that the mother does not 'have' the phallus, for instance, can only be understood as a direct extension of her penile 'lack', just as the penis is referred to when Lacan describes the woman finding 'the signifier of her own desire in the body of him to whom she addresses her demand for love – adding that 'the organ that assumes this signifying function takes on the value of a fetish'.[56] But once we accept that the desire for the phallus is dependent upon, at the very least, an analogy with its penile referent, it becomes possible to 'lift the veil' from the phallus (which Lacan has told us can only serve its function 'veiled'), and thereby, perhaps, to begin to challenge its authority and privilege as a transcendental signifier.

Jane Gallop, like Kaja Silverman and a growing number of feminist critics, has written wittily of the importance of just such a strategy.[57] But perhaps more appropriately, it is a male writer, Charles Bernheimer, who follows it through most thoroughly, exploring penile anatomy for its subversion of phallic conceit: 'The word is out: Lacan's phallus will not fly. It is too closely tied to the penis to be able to soar freely as a transcendental signifier.'[58] Once the phallus is unveiled to reveal its dependence upon a penile referent, it is possible to reflect upon just how inadequately it serves to signify that male organ, and men's personal histories of bodily experience. The problem, of course, in admitting penile reference in conceptualizing the phallus is the changing condition of that particular bodily organ, between its transient firm and erect state and its more characteristic limp and flaccid (detumescent) one. It is this only temporarily erect penis, this change in the male genital, which Lacan (and Freud) dare not risk evoking as a type of phallic lack, shifting the signification instead onto an image of female lack. The phallus, in contrast, unaffected by time, context or desiring encounter, has no such temporal changeability, symbolizing (in its veiled way) the fantasy of the fullness and generative power of the always-erect penis. Its signification calls to mind the silicone rod of penile implants – a form of surgical prosthesis sought after by hundreds of thousands of men in the USA today. Their anxiety over penile insufficiency and eagerness to pursue the fantasy of phallic wholeness is apparently undaunted by knowledge of the resulting decline in penile sensitivity, high rates of post-operative infection and subsequent mechanical malfunction.[59]

Bernheimer's argument is that male subjectivity emerges allegorically in the struggle for authority between the penis and the phallus. 'In so far as the phallus refers to the erect penis, it refers to something whose temporality is erratic, whose appearance is sporadic, and whose duration is uncertain. The phallic reference in short is not phallocentric.'[60] But Lacan refuses to discuss or even acknowledge the effect of bodily reference on the unconscious. Castration anxiety, which Lacan sees as the difference between phallic 'all' and feminine 'not all' (man has it only in so far as woman lacks it), is seen by Bernheimer as more appropriately attaching itself not to the sight of female difference, but to the sight of male lack, to categories *internal* to the penis: an anxiety which is then projected onto women. In a similar way Susan Lurie had earlier challenged the psychoanalytic notion that men fear women because she appears to be castrated, suggesting instead that men fear women and construct them as castrated because '*she is not castrated* despite the fact she has no penis', while his own experience of detumescence feels like a castrating loss of patriarchal power and masculine identity.[61] Kaja Silverman also suggests that the boy's 'horror' of female 'castration' can be explained as the effect of projection onto the female body from a source within the boy's own psychological history.[62] Although dominant representations of masculinity always work to maintain the equation of penis and phallus, existing representations of marginal male subjectivities (perhaps portrayed as 'damaged', perhaps as 'homosexual') tend to subvert it. The utopian hope Silverman holds out is that with the disassociation of the equation of penis and phallus, 'the typical male subject, like his female counterpart, might learn to live with lack'.[63]

For these particular critics, there is no denying the force of Lacan's notion of phallic privilege in language and representation. The question is whether the fear and anxiety it is seen as creating in men comes from its role as the signifier of the subject's metaphysical lack-in-being, or whether, as Bernheimer suggests, it is better theorized as coming from the social and cultural history of men's relations to their bodies, and their failure to sustain a particular symbolic attribution. It is also important to note that just as Lacan denies the anatomical reference of the phallus, so too he denies the social reference of actually existing fathers, or the significance of shifting family patterns and social relations in maintaining the timeless authority of the phallus which, through the metaphor of the 'Name-of-the-Father', has been identified as 'the figure of the law' from the dawn of history. This Father has neither bodily nor social dimensions, which is just as well for Him. Today, actual fathers are threatened not only by penile wilting and inadequacy, but by the visible decline of both their familial and wider social power, as women (still against enormous odds) become heads of households and occupy positions of status in the public sphere.

The fantasy of the all-powerful phallus remains as symbol and metaphor of idealized manhood, but however ubiquitous, it is not the only image we have of men and masculinities. In his theorizing of desire, Lacan leaves us exactly as he assumes he found us, still staring hypnotically at the phallus – even while recognizing its fraudulence. For men, such phallic thraldom will forever deny access to the possibilities of bodily eroticism and the extremities or unconditional pleasure, of *jouissance*. Men's bodily desire, as Terry Eagleton wryly comments, 'is condemned to grope its laborious way from partial sign to partial sign, diffusing and fragmenting as it goes.'[64] For women, such pleasure can occur, but it can never be articulated. Lost for words, Lacan cannot take us beyond the phallic stranglehold of loss, lack and silence. But there are alternative, if subordinate, discourses and images of masculinity: some focussing upon men's anatomical and social uncertainties, others which linger over the objectified, eroticized male body – increasingly commodified in Western advertising. There are also differences of class, race, ethnicity and sexual orientation throwing up a multiplicity of discourses about the body other than gender.[65] The Lacanian account of the unchanging structure of meaning which created the transcendental phallus today itself looks more precarious. New rhetorics of the body and its erotic potential may yet help to forge a language which does not require the repudiation of bodily experiences, interactions and pleasures (whether male or female); just as shifting gender positions inside and outside the family may yet help us find the words to acknowledge women's existence in terms other than their 'lack' in relation to men. That the human subject might remain forever frustrated in what Lacan calls its desire for imaginary 'phallic' wholeness, a *jouissance* fantasized as possible only through the impossible possession and fulfilment of the desire of its original m/other – as both the subject and object of this desire – would then serve as just another tale of the pains of love.

It has been necessary to grapple with Lacan and his influence because so many academic feminists have turned to his work in search of explanations for the centrality of phallic metaphor and meaning in Western culture and identity, freed from its traditional grounding in biology. It is necessary to try to get beyond Lacan because he has provided the most sophisticated arguments for the cheerless certainty of phallic privilege, mocking feminist hopes that it might be possible for a woman to have a sense of power, identity and desire other than for and through the symbolic attribute of manhood. Finally, it is necessary to get past Lacan before we can reconsider, one last time, the potential and limitations of psychoanalytic thinking for explaining sexual desire in ways which shed light upon its ambiguous and uneasy nature.

Women's desire and the bonds of love

Although Lacan's followers have promoted their own version of Freudian orthodoxy, centred like Freud's own work on the role of the father in the Oedipal experience, clinical developments in psychoanalysis have, for the most part, pursued a very different trajectory. They have downplayed Freud's phallic stage and the presence of the father to become 'almost entirely mother-centred'.[66] In Britain, for example, the followers of Melanie Klein emphasized the child's early experiences of mothering, and her ideas of the persistence into adulthood of the effects of the infant's early 'schizoid' and 'depressive' positions created around its love and rage towards the mother – cutting across gender.[67] Even more focussed upon the adequacies of actual maternal behaviour, the Independents of the British School of Psychoanalysis explored the early mother-infant bond. Donald Winnicott, Ronald Fairbairn, Michael Balint and Harry Guntrip all highlighted the crucial importance of the 'good-enough' mother in enabling the infant to experience a fundamental fusion, and then gradually to develop a sense of separateness, with and from her, within a warm and holding environment. In the USA, Margaret Mahler wrote similarly of the significance of the mother-infant bond, sustaining the child's growing sense of itself as it consciously becomes a separate being from the mother.

Case studies in this post-Freudian tradition, now loosely referred to as the school of 'object-relations', addressed aspects of maternal care in the assumed world of the child: identification, idealization, projection, envy, aggression, deprivation and loss became its core concepts.[68] The role of sexuality in the interactions of the child with the parents was increasingly marginalized, if not eliminated, in these new psychoanalytic tales, where what matters is always the threat of the loss of the mother. The father disappears from the theory. As Appignanesi and Forrester conclude:

> Freud's sexual mother had been ushered blushing from the analytic scene. And, with the eclipse of the sexual mother, the . . . child was itself to be desexualized, in that very British tradition which has also created *Alice in Wonderland* and *Peter Pan*.[69]

Even in the adult, in fact, any reference to sexual bodies and sensual pleasures begins to fade out of the picture – in the healthy person – replaced by the search for 'true object love' or the 'forms of transcendence' characterizing mature heterosexual love, as Otto Kernberg and others have put it.[70] This is always the search for the recovery of a primary sense of real or fantasied fusion with the mother, through orgasmic merging with another – at least in men. (Only in heterosexual intercourse, in this view, can such fulfilment be found, which explains the moral prescriptiveness of most object-relations analysis: 'without normal intercourse, there is no real contentment,' Michael Balint affirms.[71]) Here, also, the satisfactions of sexual contact for women are less complete than for men. A woman has not so much a direct as a vicarious sense of recapturing the sense of oneness with the mother, created through her identification with the man penetrating her – she thus becomes the mother.[72]

Although these post-Freudian case histories always lead back to maternal shortcomings, seen as responsible for the problems of the disturbed adult, object-relations psycho-analysis suggested new directions for understanding the tenacity and significance of gender identity and gender hierarchy to some feminists in the mid-1970s. Its focus on women and the importance of mothering inspired a second feminist reappropriation of Freudian thought, first of all in the USA, where only a few years earlier it had been almost completely rejected as quintessential patriarchal ideology by writers like Betty Friedan, Kate Millett and Shulamith Firestone.[73] The psychologist Dorothy Dinnerstein and, even more influential, the sociologist Nancy Chodorow, were its two earliest exponents.[74] Chodorow, in *The Repro-duction of Mothering*, draws upon the work of British analysts Fairbairn, Balint and Guntrip to reject Freud's notions of sexual drives and his interest in the unfolding of erogenous zones through their erotic stimulation, except in so far as they become 'vehicles for attaining personal contact': infants are first of all object-seeking rather than pleasure-seeking.[75] She also rejects penis envy as dominant in women's lives, or castration anxiety in men's, for an alternative account of how women's universal responsibility for mothering creates oppositional and unequal gender identities.

Mothered by someone of a different gender from them-selves, who recognizes and loves them as different from herself, boys must develop their sense of self in opposition to the mother, repressing and denying their early infantile 'mergence' with her. The boy will therefore construct strong ego boundaries, concealing a defensive, often fragile, masculine identity resulting from the emotional and physical absence of fathers in the social world of the child. This fuels his ongoing fear of and contempt for the 'feminine' in personal relationships, and male dominance in society generally: 'the very fact of being mothered by a woman generates in men conflicts over masculinity, a psychology of male dominance, and a need to be superior to women.'[76] Girls, in contrast, form their sense of self through merging with the mother, who in turn identifies with the daughter as the same as herself. The girl's gender identity is thus more secure and straightforward than that of the boy's, but exists always in relationship to others, with ego boundaries which are fluid and permeable, creating her capacity for empathy and sensitivity towards others and the ability and desire to mother. As long as women mother, women remain 'more open to and preoccupied with those very relational issues that go into mothering'.[77]

Unlike Lacanian feminism, Chodorow's feminist object-relations theory was inspirational both clinically and strategically for feminist psychotherapists and activists. Her argument that shared parenting could help undermine existing familial construction of gender asymmetries was widely endorsed by other pioneers of feminist therapy, like Luise Eichenbaum and Susie Orbach.[78] But Chodorow was criticized by some feminists, myself included, for narrowing down the conflicts and complexities of both the psychic and the social world, and ignoring differences between as well as within women – or men – in conformity with existing gender stereotypes.[79] Freud always said, for example, that while human activity may become comprehensible in hindsight, it is never fully predictable or determined in advance. Indeed Chodorow herself, who has now trained as an analyst, no longer sees mothering as the over-riding cause of male dominance and is more open to 'views of the multiplicities of gender(ed) experience'.[80] More significantly for my purposes here, however, is the outcome that the central motor of psychoanalytic theorizing – the dynamics of sexuality – has run itself out, replaced by other forces in the move from sexual drives to object seeking, and the attention now given over to understanding gender identity and ego boundaries. In particular, female sexuality has become a muted, 'milky' affair, an offshoot of benevolent mother-daughter bonding. As Andrew Samuels puts it: 'The numinosity of sex has been replaced by the numinosity of feeding'.[81]

The Reproduction of Mothering, for example, contains no significant discussion of either women's childhood or adult sexual experiences: their sexual fantasies or masturbatory activities are missing from the text. Chodorow does argue that the girl's bisexual potential combined with her learning of appropriate gender roles means that most women will 'become genitally heterosexual', but they will not develop 'strong heterosexual object love'.[82] They are, on this view, weakly heterosexual, because men 'tend to remain *emotionally* secondary', women rarely abandoning their earlier mother bonding.[83] Women, however, do look to and frequently idealize fathers – and subsequently other men – as a source for their own autonomous selfhood, always threatened by a dependent merger with the mother, with her apparent maternal omnipotence. Men, although more directly desiring women as replacement for the lost mother, also fear them. They are as a consequence less able to offer women the recognition and intimacy they need. 'Families', Chodorow argues here, 'create children gendered, heterosexual, and ready to marry.'[84] But men's 'lack of emotional availability' and women's 'less exclusive heterosexual commitment' mean that they are unlikely to meet each other's asymmetrical erotic and emotional needs, if and when they do.

Sexuality, when it does emerge in this perspective, is something men have learned to use, not just to find their original female object, but to consolidate their more fragile gender identities: to gain a symbolic sense of power over women, to enable the disguised expression of dependency needs and to keep primary 'feminine' identifications repressed. This is why, it is suggested, men's sexuality so frequently appears compulsive or driven. Female sexuality, however, is altogether less pressing in this account. In an influential formulation, the New York psychoanalyst Ethel Spector Person puts it like this:

> There is a wealth of clinical material to suggest that,
> in this culture, genital sexuality is a prominent feature in
> the maintenance of masculine gender while it is a variable
> feature in feminine gender. .... In men, gender appears to
> 'lean' on sexuality. . . . In women, gender identity and
> self-worth can be consolidated by other means.[85]

She, and others in her wake, have used this analysis to offer persuasive new reflections on the compulsive aspects of much of men's sexuality. Person, for instance, sees in many men's routine consumption of pornography not just their fears of genital inadequacy – derived from the threatening Oedipal father and castration anxiety – but intense oral and dependent needs for the 'omni-available woman', the pre-Oedipal 'feeding' mother, camouflaged as sexual demands. Pornography denies and reverses men's dread of female rejection, experienced from both mothers and subsequent adolescent encounter. Person also points to unconscious female self-identification in men's fantasies of lesbian sex, another staple ingredient of the pornography men consume.[86] Similarly, John Munder Ross has described the sexual practices of many heterosexual men who are so afraid of their own repressed 'feminine' identifications that any intimacy, or union, with women is terrifying: they must be 'in and out like a shot'.[87]

Since sexuality is understood as primarily a vehicle for object relations, these theorists emphasize the wide variety of non-sexual motives which it serves. They are predominantly dependent or hostile motives, particularly in what they deem its perverse or neurotic manifestations. Robert Stoller, for example, studying both pornography and his own patients' erotic fantasies and daydreams, argues that some element of hostility is *always* present in sexual excitement: 'I have found that what makes excitement out of boredom for most people is the introduction of hostility into fantasy.'[88] Erotic fantasies, he argues, are uniquely constructed in complex but precise detail to undo the traumas, conflicts, frustrations and humiliations which, from infancy, every person has experienced in their search for intimacy. Stoller's work illustrates that there is potential for reflecting upon sexual experience in object-relations theorizing (which does more than pathologize as immature 'perverse' sexual practices) – although he is certainly unusual in producing it. But in the feminist versions, as indeed in Stoller, which emphasize many women's capacity to abstain from sex 'without negative psychological consequences', there seems a danger of merely continuing Western traditions of muffling women's sexual desires and possible pleasures.[89]

Women's desire is what Jessica Benjamin, another object-relations therapist and theoretician in the USA, attempts explicitly to reclaim, as she explores the problem of male domination and female submission. She doesn't succeed, but she holds out the possibility of success in the future. In the present, the complexities of women's sexual realities once again tend to disappear behind generalizations of gender hierarchy and women's search for subjectivity. Her failure is, however, instructive. Like Chodorow, on whom she draws, her work is important in trying to connect psychoanalytic reasoning with a social and political analysis of the historical specificities of gender and power. In *The Bonds of Love*, Benjamin uses clinical data and, more surprisingly, Hegel's philosophy to explore how family life and gender hierarchy foster a desire for submission in women, and to suggest how we might change this.

She begins, unusually for someone influenced by object-relations theory, by accepting rather than downplaying the importance of the phallus and its hold on the unconscious as a symbol of power and desire. But she sees the representation of the father's penis not as powerful *in itself*, but rather in its function of representing paternal independence from the mother. Drawing upon French analyst Janine Chasseguet-Smirgel, Benjamin argues that the wish for the father's penis signifies the desire to 'beat back the maternal power', symbolizing separation from the fantasy of the all-powerful mother of infancy.[90] The girl, like the boy, turns to the father, who represents the excitement of the 'outside world', and freedom from dependence on the mother. But, unlike the boy, her struggle for autonomy and identification with paternal independence (and his status and place in the external world) is unlikely to be recognized by the father. This returns her to maternal identification, and the construction of her sense of self through the paradoxical experience of a controlling and intrusive, and yet socially demeaned and submissive mother. She is a woman, we are told, who because of gender inequality is not a subject herself, but she is nevertheless experienced as powerful.

Women's 'desire' (if, as Benjamin does, we can call it

that even though a woman still here characteristically lacks a 'desire of her own') is thus formed through alienation, submission, and idealization of a paternal power and agency that they can never possess: 'Unprotected by the phallic sign of gender difference, unsupported by an alternate relationship, they relinquish their entitlement to desire'.[91] Men's sexual desire, in sharp contrast, is seen as tending towards domination, denying and devaluing the dependence associated with the mother. Lacking any sense of their own autonomy, Benjamin continues, many women consent to relationships of domination with men, or experience fantasies of domination. Combining Hegelian dialectic with Winnicottian developmental stages, the desire for physical humiliation and abuse is presented as a desire for recognition from the other, from the He who has the power to bestow such recognition. She illustrates this with a reading of *The Story of 0*:

> Submission, as we saw in *The Story of 0*, is often motivated by fear of separation and abandonment; masochism reflects the inability to express one's own desire and agency. The masochist abrogates her will because the exercise of independence is experienced as dangerous. To the extent that the mother has sacrificed her own independence, the girl's attempt at independence would represent an assertion of power for which she has no basis in identification.[92]

There seem at least three problems with Benjamin's analysis of masochistic fantasy here, which means it falls well short of utilizing the potential of psychoanalytic reflection on sexuality (as, it must be admitted, does most contemporary psychoanalytic writing on the topic of heterosexuality). The complexity of the social is ignored, reduced to generalizations about fixed relations of power – as though to be less powerful in society, as mothers so often are, is to be, and to be perceived to be, simply submissive and powerless. The psychic is no longer layered and contradictory, but thought to mirror directly what is seen as the nature of the social – as though to fantasize submission is no different from the experience of actual social subordination. Finally, sexuality is not analysed in her account as a multifaceted but nevertheless distinct and autonomous mental experience, constructed out of the psychic representations of individual histories of bodily sensation and pleasure. Indeed, when seen by Benjamin as the enjoyment of erotic submission, sexuality is not about bodies and pleasures at all, but the search for subjectivity. Here, women's sexuality can only re-enact their total identification with 'the self-sacrificing mother': 'it is a replication of the maternal attitude itself.'[93] Women's sexual desire, it appears, has not so much been reclaimed by Benjamin, as removed. She ends up with everything to say about the construction of gender identity, but little to offer on women's complex autoerotic or inter-personal sexual encounters, nor even on women's sexual fantasy – apart from a dubious reading of *The Story of O*.

It is a dubious reading because, as Freud himself was certain, the most consistent feature of both masochistic and sadistic fantasy and practices is that they do not separate out from one another or correspond to lived relations of power and subordination, but invariably occur together in the same individual: 'A sadist is always at the same time a masochist.'[94] As we shall see in the next chapter, what is so scandalous and threatening about the growing awareness of sado-masochistic fantasies and sexualities is that they characteristically challenge rather than uphold traditional assumptions (reasserted by Benjamin) linking sexuality to gender in dominant sexual discourse: the 'masculine' as dominant and active, the 'feminine' as submissive and passive. This is precisely why the practice is so savagely condemned today, especially – where most commonly found – in consensual relations between men. When Madonna directs, orchestrates and pockets the millions she makes from the sado-masochistic theatre displayed in her best-seller *Sex*, we would be fools to read her masochistic moments as 'the inability to express [her] own desire and agency'.

Benjamin's analysis, while it may possibly tell us something about gender identity and women's acceptance of relationships of social subordination, sheds next to no light on sexual realities – either of women or of men. Indeed, it is at odds with what is now well known from the evidence of sex workers, among others, that submissive sexual scenarios are regularly sought after by men, who supposedly want erotic dominance: 'In the world of the sadomasochist, there is nothing "abnormal" about a male being passive and submissive.'[95] There is much more to sexuality than an individual's erotic replaying of gender hierarchy, at least if this is seen as the boy escaping from, while the girl internalizes, 'submissive and demeaned' maternal roles.

But there is another side to Benjamin's writing, which is more optimistic about the possibilities for women finding 'a desire of their own', which sits paradoxically alongside her account of the impossibility of any such thing. In tune with the potential complexity of psychic life and social relationships, Benjamin points to the possibilities of both girls and boys making use of their identifications with both parents – a feature, as she points out, of the pre-Oedipal years before identification becomes tied to gender identity. In Oedipal identifications, occurring with the child's knowledge that it can only be one sex, when boys and girls both chauvinistically want to valorize their own sex and triumph over the other sex, it is girls who lose out because of the cultural devaluation of women's existence as mothers. However, mothers as well as fathers *could* become figures of separation *and* attachment, Benjamin argues, but only once there is social and political change, along the lines of men's greater engagement in caring, and women's increasing involvement and status in the world beyond the family. Then and only then, according to Benjamin, could children of either sex remain identified with the sameness *and* difference of both parents.[96]

Presenting a parallel argument for the possibilities of representing women's desire, Benjamin writes of the need to think in terms of both inner and intersubjective space, of the 'containing' and 'holding' mother, as representing a type of sexual subjectivity:

> When the sexual self is represented by the sensual
> capacities of the whole body, when the totality of space
> between, outside and within our bodies becomes the site
> of pleasure, then desire escapes the borders of the imperial
> phallus and resides on the shores of endless worlds.[97]

Here the 'holding' mother is being valorized as providing a 'constituent element of desire', alongside the 'exciting' father. Today Benjamin stresses more firmly than before both the significance of the 'sexual' mother and the possibilities for cross-sex identifications, and therefore for a plurality of positions. After the Oedipal phase, she suggests, there is the possibility of a post-Oedipal developmental phase when the subject of either sex can transcend Oedipal identifications to reincorporate earlier cross-sex identifications, balancing the Oedipal polarities of masculinity/femininity, activity/passivity.[98] In this mode, Benjamin is suggestive about how we might begin to re-think women's sexual agency. But her work to date has yet to expand such a project beyond occasional fragments.

Promises and evasions in psychoanalysis

It is ironic that although sexual conflict and frustration provided the building blocks of psychoanalysis, very few adult sexualities are explored in contemporary psycho-analytic writing – least of all heterosexual fantasies and practices. Since Freud's day, as Kenneth Lewes and Henry Abelove have documented, psychoanalysts have shown, if anything, even less desire to deconstruct, rather than maintain, normative assumptions around heterosexuality.[99] A few years ago, Karin Martin surveyed eight major psychoanalytic journals over the previous decade, finding no articles directly addressing heterosexuality and a mere two on love.[100]

Chodorow now complains that there is no psychoanalytic examination of 'normal' heterosexuality to compare with the richness and specificity of accounts of the development of homosexuality. (This 'richness', it must be said, is often the result of the extreme pathologization of both homosexual and other 'perverse' sexualities, as in Chasseguet-Smirgel's grotesque association of non-heterosexual activity with murder, genocide and Nazism.[101]) In contrast, Chodorow stresses what she sees as the importance of looking for the inherent defensiveness, conflicts and identifications that shape heterosexual desires and practices, and of assuming that analysts will find, were they to look, a wide variety of heterosexualities – both 'normal' and 'perverse'. Instead, however, heterosexual eroticism is taken for granted, and the description of homosexual desire reduced to these presumed heterosexual structures of attraction: 'feminized' men and 'masculine' women. As Chodorow concludes, even as the evidence of people's fantasy life and behaviour tends to disentangle the links between gender and sexuality, psychoanalytic theory, betraying many of its own insights, continues to assume them.[102]

Although Freud found disjunctions and ruptures in the assumed links between gender and sexuality, and although he kept warning against any easy acceptance of their normative connections, he could never himself cast them aside, or suggest a way of questioning or re-conceptualizing them. Thus, what psychoanalysis seems to promise with the one hand (or some versions of it anyway), it immediately withdraws with the other. On the one hand, there is awareness of the fragile, unstable, layered, precarious, fragmentary nature of psychic life, and its autonomy (or relative autonomy) from social prescriptions of sexual difference, of masculinity/femininity. On the other hand, sexual difference is bedrock, masculinity is activity, femininity is passivity. Psychoanalysis does not transcend, undermine or subvert these binaries, ultimately it relentlessly embraces them.

It is hard to avoid the paradox of wanting to assert psychoanalytic arguments while simultaneously needing to challenge them. It is to psychoanalysis rather than to sexology that we owe the insight that sexuality can never be reduced to the genital 'sex act', nor to biology, but is from the beginning central to the development of individual identity. This is what makes it so challenging and complex an affair. It interconnects with all other aspects of human existence. As Laplanche puts it, 'human beings *spontaneously reinvest* or *recathect* . . . the whole of psychical life with sexual motivations which are to a great extent unconscious.'[103] It is to certain psychoanalytic perspectives that we owe the idea that sexuality and sexual difference is bound up with language and representation, which again loops back to identity, and to the construction of desire. Finally, it is to psychoanalysis that we owe some of our understanding of phallocentrism. Freud did not merely invent its role in human consciousness. He found the dread and the repudiation of 'femininity' in his patients (as in himself), even if his legacy has often served more to entrench than to question the cultural force behind it.

Freud could never personally surmount such repudiation or imagine a world where women were not, simply, the subordinate sex. Either women's sexuality was the 'same' as men's – active and centred upon what he saw as that 'small and inconspicuous' organ, the clitoris; or women's sexuality was the 'complement' of men's – passive and centred upon that unknown and 'receptive' organ, the vagina. Freud would always share some of the 'horror' or 'threat' of castration he attributed to the little boy's sight of female genitals, endorsing, as Linda Williams comments, the 'fetishistic misrecognition of a sensuous perceptual thing'.[104] This is the force behind Luce Irigaray's compelling critique that Freud offers us not a theory of sexual *difference*, but rather a theory of sexual *indifference*, always within 'the problematics of sameness'.[105] But then, in my view, no other psycho-analytic approach has proved any more able to meet the challenge of rethinking female sexuality and desire, without retreating from Freud's 'complicated mental processes going on in different layers of the mind', to some less nuanced form of biological or discursive essentialism.

Freud's early critics returned women's sexuality to reproductive imperatives. Half a century later, Luce Irigaray, offering a different projection of the female body, also writes that in a direct and unmediated way 'we are women from the start'.[106] She bypasses rather than explores women's complex psychic compulsions and resistance in relation to phallocentric assumptions of sexual difference; bypasses rather than contests their cultural and political backing. Irigaray encourages women, instead, to speak and write directly 'her body-sex', to dare to speak as a woman, perhaps in mimetic parody – and hence exposure – of the reigning sexual economy of 'phallocracy'.

Irigaray's utopian re-imaginings of 'woman's' bodily morphology in terms of her multiple sex organs, her preference for the tactile over the visual, her bodily fluidity, her diffuse, changing and undefinable existence, has unquestionably inspired many women to think about questions of female difference in an alternative and positive way, rather than in the phallocentric terms of defective or 'castrated' men.[107] But in presenting women's sexuality as flowing directly from her 'speaking body' (however enigmatically metaphorical or figurative the presentation), without further forms of mediation (whether of biographical individuality or cultural diversity), Irigaray closes down what we most need to open up if we are ever to tackle the psychic complexities and conflicts of women's differing experiences as subjects and objects of sexual desire. Irigaray's writing is best seen as a strategy for undermining the dominant ways of thinking and writing about the female body. It is similar to the devices for cultural subversion now pursued in 'queer theory', which will be explored in the next chapter. 'She is', as Elizabeth Grosz celebrates, 'creating a discourse to contest or combat other, prevailing discourses.'[108]

Meanwhile, as Lacan and his followers abandon the study of bodily pleasures to dazzle us instead with their linguistic display of the reign of the fraudulent phallus, and object-relations theorists, for quite different reasons, eschew libidinal practices to elevate the search for normative heterosexual bonds, the disruptive challenge of Freud's own theorizing of sexuality recedes from psychoanalytic scholarship. But even as the traces of that libidinously flexible and excessive infant disappear from psychoanalytic narratives of adult sexual life, they reappear in the altered images and sounds of contemporary culture. They surround us, whether in lurid hard-core pornography, the extravagant sexual ambiguities and trashing of gender boundaries celebrated in the lyrics of the trendiest pop music (from Madonna to Suede), or in the less stirring but equally 'perverse' texts popular researchers are busily recording and publishing of men's and women's daydreamings and night practices. 'I'm the dominant one doing all the work and he's the receptive one,' 'Sue' reports to that intrepid collector of sexual fantasies, Nancy Friday. 'All I want is to control everything,' another tells her. Bizarrely, Friday seems to feel that she can take some responsibility for creating the abundance of what she sees as the 'new' sexual fantasies of 'Women on Top'. She believes that the publication of her book *My Secret Garden* empowered women: 'overnight the rape fantasy was rejected by the women in this book who wanted to exercise total power and domination over men.'[109] Nancy Friday knows about as much about fantasy as Freud knew about sex toys (she sees it as a direct reflection of conscious wishes). But it is ironic that today it should be the analyst-as-moralist who disdains to engage in any positive way with this brave new world where sexualities publicly cavort detached from either genitals or gender.

When Charles Socarides, for example, dismisses all perverse practices as pathological, and male homosexuality in particular as governed by 'destruction, mutual defeat, exploitation of the partner and the self', one could forget that it was Freud who first introduced us to the idea of the 'polymorphously perverse', and insisted that no pathology and 'no moral judgement was implied in the phrase'.[110] One could forget, as well, that it was Freud – almost a century ago – and not some contemporary queer theorist, who declared that when 'any one has *become* a gross and manifest pervert, it would be more correct to say he has *remained* one';[111] who claimed he could point to some trace of homosexual object-choice in everyone; and who wrote of the irresistibility of perverse instincts:

> The detaching of sexuality from the genitals has the advantage of allowing us to bring the sexual activities of children and perverts into the same scope as those of normal adults . . . from a psycho-analytic standpoint, even the most eccentric and repellent perversions are explicable as manifestations of component instincts which have freed themselves from the primacy of the genitals and are now in pursuit of pleasure on their own account as they were in the very early days of the libido's development.[112]

And one could certainly forget it was Freud who questioned the high price of 'civilized sexual morality', offering a picture of heterosexuality, as John Fletcher recounts, 'as a casualty ward of psychic cripples and walking wounded, of male impotence and female frigidity'.[113]

Despite the ubiquity of perverse fantasies and activities at the very core of Freud's writing, which confounds our ideas of what it means to be 'masculine' or 'feminine', the radical failure of his legacy is that it still, for the most part, simply follows his lead, 'takes over [these] two concepts and makes them the foundation of its work'.[114] If psychoanalysis is to liberate itself from its idea of the 'normal' woman's renunciation of active sexual aims, or from its idea of the 'normal' man's renunciation of passive sexual aims, then it must abandon its bedrock of oppositional sexual difference.[115] It may, or may not, take longer to liberate actual women and men from the ambivalence, confusion and pain of living out the effects of such cultural myths of difference – the idealization of the phallus and the disavowel and denigration of the feminine – but challenging their place in psychoanalysis could assist that process. After all this time, we have still to keep drawing attention to the ahistoricism of psychoanalysis. We have still to keep forcing it to accept that while our sexuality is formed in the shadow of the phallus, although never all-encompassingly, there exists no timeless decree that it must always be so formed. On the contrary, today, phallic distortion of the potentialities and diversities of human experience could hardly be more obvious.

Is it really impossible to reconcile sexual 'activity' with the acceptance of 'feminine' identity; or sexual 'passivity' with the acceptance of 'masculine' identity? There is a space in the psychoanalytic narrative of development, a space exemplary for all subsequent human sexual experience, where both girls and boys each easily reconcile the two, when active aims simply emerge out of prior passive aims:

> The first sexual and sexually coloured experiences which
> a child has in relation to its mother are naturally of a
> passive character . . . A part of its libido goes on clinging to
> those experiences and enjoys the satisfactions bound
> up with them; but another part strives to turn them into
> activity. In the first place being suckled at the breast gives
> place to active sucking.[116]

There is, as Freud puts it, no inevitable obstacle to a 'woman loving in a masculine fashion'. She has only to draw upon her early identification with the mother (or, of course, possible identifications with the father, or other intimate care providers), when that mother (or other) was experienced as the *active* provider of bodily pleasures of all sorts.

It is this active side of all girls' sexuality, however, which Freud believed, and cultural meanings of gender ordain, *must* be forsworn in the switch to heterosexual object love: 'A woman who has loved in the masculine way', he tells us, concluding the case study of his briefly analysed young lesbian patient, 'will hardly let herself be forced into *playing the part of a woman.*'[117] But why not? Why would anyone *not* want to enjoy both sides of sexual pleasure – that which Freud and our culture generally assigns to the passive or 'feminine' ('*playing* the part of a woman') and that which it assigns to the active or 'masculine' ('*playing* the part of a man) – when the latter, on his own analysis, *is but an inevitable progression from the former*? Like so many hierarchical binaries they are interdependent. A woman may certainly actively desire a man's (or woman's) body, and actively seek and stimulate the penis (as well as passively wait to receive and enjoy it). What we need to recognize, however, are the deep cultural obstacles, always at least partially psychically inscribed, to claiming as our own those experiences which reverse the dominant phallic presciption which insists that 'masculinity', and *only* masculinity, must be forever active, and femininity, as a consequence, and only as a consequence, must be forever passive.

Recognizing the cultural and psychic source of our experiences of the body and its relations with other bodies puts phallic pretension on display, exposing – and perhaps thereby subverting – the linguistic edifice of a sexual division which would conflate biological sex and sexuality. It can be further subverted by insisting upon the ease with which our fantasy life (and much of our reported experience of sexual pleasure) refuses to conform to conventional patterns of supposedly feminine or masculine ways of loving. Nothing is more common, in fantasy, than for us to be experiencing ourselves as the person we desire to possess, or to be – often someone of the 'opposite' sex. 'I was always the Scarlet Pimpernel myself, as well as his adored wife,' Elizabeth Wilson recalls in her autobiographical writing.[118] We could all provide our own examples. Nin Andrews describes her phallic fantasies in her poem 'The Dream', which feel all too familiar to me:

> as a child I would dream I was discovered behind the green flowered couch . . . I would look down and see there, resting between my white and freckled thighs, a little boy's penis . . . hopping about in search of good company, personal attention, growing larger by the minute, becoming quite a towering young fellow, the kind with a future . . . the penis would rise again, night after night . . . I wouldn't tell this to anyone for fear of what it might mean.[119]

They are as familiar as the ecstatic delights of erotic submission, expressed so memorably in the spiritual ecstasies of John Donne, or here, by Thom Gunn, in 'The Stealer':

> I lie and live
> my body's fear
> something's at large
> and coming near
>
> . . .
>
> Fear stiffens me
> and a slow joy
> at the approach
> of the sheathed boy
>
> Will he too do
> what that one did
> unlock me first
> open the lid
>
> and reach inside
> with playful feel
> all the better
> thus to steal[120]

In fantasy, as Laplanche and Pontalis argue in their classic essay, all kinds of 'permutations of roles and attributions are possible'.[121] We insert ourselves, whatever our sex, at one and the same moment as both active and passive, powerful and powerless, giving and receiving: desire flows through binaries in all directions at once, all of the time. We can illustrate the difficulty psychoanalysis has in tying in masculinity/femininity with activity/passivity when Freud observes, in a letter to Jones, that 'the first representation of sexual intercourse [for women] is an oral one – sucking the penis, as earlier, the mother's breast.'[122] Just who, or what, is active or passive here? The binaries masculinity/ femininity, activity/passivity, with their privileging of the first and dominant term, may appear linguistically secure, but they are far from psychically so. It was never really so hard for women to find images of active loving, whether that of kissing, sucking, licking, touching, rocking, or eagerly embracing, encircling or enclosing, even though such eroticized sexual imagery is everywhere surrounded by the stridency of that active imagery of sexuality which happens to be seen as phallic.

Another way of collapsing existing binary oppositions into relational interdependence has been suggested in the philosophical reflection that it is, fundamentally, the nature of the human body and hence of human experience to be at one and the same time an object and a subject, for others and for itself, as the philosopher Maurice Merleau-Ponty argued in *The Phenomenology of Perception*.[123] What distinguishes the human body is that it can transform itself in the process of transforming and being transformed by the material bodies which surround it. Being self-transformative the body is always a kind of 'surplus', something over and above its existence at any moment for itself or others. Although a material object, the body is never *simply* an object, although it must be treated as an object for others to recognize and relate to it. Indeed, the significance and intensity of sexual activity, Merleau-Ponty believed, making critical use of Freud, derives from its pre-eminent role in our experience of the inevitable ambiguity of bodily existence, a drama in which we are necessarily always *both* subject and object, *both* autonomous and dependent. Moreover, every aspect of human life, he continued, 'breathes a sexual atmosphere without it being possible to identify a single content of consciousness which is "purely sexual" or which is not sexual at all.'[124]

What Merleau-Ponty did not do, though Simone de Beauvoir did, in her groundbreaking text *The Second Sex*, was to observe how gender is mapped onto this essential ambiguity of bodily experience, fracturing it to make of 'maleness' pure subjectivity and of 'femaleness' pure objectivity: 'He is the Subject, he is the Absolute – she is the Other . . . he sets himself up as the essential, as opposed to the other, the inessential, the object.'[125] Despite the tenacious hold of this duality attaching itself to sexual division throughout the history of Western metaphysics, from Aristotle and Augustine to Descartes, Rousseau and Sartre,[126] such dualism was precisely what Merleau-Ponty was rejecting in his account of how subjectivity necessarily 'draws its body in its wake', making it possible for any two people to be both subjects and objects for each other.[127]

Such a philosophical framework makes it easier to perceive how women can and do actively seek and embrace the penis and, in a potential infinity of other erotic variations, pursue their loving 'as a man', just as men can and do experience the varied delights of passive stimulation. Whether it is the penis, the mouth, the anus, or any other eroticized surface of the male body receiving the sensual arousal which can break through the phallic armour of the largely desensitized phallic body, it does not necessarily, despite men's fear that it might, destroy whatever claim they think they have on 'manhood'. (Although it did, we know, in the case of Daniel Paul Schreber who, faced with his own passive eroticism towards men, was pushed into the paranoid delusion that he had been transformed into a woman, with what he described as a woman's kind of dispersed all-over bodily 'nerve endings', because God required of him 'the greatest possible generation of spiritual voluptuousness'.[128])

For most of us, however, is it not precisely in sexual experiences that we most often, most inevitably (and without succumbing to serious psychotic delusion), break through the male-as-subject female-as-object absurdity of gendered positions? Is sexual encounter not so intense and significant, *when* it is intense and significant, just because of its contradictions and ambivalence, just because it takes us back to a powerful helplessness, an active passivity, a defenceless omnipotence, which is at least partially sexually undifferentiated? Elizabeth Wilson comments again on the confusions of her first experiences of love as a young adult, when despite having 'positively courted femininity' she no longer '"felt" feminine or masculine': 'Sexual feeling seemed to destroy gender identity, and I was just a raging "I".'[129] Or, as Roland Barthes reflects, 'I want to be both pathetic and admirable, I want to be at the same time a child and an adult.'[130] Of course, of course; that is the excitement, the danger, and the joy, of sexual love. 'Being in love', Freud had said, 'has the power to remove repressions and re-instate perversions . . . [it] occurs in virtue of the fulfilment of infantile conditions for loving. . . .'[131]

Parveen Adams, in one of the many recent compilations reclaiming Freudianism for feminism, presents lesbian sadomasochism as a new type of transgressive sexuality which, existing in a complex and as yet unclear relation to external reality, uniquely separates sexuality from gender.[132] It is not pathological, she tells us, drawing her knowledge from narratives collected and edited by lesbian feminist Pat Califia, because the lesbian sadomasochist is not compulsive, nor fixated upon the genitals, and she engages with women:

> there is an erotic plasticity and movement: she constructs
> fetishes and substitutes them, one for another; she
> multiplies fantasies and tries them on like costumes. All
> this is done quite explicitly as an incitement of the senses,
> a proliferation of bodily pleasures, a transgressive
> excitement; a play with identity and a play with
> genitality.[133]

But existing as it does in an unspecified relation to 'external reality', what is it that restricts this trangressive play with phallic signification to lesbian s/m practices?

Psychoanalytic thinking, one might have thought, with its stress on psychic inconsistency and contradiction, could do better than this. When Freud suggested from his findings that 'libidinal attachments to persons of the same sex play no less a part as factors in normal mental life . . . than do similar attachments to the opposite sex',[134] he laid the seeds for something altogether more ambitious: reclaiming not just what we now call 'transgressive' sexualities, but 'normal' heterosexualities as well, as problematic exchanges which can and do challenge the existing ideological binaries masculinity/femininity, activity/passivity, dominance/subordination. But to sprout these seeds we will have to move well beyond the circular pathways traversed by psychoanalysis, as it liberates sexuality from gender, only to chain it the more securely later.

5. Gay and lesbian challenges: transgression and recuperation

I always wince when . . . lesbian culture celebrants downplay lust and desire, seduction and fulfilment . . . Being a sexual people is our gift to the world.

Joan Nestle[1]

Queer culture and politics herald a lesbian and gay sexuality that is SEXUAL, SEXY and SUBVERSIVE – not only of heterosexual notions of being, but of former lesbian and gay orthodoxies.

Cherry Smyth[2]

It's Hip to be Queer, It's Hot to be Queer, It's the Gay Nineties.[3]

Neither sexology nor psychoanalysis provides us with an account of sexuality which explains either its varied historical forms or its potential for change in the present. It was listening to an afternoon radio programme on which a sexologist and a psychoanalyst were confidently advising a caller on his sexual problems that finally goaded Michel Foucault to elaborate his own approach, the ambitious *History of Sexuality*. 'The only thing they would ask the poor man', Foucault complained, 'was "Can you get an erection or not?"'[4]

What Foucault heard, and undertook to analyse, was the way in which people's sense of their own bodies and behaviours is experienced through a multiplicity of historically specific discourses, constructing what we call 'sexuality'. His goal was not to 'liberate desire', which he saw as more incited than repressed by popular discourses, but to create new ways of relating to bodily pleasure which would go beyond existing understandings of sexuality. It was no accident that Foucault was himself a gay man, whose own sexual practices had early on intruded on his career – in his forced retreat from his post as French cultural attaché in Warsaw after an incident of homosexual entrapment.[5]

In this chapter I will be assessing the shifting impact of the lesbian and gay politics of the last twenty-five years on theories of sexuality. From gay liberation and political lesbianism to queer theory, the meaning and significance given to same-sex practices have played a central role in shaping feminist perspectives on sexuality – including heterosexuality. In particular, we will see the relevance of Foucault's work for any understanding of modern sexualities. But his legacy is complex and contradictory. People have drawn different conclusions from it, especially in relation to the challenge offered by the proliferating diversity of sexually oppressed minorites to established sexual norms. It was the thinking and activities of gay men and lesbians which lay behind this challenge, as they set off to liberate themselves – at first, without any help from Foucault.

Coming out, fighting back

Gay liberation was born with the rioting which erupted in June 1969 during a routine police raid on the Stonewall Inn, a small gay dance bar in Manhattan. Occurring on the day of Judy Garland's funeral (that self-destructive but determined fighter worshipped by many gay men), it was led by Latino 'drag queens' and butch lesbians, people who were still embarrassed and ashamed of their sexuality, who were neither confident nor politicized – at least, as Edmund White later poignantly recalls:

> I suppose the police expected us to run away into the night as we'd always done before. . . . I had an urge to be responsible and disperse the crowd peacefully. . . . After all, what were we protesting? Our right to our 'pathetic malady'? . . . But in spite of myself a wild exhilaration swept over me. . . . Someone beside me called out, 'Gay is good', in imitation of the new slogan, 'Black is beautiful', and we all laughed. . . . We were all chanting it, knowing how ridiculous we were being in this parody of a real demonstration but feeling giddily confident anyway. Now someone said, 'We're the Pink Panthers', and that made us laugh again. Then I caught myself foolishly imagining that gays might some day constitute a community rather than a diagnosis.[6]

A new era of politically active gay men and lesbians burst upon the scene. In its early years, the 1970s was a time when many individual radicals and oppressed groups came together to consolidate alternative communities of eager young revolutionaries – no longer inspired, as they had been, by male leaders (black or white), but seeking to connect their politics to their lives, and working, in particular, for the liberation of women, gay men and lesbians.

'Coming out' as gay or lesbian meant both a positive affirmation of an identity and a sense of belonging to a movement: 'We believed everything would change, even ourselves.'[7] Yet, strange as it may now seem, there was little discussion of sexual practices or desire in the early Gay Liberation Front (GLF) – as the movement was called. There was, instead, a great emphasis on constructing 'a liberated life-style' and aggressively 'confronting straight society' – especially discrimination in the workplace, and the hostile attitudes of the medical, legal and media establishments to gay men and lesbians. The British GLF *Manifesto* of 1971 explains that gay liberation, like women's liberation, means ridding society of 'the gender-roles system which is the root of our oppression' and replacing 'the family unit' by more flexible collective living patterns: '*We have to get together, understand one another, live together.*'[8] Gay men and lesbians were to use their 'righteous anger to uproot the present oppressive system', in alliance with women generally and oppressed groups everywhere.[9] As work, sex and politics came together for a few brief, exciting if exhausting years, gay liberation was less about exploring one's sexuality (for which there was little time, and homosexuality anyway tended to be seen as a natural capacity in everyone) than about building a community and recognizing the need for social change in which different life-styles and relationships could flourish. As Jeffrey Weeks reflects:

> I wrote a lot about gay politics in the seventies . . . [but] I don't actually talk about sex at all. My work has been mainly about the development of a sense of identity and sense of community. . . . Yet in the States at this time there was a real explosion of sexual activity, of public sexual activity, the development of gay saunas, the development of sexually explicit magazines . . . a whole burgeoning of a literature and expression of new sexual activities which I don't think was really echoed to the same extent until quite late in the seventies in this country.[10]

In fact, GLF in Britain was a perfect replica of GLF in the USA, which had, a year or so earlier, also set out to transform society and liberate everyone from sex-roles and the indoctrination of the nuclear family: 'The artificial categories "heterosexual" and "homosexual" have been laid on us by a sexist society. . . . As gays, we demand an end to gender programming. . . . [O]ur understanding of sexism is that in a free society everyone will be gay.'[11] In the USA revolutionary zeal died, almost as suddenly as it had begun a few years earlier. On the one hand, it was superceded by reformist civil rights pressure groups (which stressed the notion of fixed sexual orientation rather than the revolutionary potential of the liberation of homosexual desire). On the other hand, more spectacularly and far exceeding anything which occurred in Britain, it was replaced by the swift commercialization of the gay male subculture, with gay consumers targeted in a new commodity boom feeding off sexual permissiveness.[12] As Dennis Altman reflected in the early 1980s: 'We did not foresee the extent to which much of the new gay culture, especially for men, would be no more than the development of a new market based on the provision of luxurious entertainment and commercial cruising grounds.'[13]

There had been a significant, if minority, group of lesbians in GLF in both Britain and the USA. But the attraction of the emerging Women's Liberation Movement was soon to highlight the dissatisfaction of working in a predominantly male group, particularly once some of them took to donning women's clothes or 'radical queenery' as a form of 'revolutionary' provocation: 'We must be "rotten queers" to the straight world . . . [and] "freaks" to the gay ghetto.'[14] Fed up and offended by the 'tawdry theatricality', angry that it was still men who dominated GLF meetings, the women were also critical of a politics they saw as more about 'life-style' than challenging the underlying structures of gender hierarchy.[15] In London most of the women abandoned GLF in 1972, hastening its demise. They were now immersed in the somewhat less conflictual terrain of the women's movement – despite often finding there a concern with motherhood and childcare which seemed to exclude their own needs. Yet for all its radical posing, Elizabeth Wilson would later reflect:

> Gay liberation did . . . make me conscious of the massive contradictions we all have to endure throughout our lives. It heightened my awareness of this not in its sober and more reasonable moments, but when it was at its maddest, at its most surreal and bizarre.[16]

Any woman can: reconstructing the lesbian

Meanwhile, within the autonomous feminist milieu, where women were busy linking their personal lives, work and politics into a new sense of passionate sisterhood, many were becoming ever more critical of their sexual relations with husbands and male lovers. Men who were not threatened by and hostile to women's liberation – and feminists' growing sense of independence and confidence in solidarity with each other – had often complacently assumed that it would merely 'liberate' more women into the arms of men, and their ideas of carefree sex: 'there is as yet no widespread sign of boycott . . . at least, on the *girl's* part', Richard Neville had chirped in 1971.[17]

It was hardly surprising that new forms of politicized lesbianism should grow stronger throughout the 1970s. This was in part simply an aspect of an exciting social scene where women were becoming more and more involved with each other, and more and more critical of a world which defined them in terms of their appeal to and relationships with men – whether as wife, mother, mistress or secretary.

From the USA Rita Mae Brown offered feminists a self-loving portrait of the lesbian feminist dispatching foolish men, shallow women and menial jobs on her triumphant pathway to glory in her best-selling *Rubyfruit Jungle* – its title a celebration of female genitals.[18] And before long some feminists would come to see lesbianism as a key tactic for undermining male dominance. While one feminist might report that she was attracted to other women because she saw 'lesbians as the elite of the movement' ('more exciting and more glamorous' than either her husband or other men), others would offer a more political rationale for their lesbian identification acquired 'through the movement'.[19] The latter were concerned not so much about sexuality or desire, as about bringing their sexual feelings into line with their goal of creating strong women's communities of resistance. As Lynne Harne recalls:

> Many women including myself were to make the connections between women being *for women*, and being sexually, emotionally and as far as possible economically independent of men in order for women's liberation to succeed. But of many who embraced political lesbianism at this time a number were to go back to men, when unrealistic expectations of lesbian relationships were not met (women are not always nice to women) or when the extent of lesbian oppression was fully experienced.[20]

Certainly, Harne's account of life in the lesbian collective (in contrast to Rita Mae Brown's hedonistic heroines) is silent as the grave about pleasure: 'I moved into a lesbian collective in Hackney where everything in our lives was collectivized from childcare to clothes. We were actually living the revolution, and taking control of our lives now.' Might this grim revolutionary zeal have something to do with why, having 'spent years in women's health groups and later teaching women's health classes (persuading women by indirect means that heterosexuality was bad for their health)', she felt 'betrayed and let down by heterosexual women whose loyalties in the end were to men'?[21]

Other feminists were a lot less dour, but no less politically correct, recounting their move from 'a strong person, to a feminist to a lesbian' as just 'a very logical progression'.[22] In 1980 Adrienne Rich had summarized the new approach which made 'lesbianism' more or less synonymous with 'feminism' in her classic essay on 'compulsory hetero-sexuality'. Here, boldly turning on its head all previous and prevailing ideas of the 'natural order', she argued that heterosexuality 'had been forcibly and subliminally imposed on women', even though 'everywhere women have resisted it, often at the cost of physical torture, imprisonment, psychosurgery, social ostracism and extreme poverty'.[23] Every woman could be, and most were, part of 'the lesbian continuum', a continuum based not necessarily on sexual desire or engagement but on the intense emotional ties of 'woman-identified experience': women sharing their 'rich inner life', caring for each other and 'bonding against male tyranny'.[24]

As we saw in Chapter 2, with the lesbian defined as 'woman-identified woman', and 'heterosexuality' seen as an institution enforced by men to ensure male dominance, straight feminists fell silent over the pleasures and not infrequent pains of sexual desire and experience. But with lesbianism seen as an unproblematic choice for feminists, lesbian feminists also fell silent about sex and sexuality, except in their forceful critique of women 'sleeping with the enemy'.[25] Certainly, by the early 1980s, some lesbians were complaining that their sexuality was not being seen as a sexuality at all, but as a political practice, gutted of its history, passion, sexual meaning and significance.[26] Joan Nestle, who helped found the Lesbian Herstory Archives in the USA to record 'the complexity and diversity of resistance, the nonchalance of courage, and the tenacity of those who are different', would later sum up their feelings:

> We lesbians made a mistake in the early seventies: we allowed our lives to be trivialised and reinterpreted by feminists who did not share our culture. The slogan 'Lesbianism is the practice and feminism is the theory' was a good rallying cry, but it cheated our history. . . . In some sense, lesbians have always opposed the patriarchy; in the past, perhaps most when we looked most like men. . . . When we broke gender lines in the 1950s, we fell off the biologically charted maps.[27]

And ironically, while the pre-feminist lesbian (representing a minority of women) had been of great sexual interest to feminists – whatever their sexuality – the new lesbian feminist, defined as a 'woman-identified woman who does not fuck men'[28] (representing a type of universal woman), helped destroy much of the sexual subversion and allure which lesbianism had held for many straight women. The 'political lesbian' was no longer any challenge to traditional definitions linking sexuality and gender – as the 'mannish lesbian', the sexual outlaw, had been. She was the genuinely womanly woman. Her sexuality was egalitarian, nurturing and loyal, in contrast to the dominating, objectifying and exploitative nature of 'normal male sexuality'. Gay men, once the political and social allies of lesbians and traditionally seen as 'feminine', were now declared quintessential representatives of oppressive male sexuality by the new vanguard of political lesbians: 'dominant modes of male sexuality are actively maintained and promoted rather than challenged by gay men.'[29]

Combatting cultural compulsions for heterosexuality with feminist denunciations against it (as intrinsically coercive for women or 'bad for their health') thus not only closed down dialogue between heterosexual women and lesbians over the similarities or contrasts between their diverse sexual experiences, but it undermined the actual challenge and interest of lesbian experience for all women – regardless of their sexual preferences. Whatever emotional transcendence, tears, or laughter self-identifying lesbians, bisexuals and straight women were having between the sheets (together or with men), sex as pleasure had fled from feminist platforms by the close of the 1970s, and some of the joy of early women's liberation went with it.

However, the battles over 'lesbian existence', its meaning and significance for dismantling male domination or contesting the sexualized nature of gender boundaries, were far from over. In Britain today, for example, there is a resurgence of political lesbianism within the 'feminist' wing of mainstream psychology, where Sue Wilkinson, Celia Kitzinger and Rachel Perkins have been waging a protracted assault on 'the heteropatriarchal order' by 'accepting the label "lesbian" [in] a defiant act of self-naming'.[30] 'Lesbianism', they insist, is a 'political identity for lesbian feminists'. One of the most important achievements of feminism, Kitzinger argues, has been the redefinition of 'lesbianism' in terms of a 'blow against the patriarchy' rather than in terms of 'sexual/emotional preference'.[31] Here, obviously, lesbianism is a purely voluntaristic choice, dictated by one's politics.

At the same time, often in sharp contrast, other feminists have been researching the historical continuities and discontinuities in lesbian lives, wondering whether there has not been an imperious dismissiveness of varieties of lesbian experience, and women's ways of understanding

it, in certain feminist reconstructions of women's relationships with each other. The pioneering research of Lillian
Faderman, *Surpassing the Love of Men*, had certainly
presented a history of Western women in harmony with
lesbian feminist beliefs, one where 'passionate love between
women was not atypical'.[32] Without fear of public censure,
Faderman argued, women had for centuries shared the most
intense 'romantic attachments', and these had continued
up until the time when they began to seek and to gain
greater economic independence, in the late nineteenth
century, when male sexologists had invented, sexualized and
stigmatized the 'lesbian': 'to frighten women away from
feminism and from loving other women by demonstrating
that both were abnormal and were generally linked together.'
These sexologists were seen as drawing upon a pornographic
imagination depicting the bizarre sexual practices of
'the lesbian', like flagellation – a male literary genre.

Faderman's account of women's intimate relationships, as
intense and supportive, although not necessarily sexual
or genitally focussed, affirmed the feminist redefinition
of lesbianism which, at the time, she endorsed: 'Women
who identify themselves as lesbians do not view lesbianism
as a sexual phenomenon first and foremost.'[33] But in sexually
segregated Victorian society, female romantic friendships
were far from any rebellion against male domination. On the
contrary, as Carroll Smith-Rosenberg argued, they were
open and accepted, flourishing in the nineteenth-century
bourgeoisie as part of the 'rigid gender-role differentiation'
characterizing the 'female world of love and ritual' preparing women for marriage, childbirth and domesticity: 'Most
eighteenth- and nineteenth-century women lived within
a world bounded by home, church and the institution of
visiting.'[34]

There was a certain wish fulfilment in contemporary

feminist reclaimings of women's romantic friendships in Victorian times as resistance against 'patriarchy'. (Some lesbian feminists always distrusted the universalizing dilution of the specificities and intensities of lesbian desire present in Faderman or, in this country, in the historical reconstructions of Sheila Jeffreys.)[35] There was, equally, disavowal in that same feminist tendency's disclaiming of the significance of those women in the past who lived and passed as 'men', cross-dressed, became 'female husbands', or, like George Sand, were intermittent cross-dressers and lovers of women.[36] This connects with a similar disowning of twentieth-century 'butch–femme' lesbian rituals as a possible source of information on women's sexual lives. Women who (usually in secret) 'passed' as men to take female lovers seem neither in line with Adrienne Rich's notion of 'the lesbian experience as being, like motherhood, a profoundly *female* experience', nor to serve as a model for resisting 'patriarchy'.[37] Feminists like Rich have seen women who 'transformed themselves into men' as forced into such 'role-playing' by existing heterosexual assumptions, in the absence of any alternative understanding or acceptance of lesbian behaviour and relationships.[38] We can only speculate, in hindsight, upon the different motivations which may have fed into such 'male' impersonations, one of them obviously being the desire to transcend the many restrictions surrounding women's lives in the past, and the forceful confinement of their sexual activity to marriage. It would seem rash, however, to insist that such sexually 'dominant' behaviour and life-style, although usually attributed to men, was 'merely' an enforced 'copying' of heterosexual patterns.

It was Joan Nestle who first most passionately complained as a feminist that although it was all right to analyse (and dismiss) butch–femme relationships in the past, to discuss them in any positive way in the present was to be labelled 'reactionary', a 'heterosexually-identified lesbian' and 'believer in patriarchal sex'.[39] In contrast, drawing compellingly upon her own engagement in butch–femme relationships a generation earlier, she had argued (at the explosive Feminist Scholars Conference on Sexuality in New York in 1981) that a butch lesbian was never simply imitating men, but rather – with extraordinary courage and defiance – she was 'a woman who created an original style to signal to other women what she was capable of doing – taking erotic responsibility'.[40] This is a debate to which we will keep returning. It was around this time that Pat Califia and certain other lesbian voices in the USA initiated the s/m (sadomasochistic) debates, preceding most contemporary gay male and heterosexual theorization of s/m. They encouraged women to explore rather than deny or repress the role of fantasy in sexual desire – in particular the excitement of fantasies of dominance and submission. Califia herself wrote and collected erotic/pornographic narratives of strong, self-defining, mutually supportive lesbians engaging in s/m practices, explaining:

> I have always been titillated by sexy images and stories. . . . The images of capture, helplessness, and torture (reassuringly followed by miraculous escape and revenge) were the most exciting.[41]

It would now seem hard to disagree with Martha Vicinus when, after surveying the differing contemporary feminist reclaimings of 'the lesbian', she cautions: 'Rather than raiding the past to find satisfactory models for today, we should look to the difficulties, contradictions and triumphs of women within the larger context of their own times.'[42]

Following Foucault: resisting homosexual identity

Gay liberation embraced a new theoretical paradigm for understanding and explaining sexuality as mediated by society, rather than as biologically given. What gay men and lesbians shared, in this 'social constructionist' account, was not any inner essence of desire or personality, but rather the harsh experience of social discrimination and prejudice – co-ordinated by church, state and media. Connected to the radical deviancy theory of the 1960s, its take-off in Britain was an article by Mary McIntosh, 'The Homosexual Role', in 1968. Pointing to the historical and anthropological evidence that homosexual acts and orientations are understood in very different ways across time and place, she suggested that 'the homosexual should be seen as playing a social role rather than as having a condition.'[43] Despite our contemporary idea that people are either 'homosexual' or 'heterosexual' by nature, she reminded us, research like that of Kinsey revealed that such terms do not necessarily fix who or what has triggered sexual desire over a lifetime – although men and women tend to adopt specific sexual identities as they grow older. The important thing to study, given the immense variations in what type of person and what type of practices those who engage in same-sex acts desire and enjoy, is how the social creation of 'homosexuality' as a stigmatized identity or condition maintains heterosexual norms and institutions – keeping 'the bulk of society pure'.[44]

From the USA, the increasingly influential symbolic interactionist perspectives of Gagnon and Simon lent further support to this social control or 'deviance' approach. They argued that sexuality is always 'socially scripted behavior', including the importance we attach to sexuality in our culture: 'It is not the physical aspects of sexuality but the social aspects that generate the arousal and organize the action.'[45] Gender identity, they stressed, is prior to and determining of the sexual scripts which shape boys' and girls' conscious entry into and experience of sexuality – sexual performance serves as a central confirmation of 'masculinity'; marriage or relationships serve as a central confirmation of 'femininity'.

These new sociological approaches to sexuality were subversive of dominant assumptions in their claim that sexuality, although thought of as a most intensely private and individual experience, was in fact socially constructed and predetermined 'to a degree surpassed by few other forms of human behavior'.[46] Psychoanalysis had challenged the idea that human sexuality could be reduced to biological or instinctive behaviour, because of the psychic significance attaching itself to all bodily experience from birth onwards. Sociological analysis now challenged the idea that sexual experience could be reduced to an individual or private affair, because of the shared social meanings which inevitably define and determine it. (There are parallels here with Lacan's emphasis on the function of the symbolic, but without the transcendental role of the phallus as privileged signifier, or the inevitability of absence, alienation and lack at the heart of desire.)

With the emphasis on the social construction of 'the homosexual' as one who fails to conform to the normative links between sexuality and gender, it was easy for lesbians and gay men to see themselves as part of a subculture of resistance to heterosexist norms. Tracing the history of their own marginalization and exclusion has led to an increasingly rich and sophisticated expansion of gay and lesbian studies since the mid-1970s – far exceeding any equivalent developments in the study of heterosexuality.

It was the French philosopher and cultural historian Michel Foucault, however, who increasingly provided the academic authority and political inspiration for much of this work. Foucault wrote graphically of the emergence of 'homosexuality' in the nineteenth century, 'when it was transposed from the practice of sodomy onto a type of interior androgyny, a hermaphroditism of the soul.' 'The sodomite', he famously quipped, 'had been a temporary aberration; the homosexual was now a species.'[47] There is irony in Foucault's overwhelming influence on gay and – to a slightly lesser extent – lesbian and feminist theorizing. His key idea is that there is no inner essence of sexual being, sexual drives or sexual identities. The only possible liberation is not 'sexual liberation' but freedom from all existing discourses of sexuality and sexual identity – including the 'dissemination and implantation of poly-morphous sexualities'. It is these sexual discourses, produced by different Western professional and state institutions in the late nineteenth century as a way of administering power over people's 'bodies and their pleasures', which create 'the imaginary element that is "sex"'.[48] The modern concept of 'sexuality' is thus a recent invention, as are all its categories organized around the heterosexual/homosexual polarity tied in with the 'normal' or 'inverted' masculine/feminine gender polarity:

> Sexuality must not be thought of as a kind of natural
> given which power tries to hold in check, or as an obscure
> domain which knowledge tries gradually to uncover. It is
> the name that can be given to a historical construct: not
> a furtive reality that is difficult to grasp, but a great
> surface network in which the stimulation of bodies, the
> intensification of pleasures, the incitement to discourse,
> the formation of knowledges, the strengthening of

controls and resistances, are linked to one another, in
accordance with a few major strategies of knowledge and
power.[49]

This colonization of the body has been possible because
over the last two centuries we have come to see in 'sex' the
truth of who and what we are: 'the project of a science of
the subject has gravitated, in ever narrower circles, around
the question of sex.'[50]

Foucault identified four chief domains which became
the objects of new strategies of classification and control,
producing four privileged targets of knowledge and manipulation: 'the hysterical woman, the masturbating child, the
Malthusian couple, and the perverse adult.'[51] It is from
the identities produced by these discourses that people
have to free themselves if they are ever to escape 'the hold
of power' over bodies and pleasures: 'Pleasure is something
which passes from one individual to another; it is not
something secreted by identity. *Pleasure has no passport, no
identity*.'[52] But freeing ourselves from the invigilating
and classifying mechanisms which have 'implanted' our
sexual identities – whether as wailing women, wanking
children, breeding couples or pathological perverts – can
never be a straightforward or simple matter. We can talk
back to or resist power, demanding our liberation from
its pathologizing scrutiny. But we always do so in the name
of similar categories, through the same discourses which it
has given us: we can only resist from 'inside' power, there
is no escaping it. This is because power is everywhere, it
does not exist in any one place, to be seized or overthrown,
but 'runs through the social body as a whole'.[53] It is for
this reason that Foucault bypasses accounts of individual
experience or motivation: such accounts are always already
impregnated with the discourses of power.

Foucault's anti-naturalism and anti-essentialism was popularized in Britain and the USA by leading gay and lesbian theorists, alongside influential feminist scholars.[54] They welcomed, most of all, his focus on the body as a key site and vehicle of 'disciplinary practices', but also as a site of resistance to such practices. Using his discursive analysis, they highlighted the element of social control in the construction and maintenance of both 'normal' and 'deviant' sexual identities – especially in the disciplines of medicine, psychiatry and criminology. They too emphasized the centrality – yet complexity and multiplicity – of modern discourses of 'sex', which have produced it as the core of our being. Combining Foucault's recognition of the heterogeneous elements constructing the 'truths' of sexuality with Jacques Derrida's deconstructive account of the hierarchical or 'violent' nature of binary oppositions, they explored the dominant Western polarities normal/perverse and natural/unnatural to show their necessary interdependence. These terms gain their meaning, they showed, only in relation to each other in each instance, rather than through any set antithesis. It is this contingency of meaning which, as we shall see, would soon be developed into strategies of 'transgressive resistance', where the deliberate proliferation of oppositions – for example, in s/m relationships – was thought capable of undermining the hegemony of binary opposition itself.

Foucault's analysis of power as productive rather than merely repressive informed all these new approaches, and his emphasis on studying the 'genealogies' of existing knowledge in terms of power suggested to some the possibility of liberating individuals from their socially inherited identities and values. 'Freedom' for Foucault, John Rajchman comments, was a 'constant attempt at self-disengagement and self-invention'.[55] And it was drawing upon Foucault that

Jeffrey Weeks would suggest, in optimistic mode, that since sexual definitions are historically formed and contested through a multiplicity of institutional sites: 'the road is open for developments of alternative practices and definitions of sexual behaviour, definitions which would owe more to choice than to tradition or inherited moralities.'[56] The problem, he hastened to add, was the question of who would produce these new definitions, and how they could be articulated and attained.

Nevertheless, following Foucault – and the methods of discourse analysis and deconstruction – in pursuit of the 'fields of power' constructing our sexual identities, did not please everyone engaged in sexual politics – whether gay, lesbian or feminist. Despite the growing prestige of Foucauldian theory, it had (like social construction theory more generally), many contradictions of its own, both as an explanatory tool and a political vehicle for enabling resistance and struggle. Foucault addressed the body and its pleasures as the target of technologies of surveillance and control, but he had next to nothing to say about those bodies, or the pleasures which were being controlled. This creates, as his critics complain, only a disembodied, unstable or empty space around which to frame any alternative understandings or politics. Foucault provided few clues on how to reflect upon bodily sensations, bodily functions, bodily pains and pleasures other than as objects of external manipulations of power, which always threaten to wipe away the significance of individual biographical narratives – whether pieced together from consciously or unconsciously manifested behaviour.

Moreover, in its generalized and anonymous abstractions, Foucault's Nietzschean analytics of power seems to remove the need for any more developed account of the specificities of social relations, contexts and structures, or cultural formations, in the domain of the sexual.[57] His ubiquitous surveillance strategies can be likened, John Fletcher suggests, to 'a paranoid Gothic theory of power ... where all are subject to a structure which internalises the gaze of power whether the warders are watching or not'.[58] In his reduction of the formation of subjectivity to an inevitable subjection to power, Foucault rejected any theorizing at the level of the physiological or the psychic, on the one hand, or at the level of the concrete specificities of social relations and cultural processes, on the other. As the sociologist Bob Connell argues in exasperated criticism of the fashion for Foucauldian writings on the 'body' which confine themselves to analysing discourse (and subject positions in discourse), it is not necessary to retreat from social analysis when attempting to grapple with concrete bodily processes and our experiences of them:

> This evacuates, rather than resolves, problems about bodies: which are certainly surfaces to be written on, but are also busy growing, ageing, reproducing, getting sick, feeding well or badly, getting aroused or turned off, and so on. All these are social processes, and all are hard to separate from sexual practice and sexual signification.[59]

It is residual doubts over reducing the theory and politics of sexuality to battles over meaning and representation that have led many theorists to make only selective use of Foucauldian insights, presenting the body as the *interface* between internal forces (whether conceived of as psychic, libidinal or whatever), and the external social forces which mould and give meaning to them. Thus Jeffrey Weeks, in his excellent overviews of the formation of modern sexualities, has always combined his use of Foucault with an eclectic interest in psychoanalytic perspectives – seeing sexual identities as highly problematic social products: the biological possibilities of the body become meaningful through psychic activity framed within a multiplicity of external definitions and regulations. 'No theory of sexuality', he insists 'can be complete which ignores the lessons of the discovery of the unconscious.'[60] Less eclectically, John Fletcher draws upon Jean Laplanche's psychoanalytic notions of a 'fantasmatic self-inscription' by the child, through 'implantations' of highly charged and enigmatic parental significations and messages, to convey how 'the policing norms of a heterosexual culture are incorporated as intensely weighted representations, not as discursive ruses and strategies of an anonymous and conglomerated power.'[61] Connell offers his own nuanced sociological reflection on gay and straight men's sexual biographies, suggesting that sexual agency should be seen as neither simply an effect of individual dynamics, nor of abstract regulation, but part of the shifting mobilization of distinct social collectivities.[62] Such accounts look simultaneously for external and internal self-constructions of sexual identities, stressing that the social is already a part of the sexual domain, and *vice versa*. In a significant essay for gay and lesbian studies, Carole Vance has surveyed the range of criticisms of those perspectives which focus exclusively upon the cultural or institutional frames currently constructing 'sexuality', while insisting upon their strengths in the face of still reigning biomedical assumptions of bodily imperatives:

> to the extent that social construction theory grants
> that sexual acts, identities and even desire are mediated
> by cultural and historical factors, the object of study –
> sexuality – becomes evanescent and threatens to

disappear. . . . More to the point in lesbian and gay history, have constructionists undermined their own categories? Is there an 'it' to study?[63]

Foucault's warning that oppositional discourses themselves inevitably echo, however contrarily, the relations of domination they are resisting, has been important in highlighting the traps facing emancipatory movements – of extending rather than transcending traditional frameworks of subjection. But it also threatens to subvert the basis of their solidarity, as itself an accommodation to power. Deconstructing or rejecting what has made meaningful our conceptions of 'our bodies/ourselves' leaves little to empower those who have always felt marginal and disempowered – as 'feminine' or 'perverse'. Yet ironically, though unsurprisingly, it has been lesbian and gay scholars – rather than the more mainstream authorities in the social sciences or humanities – who have been most open to Foucauldian analysis and rhetoric. In response, some lesbian, gay and feminist writers have been promoting a revival of more essentialist discourses – like Liana Borghi calling for an analysis of the lesbian mythology in contemporary North American feminist poetry: 'We need this mythology too, the way we need all new formulations that show our communities to be fluid, heterogeneous, multivocal and authoritative.'[64]

More generally, what Foucault's male critics have been arguing is that gay men and lesbians were not simply passive objects of an all-pervasive surveillance, but were themselves searching for ways to describe their experiences and claim an identity which, however socially stigmatized, they helped to mould. Thus gay historians Randolph Trumbach and Frederic Silverstolpe have shown that doctors were not simply 'creating' the behaviour – like that of 'the effeminate sodomite' – which they tried to control and regulate in 'the categories of their science', but were inadequately describing behaviour which had already existed in marginalized subcultures for hundreds of years.[65]

At times, Foucault was willing to endorse a role for what he called the 'subjugated knowledges' of resistance, which are 'located low down on the hierarchy, beneath the required level of cognition or scientificity'.[66] But his more fundamental resistance to any form of identity politics for what he once described as the 'happy limbo of non-identity', and his consistent anti-humanist portrayal of *all* self-identity as imprisoning 'the reality of the body and the intensities of its pleasures', would have kept him, at the very least, highly sceptical of any assertions of a more consciously interactive history between 'homosexuals' and those who apparently so ubiquitously surveyed and labelled them.[67] The problem, as Foucault saw it, was not 'to discover in oneself the truth of sex but rather to use sexuality henceforth to arrive at a multiplicity of relationships'.[68] The problem, as many gay men saw it, was that they wanted an identity of their own to fight a straight society, and its vicious, at times murderous, dismissal of their right to exist. In coming out and telling their own stories in the face of a hostile world, they need to believe, as Edmund White puts it, that they are not just recalling the past but shaping the future, 'forging an identity as much as revealing it'.[69]

But if gay men sometimes baulk at Foucault's freedom from identities, some feminist critics more aggressively attack the neglect of gender in his discursive analysis. His strategy of self-refusal, they complain, conveniently for men, questions the foundations of emancipatory struggles, when women have barely begun to find the confidence, authority, and sense of self-worth to articulate them.[70] His analysis of the multiplicity of discursive formations of power at the microlevel, they add, diverts attention from any analysis of overall structures of male domination, just when feminists had highlighted the systemic ways in which they are organized – especially at the level of the state, the economy and the family.[71]

Other feminists, however, equally firmly assert the importance of Foucauldian frameworks for thinking strategically about the programmes they endorse, stressing that identity formation is always both 'necessary and dangerous'.[72] An emphasis on identity as alien, incoherent and unstable does not, as Diana Fuss argues, undermine the possibility of political agency, but can 'produce a more mature identity politics by militating against the tendency to erase differences and inconsistencies in the production of stable political subjects'.[73] It is such theoretical speculation which now inspires the burgeoning productivity of 'queer theory' in the recently thriving lesbian and gay scholarship. Rooted in strategies of disruptive resistance rather than identity, it seeks to transcend and erode the central binary divisions of male/female, heterosexual/homosexual in the construction of modern sexualities.

Who's a pervert?: queer theory and gender sabotage

When Susan Sontag wrote her 'Notes on "Camp"' in 1964, she saw 'Camp' sensibility as preserving a determined but detached, ironic, extravagant, playful and creative aestheticism in the face of mass culture. It is a style and taste, she wrote, peculiarly linked with homosexuality, one which sees life as theatre, understands 'Being-as-Playing-a-Role': 'Camp is the answer to the problem: how to be a dandy in the age of mass culture.' It is also, Sontag believed then, essentially 'apolitical'.[74] Soon, however, camp would find itself heavily politicized, occupying the paradoxical position where its significance and meaning would be fought over with an engaged and committed seriousness quite at odds with its traditional frivolity and aestheticism.

For most gay men and lesbians moving into the Western gay liberation and women's movements in the 1970s, camp humour and drag suggested only the self-mocking, misogynist expression of internalized oppression, reproducing rather than challenging the gender stereotypes of dominant culture. The 'butch shift' in male gay subcultures in the USA and Britain in the 1970s, as pre-Stonewall drag queens were overtaken by 'macho men' – the short-haired 'clone', men in uniforms, all-leather or denim-men – was even more problematic for some gay activists. John Marshall suggested that the shift served merely to illustrate 'the extent to which definitions of male homosexuality continue to be pervaded by the tyranny of gender divisions.'[75] Gay machismo, Andrew Britton argued, allowed men to hold on to their privileges, while enjoying the illusion of flouting them, and it undermined the political role David Fernbach had asserted on behalf of gay men who, he claimed, 'really are effeminate', and therefore women's closest allies.[76] But other gay men at the time, like Jack Babuscio or Gregg Blachford, were already suggesting that the capacity to either 'camp it up' or 'butch it up' at will, served, albeit mildly, to mock and ridicule traditional gender imagery, while helping gay men to survive in a hostile world.[77]

Camp, drag and machismo may have initiated ongoing debate between gay male activists, but it provoked public warfare in lesbian communities. While most lesbian feminists at the close of the 1970s were inclined to damn any signs of 'butch' (or 'femme') display – in men or women – as participation in patriarchal domination, those lesbians who expressed dissent would find themselves embroiled in conflicts far sharper and deeper than any disrupting gay men's politics. This is perhaps why it has been, predominantly, dissident lesbian feminists, embattled alike from within and without as they resist gender and identity categories (while also seeking strategies to combat both heterosexual and male privilege) who have most comprehensively theorized the new queer project.

Judith Butler has become one of the more prominently cited lesbian theorists who, following Foucault, calls into question the need for a stable 'female' identity for feminist theory, exploring instead the political possibilities of a radical critique of all categories of identity. In *Gender Trouble* she offers an analysis of gender and sexuality not in terms of inner capacities, attributes or identities, but in terms of a set of repeated performances 'that congeal over time to produce the appearance of substance, of a natural sort of being'.[78] These enforced cultural performances or productions, enacted by subjects who are always endangered by their own intrinsic fragmentation, achieve what stability and coherence they have, Butler argues (drawing upon the work of Monique Wittig), in the context of 'the heterosexual matrix': 'The heterosexualization of desire requires and institutes the production of discrete and asymmetrical oppositions between "feminine" and "masculine", where these are understood as expressive attributes of "male" and "female".'[79]

Gender identities are thus both necessitated by and dependent upon the production of 'sexuality' as a stable and oppositional 'heterosexuality': '"gender" only exists in the service of heterosexism.'[80] But in this account of the discursively produced chaining of gender to sexuality, where both are 'always a doing', subversive possibilities arise for making 'gender trouble', or transcending binary restrictions, from within the power dynamics of sexuality itself. The multiplicity of possible sexual acts which occur in non-heterosexual contexts cannot themselves overturn dominant heterosexual/reproductive discourses (being produced and understood from within them), but they can nevertheless disrupt and disturb them, 'through hyperbole, dissonance, internal confusion, and proliferation'.[81] Thus, Butler suggests here, it is precisely the 'butch' lesbian and drag queen (as well as the 'femme' lesbian and 'macho' gay), whose performances radically problematize sex, gender and sexuality in their parodic repetition of the heterosexual 'original'. Since heterosexuality is itself only produced through its connection to the repeated signifying practices of gender, gay is to straight not as copy is to an original, but rather as 'copy is to copy': '*In imitating gender, drag implicitly reveals the imitative structure of gender itself – as well as its contingency.*'[82]

Butler's thoughts are in some ways reminiscent of those of Luce Irigaray who, in declaring the unrepresentability – and hence repudiation – of women in phallogocentric discourse, proposes a strategy of '*disruptive excess*'.[83] Irigaray writes a rich and extravagant poetics, seeking to embrace all the metaphors of the feminine in order to construct a language for the feminine body, to explore the 'distinction of the sexes in terms of the way they inhabit or are inhabited by language'.[84] She argues that in *deliberately* taking on the feminine role, women 'convert a form of subordination into an affirmation, and thus . . . begin to thwart it.'[85] But Butler, not surprisingly, is critical of Irigaray in so far as she uses this strategy not just as a type of parody – or subversive mimesis – of dominant phallocentric discourses, but to characterize (however metaphorically) a specifically feminine pleasure, most memorably, of course, in her account of women's eroticism in terms of genital morphology: 'two lips in continuous contact.'[86]

Despite its influence and interest for many feminists, others respond only with bewilderment or exasperation to Butler's claim that both sex and gender, including any notion of the 'female' or of 'women', are but regulatory fictions. Disconcertingly she admits no limit or constraint emerging from anatomical bodies (such as a capacity for impregnation and child-bearing) on the fictions, or inscriptions, which discourses have been able to produce or implant in their construction of 'women' and 'female embodiment'. Butler's radical Foucauldianism could thus be described as a new kind of philosophical behaviourism, where there is no being, but only a doing. Paradoxically, in *Gender Trouble*, her anti-humanist pragmatism seems to point to individualistic transgressive 'performance' as the most relevant politics for undermining 'women's' oppression, in a feminism reduced to struggle over representation – 'semiotic guerrilla warfare'.[87] Yet, as Alan Sinfield worries, 'when you are coming from the subordinate position, everything you attempt is recuperable'. Drag, for example, is popular with both reactionary and radical audiences, and however artful or skilful its performance, dominant culture 'is not so easily subverted, so intricately is it installed in the conceptual structures that we inhabit.'[88]

Moreover, as some of Butler's critics suggest, the eroticization accompanying lesbian and gay mimicry or parody of straight gender roles may do more to reinforce them than to provide what she calls 'the inevitable site of the denaturalization and mobilization of gender categories'.[89] (This is a point which Butler partially concedes in her interesting sequel to *Gender Trouble*, where she addresses what she sees as the misconceptions accompanying both the popularity and notoriety of that book.)[90] Thus Leo Bersani has argued that gay-macho style displays a 'profound respect for machismo itself' and, despite and indeed because of its eroticized connection with homosexual desire, can be seen by straight men and women not so much as a subversion of, as a 'worshipful tribute' and '*yearning* toward' socially pervasive definitions of masculinity.[91] Nevertheless, Bersani suggests, *if* as Jeffrey Weeks – like Butler and others – claim, gay men do 'gnaw at the roots of male heterosexual identity', it is not in their exposure or parody of its constructedness. It is rather because, in their 'nearly mad identification with it, *they never cease to feel the appeal of it being violated*.'[92] What gay men can and do display, Bersani believes, against the fearful male defences and denials constituting phallocentric masculinity, is the value and significance of powerlessness, the loss of control and the exuberant self-shattering that lie at the heart of sexual pleasure: 'the seductive and intolerable image', for example, 'of a grown man, legs high in the air, unable to refuse the suicidal ecstasy of being a woman.'[93] In its knowledge of the 'demeaning' joys of 'so-called passive' or 'feminine' sex, the dangerous allure and threat of gay male sexuality – for which it is so murderously policed – is that 'it never stops re-presenting the internalized phallic male as an infinitely loved object of sacrifice'.[94]

It is this threat from *within* heterosexual structures of gender and power, created by its internal instabilities and the erotic appeal of violating its own sexual and gender binaries, that Jonathan Dollimore describes as the power and the paradox of 'the perverse dynamic'. Dollimore, in an analysis similar to that of Eve Sedgwick, claims that homosexuality is integral to the heterosexual cultures which obsessively denounce it: 'the negation of homosexuality has been in direct proportion to its actual centrality; its cultural

marginality in direct proportion to its cultural significance.'[95] As he points out, it is not only Foucault who
places perversion at the centre of the construction of
a heterosexual normality. Freud too, as we saw in the
previous chapter, places the existence of perversion at the
centre of his account of sexuality, although looking,
he believed, inwards to psychic life rather than outwards
to social regulation. Describing the perilous pathway
from infantile 'polymorphous perversity' to heterosexual
object choices, 'one could . . . define human sexuality as
essentially "perverse" inasmuch as it never fully detaches
itself from its origins.'[96]

Dollimore and Sedgwick provide, perhaps, the most
complex and original of the recent texts of queer theory,
although each – Dollimore primarily, and Sedgwick
exclusively (to the irritation of many lesbians) – addresses
male same-sex desire. Sedgwick uses her challenging
analysis of the Western literary canon (from the end of the
nineteenth century) to conclude that *all* men, in pursuing
the pathways of male entitlement, form intense male bonds
which necessarily create at one and the same time the
uneasy if not explosive combination of homosocial desires
(a preference for the attention of men over women) and
'homosexual panic' (a fear of such preference shading over,
as it always threatens to, into homosexual desire). The
notion of the 'homosexual' as an intensely stigmatized male
role entered Western culture towards the end of the nineteenth century because, Sedgwick argues (in agreement
with many other commentators on the period) it was
needed 'not only for the persecutory regulation of a nascent
minority of distinctly homosexual men but also for the
regulation of the male homosocial bonds that structure *all*
culture – at any rate, all public or heterosexual culture.'[97] It
is the internal incoherence of this homo/heterosexual

divide, as 'the presiding master term' for modern Western identity, which creates what she describes as the 'now endemic crisis' of modern sexual definition.[98]

Moreover, Sedgwick reminds us (worryingly for the ultimate success of queer or subversive strategies of resistance) knowledge of the instability of this supposedly 'oppositional' sexual divide, crucial to stabilizing our notions of gender identity, has been continually available to us for at least a century – from Freud, through Kinsey to the present. But this has done little to dismantle it: 'the nominative category of "the homosexual" has robustly failed to disintegrate under the pressure of decade after decade, battery after battery of deconstructive exposure – evidently not in the first place because of its meaningfulness to those whom it defines but because of its indispensableness to those who define themselves against it.' Indeed, its very instability still emerges most clearly, as Sedgwick and Dollimore agree, in 'straight' men's paranoid and violent disparagement of 'homosexuality' as a condition of their own 'manhood'. Most educated Western people today, Sedgwick suggests, hold two contradictory beliefs about male homosexuality. They think that some people 'really are' gay, on the one hand, while also agreeing that sexual desires really are unpredictable and fluid, and that male heterosexual identity and dominance are maintained only through the suppression and scapegoating of a potentially widespread and internally generated homosexual desire and activity, on the other.[99]

Certainly, it is now commonplace to recognize that those most passionately eager to promote heterosexuality, and most fearfully apprehensive about imagined threats to masculine virtues and power, from D.H. Lawrence to Norman Mailer (both of whom wrote and later suppressed ambivalent thoughts on homosexuality) are also those most centrally obsessed with homosexual imagery and desire. The imagined threat to manliness always attaches itself to the image of male passivity, conceived 'in terms of a denigrated and denigrating femininity at once utterly alien to yet strangely inherent within the male'.[100] The inevitability of sexual dissidence, and the possibilities for what Dollimore describes as 'transgressive reinscription' – 'a *turning back* upon something and a perverting of it typically if not exclusively through inversion and displacement' – reside in the uncomfortable familiarity of this constant return, whether in dreams, fantasies or intentional sabotage, of what is produced as most excluded and alien in dominant sexual culture. It is this, for example, which frames the subversive knowledge of Oscar Wilde, with his gentle inversions and wit, or the savage mockery of Jean Genet and Joe Orton, with their dramas of masquerade, transvestism and general 'gay non-sense'.[101]

But Dollimore, like Sinfield, also points to the limitations of deconstructive or transgressive inversions, theoretical or performative, as necessarily subversive. Contemporary academic interest in the political potential of discursive ambiguity, like Butler's strategy for displacing sexual and gender binaries through their subversive repetition in non-heterosexual frames, can succeed only if it can be *seen* as a collective struggle over representation: context, reception and, above all, articulation within wider political struggle makes the difference.[102] This returns us to where gay politics began, not merely to trangressive performances, which may or may not be read, or vaguely felt, as subversive of gendered meanings, or at least as unsettling of the comfortably familiar 'known', but to the subcultures which create and sustain them.

Today, the gay and lesbian Mardi Gras in Sydney, Australia, with its diverse, year-long preparations, negotiating with police, press and public, provides perhaps the most spectacular merging of the two: a hyperbolic condensation of transgressive reinscription or gender sabotage – exploding out into the wider world – for just one day. Like Mikhail Bakhtin's notion of the 'carnivalesque', the Mardi Gras procession of flamboyantly festive, gender-ambiguous bodies might be thought to oscillate around poles of subversion and recuperation, parody and containment: in part, a clearly demarcated safety-valve and condoned spectacle of the necessary 'Other' in the service of dominant sex/gender binaries (at least for many of the thousands of straight families who come to watch it); in part the creation and occupation of a subversive space, not just transgressing but refusing normative constructions (at least for some of the performers).[103]

For just one day, perhaps, the perverse may parade, socially sanctioned and police protected, but that day is always looming, just beyond the horizon, provoking pleasure, horror, vengeance, violence, but rarely indifference. The point of a recent wave of historical research has been to illustrate that there is nothing new about gender blurring – except the surgical procedures now available for 'gender reassignment' (with their accompanying medicalized categories of 'gender dysphoria' and 'transsexualism') and the academic interest it currently attracts in an effort to disrupt the hierarchical binaries through which we conceive and experience gender identity and sexual desire.

Analysing the recurrent allure of cross-dressing, presently presiding over Western chic wherever we look – from Iron Maiden to k.d. lang – Marjorie Garber presents the transvestite as a figure representing the permanent crisis of binary thinking at the heart of every culture her erudite research explores.[104] 'The seduction emanating from a person of uncertain or dissimulated sex is powerful,' as the French novelist Colette knew and narrated.[105] And – to capture just some of the magnetic power of sexual ambiguity – there is the record of Sarah Bernhardt on stage, Garbo and Dietrich in film, Mapplethorpe in photographs, and Michael Jackson who, throughout his lifetime has tried so fastidiously, so 'innocently', to embody it (in order to remain, in the estimation of *Life* magazine, the most popular rock star since Presley and 'the most androgynous folk hero' since Peter Pan) – till someone whispered, 'paedophile'! Garber concludes that the centrality of cultural cross-dressing and androgyny expresses not just the permanence of gender confusion and the recognition of 'otherness' as loss, but also the ineradicable threat to what is produced at the very centre of the meaning of human existence as we know it, the founding binary of sex.[106]

Reading through this radical outpouring of cultural history it becomes hard to propose a single Western icon, from Valentino to Elvis, from Mae West to Madonna, who does *not* emanate a type of sexual ambiguity (often both as feminized *and* hypermale, or vice versa), giving it a 'normality' – as theatrical performance. Even the macho Hollywood movies of the Reagan eighties, dedicated to the celebration of male bonding and violence, like *Top Gun* and *Lethal Weapon I* and *II*, confidently flaunt their masochistic homoeroticism along with their racism and misogyny: '"Give us a kiss",' the bruised and battered hero played by Mel Gibson demands of his black buddy, played by Danny Glover, in *Lethal Weapon II* – as the credits roll.[107] In Britain, Mark Simpson provides the latest witty exposure of the homoeroticism, passive anality and masochism at the quivering base of popular cultural representations of masculinity. From football and body building to shaving and Levi ads, he notices that men's bodies – naked, passive and desired – are now on display as never before: 'Traditional heterosexuality *cannot survive this reversal*,' he writes hopefully.[108] Sadly, however, sex and gender hierarchies seem to manage to thrive on their own contradictions.

Flaunting it: lesbian chic and the gay nineties

Without doubt, the ongoing theoretical confrontation between a hegemonic heterosexuality (filtered through the masculine/feminine binary) and the dissidents who would re-write and re-figure them (filtered through deconstructive analysis and subversive performance) has suggested new frameworks for contemporary sexuality. But queer theory, often sceptical of the comforts of former gay and lesbian identities – if not foolishly dismissive of seventies liberation politics – would have little impact today without the great wave of pride and purpose which accompanied the gay, lesbian and feminist activists busy building their networks and communities. It was these networks and communities *alone* which responded to the catastrophe of AIDS with grass-roots self-help, safer-sex campaigns, lobbying and fund-raising when – in the West – it struck the male gay community to, at best, the indifference – and often the vindictive delight – of much of the wider society. Today it is a politics of provocation and diversity which inspires a new generation of both activists and theorists, mocking a straight society apparently blind to the sexual ambiguities of its own favourite heroes.

But what do we find alongside popular fascination with ambiguously seductive heroes of screen and stage? Signs of gender or sexual ambiguity remain viciously policed and punished. From endemic 'queer bashing' to the denial of parental, fostering and other civil rights to homosexuals, from media vilification and rejection of positive gay and lesbian images to general harassment and the further criminalizing of consensual gay erotic practices (as in the notorious 'Spanner' case where gay men were jailed for consensual sado-masochistic acts in Britain in 1991), punishment of non-familial sex has been encouraged and resignified by the popular rhetoric of AIDS: 'for gay men with AIDS', as Simon Watney commented, 'there has been nothing but hatred, fear, and thinly veiled contempt.'[109]

The upsurge of virulent fear and hostility centring, as always, on the idea of any 'feminized' male sexual 'passivity' (such as the enjoyment of anal penetration) was indeed fanned by the tragedy that the Human Immunodeficiency Virus (HIV) responsible for AIDS first struck down gay men in the West – with unprotected anal sex proving the riskiest sexual practice. But I am sure that the hostility was and remains partly envy, which is unconsciously tied in with the growing suspicion around by the 1980s that gay men were having more fun and better sex, perhaps even better relationships, than straight men. As Alan Sinfield – with only minimal boasting – suggests:

> We seemed to have learnt a few tricks that straights had yet to develop. Gay men had organised genial ways of meeting for casual sex, and also loving couples that might manage, even, to evade gendered roles. They knew how to see other men without falling out with their partners. . . . They were at ease experimenting with kinky games; they were getting the fun back into sex. For the rightwing bigot AIDS was a godsend. It countermanded that allegedly gay advantage. It had all been a fantasy, 'the family' should set the limits of human experience.[110]

The combination of 'virtue', fear and envy is a terrifying and lethal one. And meanwhile, outside cultural studies and

related disciplines, there are still few faultlines in the hegemony – sometimes even the extension – of the dominant
sex/gender binaries shaping knowledge production. In a
seemingly unshaken and unshakable conflation of sexual
orientation and gender, scientists try to track down the 'gay
gene', and nonchalantly project their ideas of human sexual
dimorphism not only back on to animal behaviour, but
onto bacterial cells and macromolecules as well.[111]

'Have they found the gay gene, at last?' 'If so, what should
we do with it?', press, TV and even supposedly thinking
public earnestly ask themselves, usually mulling over the
ethics of choosing to abort it. Despite what we already
know of the complexities and instabilities, not to mention
the historical contingencies, of sexual desire and identities,
we rarely hear the only relevant question to claims of
correlations between gene clusters (or hypothalamic cellular
structures) and 'homosexuality': *what could it mean to
make such a claim?* Same-sex desire (like cross-sex desire)
is, on the one hand, very specific (typically narrowing
down to the erotic appeal of individuals with particular
attributes – of age, race, class, education, style, status, and
any number of specific physical attributes) and, on the other
hand, immensely diverse (typically consistently pursued
in its own significant contexts – in relationships, with
strangers, accompanying affection/ exploitation/aggression,
involving lingering contact/quick release, and so on, and on).
Sexual desire is never attraction to or engagement with
all members of the 'same' (or the 'opposite') sex. What
biological narrative, we can but wonder – because it is never
even remotely touched upon – would really enlighten us
about people's *distinctive* sexual experiences and behaviour?
Except for society's relentless and selective focus upon it,
the anatomical sex of who or what we desire and fantasize
about might seem one of the least significant features of

our extremely differing and very particular sexual biographies. The obvious flaw in genetic studies, as Alan Sinfield
summarizes, is the assumption of an already-known 'gay'
subject, when not all people who engage in same-sex
practices either see themselves or are seen as homosexual,
while others who do not engage in same-sex practices do
see themselves and are seen as 'homosexual': 'Trying to
decide who the real homosexuals are, therefore, is to join the
ideological circus, not to gain a vantage upon it.'[112]

Popular attachment to the biological determination of
sexuality and gender clearly remains culturally significant,
yet sexual dissidents have been consciously waging war
against the discourses which produce it for at least twenty-
five years now – with the growing resources of a 'pink'
economy on their side. As a war not only of signification,
but also of survival, it has been a drama in which the failure
to vanquish the weaker side has brought a new, even
swaggering, confidence to the less powerful but visibly
resilient rebels: 'Forced to define itself against the prevailing
negative definitions, homosexuality has found more and
more to say about love, gender and desire, while the media
are burying heterosexuality in an overkill of tired tabloid
cliches.'[113] It is this explosive combination of confidence
and anger which now feeds a heady, more inclusive mixture
of queer politics and culture. Attempting to capture its
significance, Cherry Smyth writes:

> The huge wave of energy unleashed by queer politics has
> enabled powerful alliances between lesbians and gay men,
> defying the separatism of the lesbian feminist movement
> and the misogyny of the gay male community . . . it
> provides a way of asserting desires that shatter gender
> identities and sexualities, in the manner some early Gay
> Power and lesbian feminist activists once envisaged.[114]

There's confidence for you! And from the late eighties, within a seemingly terminally fragmented and discouraged white urban radical milieu, 'perverse politics' provided almost the only new dialogue to be heard.

Lesbian artists and critics, in particular, were becoming prominent as they enthusiastically explored female sexuality anew. This time around, they were seeking not to delineate the correctly woman-identified feminist (now viewed as the 'repressive mother' figure sweeping lesbian sexuality under the rug of female friendship and mother-daughter bonding), but to parade the contradictory, politically incorrect but subversive identifications and desires of the eroticized lesbian.[115] In the closing years of the 1980s, lesbian sexual activities were on display in ways they had rarely been before. Jill Posener was producing her 'Dirty Girl's Guide to London', sabotaging its most sacred public monuments, and its most familiar commercial bill-boards, with images of lesbian sex. Nearby, Della Grace was photographing the 'lesbian cock', her dykes with dildos designed as parodies of phallic power, their 'penis envy' safely soothed by the knowledge that the lesbian spectator 'likes her boys to be girls'.[116] The US theatre troupe Split Britches began touring Western capitals with *Beauty and the Beast* (and *Paradykes Lost*), portraying butch and femme lesbian roles: the Butch – as Beast – representing through her style and clothing both the desire for other women and the terror and taboo directed against what is always seen as her 'predatory' desire; the Femme – as Beauty – representing the one who actively 'aims her desirability at the butch'.[117]

Sheila McLaughlin's controversial film, *She Must Be Seeing Things*, was screened, applauded and attacked in most Western capitals. (In London some women stormed the stage, while others tried to rip the film from the projector, labelling it 'pornography'.) The film attempted to confront lesbian and feminist taboos by showing how heterosexual codes shape lesbian sexuality, even as lesbians move beyond them.[118] Meanwhile, North American sex radicals were happily posing as – or eagerly viewing – phallic leather-clad 'tops', silk and lace-clad 'bottoms', or a bit of each (crew cuts, with frosted lipstick) in their favourite porn mags *On Our Backs*, *Bad Attitudes* or *Outrageous Women*. Declaring the eighties the age of the 'lesbian renaissance', Susie 'Sexpert' was seductively urging her readers on to join the (safe) sexual adventurousness of the Erotic Literary Society, pronouncing 'penetration' to be 'only as heterosexual as kissing', and celebrating 'genderfuck' over the faded 'zero femininity and milk toast butch' of androgyny.[119] Madonna was frequenting New York City dyke bars, consciously incorporating gay subculture's drag, masquerade and vogueing into her videos and performances. 'Are you ready for the gay nineties?' asks Susie Bright, at the close of '89. Ready and eager, the media responded, with its endless craving for the titillation of something 'new'. But could new forms of self-display really weaken the old heterosexist framings – always to hand?

Lesbian play with 'butch'/'femme', 'active'/'passive' 's/m' imagery, inevitably, these new voices were now proclaiming, interprets and portrays lesbian desire and experience filtered through the symbolic discourses of dominant heterosexual and gender codes. But it gives them new meanings. There does seem little doubt that, *within a lesbian space*, such work and imagery provoked recognition, pleasure and delight (at least from younger lesbians) as well as some hostility and anger. 'The marvellous revival of butch-femme erotics', Cindy Patton comments, 'reminded us that we knew how to turn masculinity on its head, and that we did not have to be afraid of these powerful transgressions.' She sees 'masculinity' reduced to the 'secret agent' of one form of lesbian desire, which cannot be read as strengthening the heterosexual male so definitively excluded from it: 'Paradoxically, macho dykes in leather have undone the phallus with their collection of dildos.'[120]

With camp wit and humour, Sue-Ellen Case had argued along the same lines in her much-cited essay, 'Towards a Butch-Femme Aesthetic'. Here, she presents the dynamic butch–femme duo as a coupled and empowered sexual position, where both partners are performers so neither 'impale themselves on the poles of sexual difference or metaphysical values, but constantly seduce the sign system through flirtation and inconstancy into the light fondle of artifice, replacing the Lacanian slash with the lesbian bar.'[121] Butch– femme role playing, Teresa de Lauretis adds (referring to McLaughlin's film), is exciting not because it represents heterosexual desire, but 'because it doesn't', because the gendered masks never quite fit, the masquerade is never quite successful. It therefore highlights the performers' investment in fantasy, where it always takes two to make a lesbian – two women.[122] This, they all agree, is why lesbians can 'play on the phallic economy rather than to it': their performance, unlike that of heterosexual female masquerade, is not recuperable by heterosexual men. Of course such confident lesbian lust remains, sadly, far removed from the consciousness of the typical self-proclaimed heterosexual man, and there is grim comedy in his ignorance of it, exquisitely captured in the consoling machismo Roger Scruton was clinging to around this time:

> The lesbian knows that she desires someone who will
> not typically make those advances that are characteristic
> of a man, even if she wants to; nor can she make
> these advances herself without compromising the

gender-identity which (she wishes to believe) is integral to her attractiveness. She can only wait, and wish, and pray to the gods with the troubled fervour captured by Sappho in her hymn to Aphrodite . . .[123]

Oh happy man!

Some lesbians, especially in California, moved towards sex radicalism through therapeutic and individualized sexological concerns, rather than with any specific political goal, other than sexual tolerance and pluralism. They wanted to promote lesbian sex education, and the diverse routes to orgasmic pleasure, to fight off 'Lesbian Bed Death', especially following widely reported statistics in the early 1980s that lesbians in general, and long-standing lesbian couples in particular, have far less sex than either gay men or heterosexual couples.[124] Gay girls were being urged to keep up with the boys.

But the lesbians rejecting Lesbian Nation for Queer Nation, or 'in-your-face' erotic culture, had higher political – as well as sexual – ambitions. Like other lesbian writers and artists before them who had sought variously to escape, deny, transcend or parody gender, they aimed, through their self-conscious play with it, to undo or de-centre hegemonic heterosexuality.[125] Yet I fear that the political edge of lesbian queer productions or performance, as we saw in the previous section, may well blunt (if not cut another way) before audiences who don't know how to 'read' them. If 'queer' still looks queer, however titillatingly 'wild' and deviant, it may mystify and muddle more than threaten and trouble its straight audience.

That this is far from unlikely is indicated by the frequent lesbian perplexity greeting the new queer productions, particularly from an earlier generation of lesbian feminists – at least, before they have been re-educated into queer readings. They worry that a queer politics, *if* it defines itself against feminism, may make a premature or shallow separation between sexuality and gender. However transgressively manipulable, at present the chains which bind a large part of women's sexual experience to their subordinate gender position remains an all too solid reality. Even when taught new and subversive ways of seeing, some women may notice, as Katie King or Jackie Goldsby in the USA remind us, that the radical risk-taking around gender has rarely extended to reconceptualizing race or class dynamics. Black lesbians still tend to be coded as 'butch', and the 'gorgeous femme' remains white – and usually blonde – in line with dominant white racist aesthetics (another criticism made of McLaughlin's film, *She Must Be Seeing Things*).[126] With black bodies (male and female) popularly portrayed to suggest the titillating promise and threat of the 'wild', 'exotic' and 'hyper-sexual' – always tied up with images of the 'primitive' and 'degraded' – the huge difference which race makes cannot be adequately addressed in any queer performance which addresses sex, gender and the heterosexual matrix in isolation from other structures of domination.

More generally, the fashionably 'post-modern' attention to surface, style and performance in re-staging and de-centring the gendered basis of power may be useful in reminding some of us of its social constructedness. But all too many lesbians and gay men, single mothers, battered and burdened women (in ways overdetermined by race and ethnicity) are already much too far out in the icy seas of economic and social disadvantage, much too endangered by their contaminating poisons of media and interpersonal hostility, to swim back in on a lifeline of subversive performance – whatever its effect on its audiences. Keeping his feet firmly on the hostile turf where most gay men and lesbians stand, Alan Sinfield comments that although as a salaried intellectual he is well cushioned from tabloid bile: 'I shudder to contemplate how other men and women cope with exposure to a sustained hate campaign, directed not just at our ideas, or actions even, but at our very selfhood.'[127] Sinfield stresses the overwhelming priority which he feels must be given to subcultural consolidation of a rich and supportive lesbian and gay milieu (while keeping alive hopes for the resuscitation of a renewed socialist project) to help sustain the dissident lives of the millions currently outside the protection which social privilege can offer from the threat of daily insult, violence and the denial of civil rights.

Studying how we live our sexual and gender identities as highly regulated performances does tell us something which is useful about the instabilities of both categories, beginning with the impossibility of insisting, without a brutalizing blindness, on their definitive connection. But we are not free to choose our performances or masquerades at will – like a type of 'improvisational theatre' (though some have, mistakenly, as she subsequently clarifies, cited Butler as licensing just such an analysis).[128] Mostly, we can only enact those behaviours which have long since become familiar and meaningful to us in expressing ourselves. This remains so however much we realize that our self-fashioning was formed through the policing norms and personal relations of a sexist heterosexual culture; indeed, however fulfilling or frustrating our routine performances may prove. Challenge to our gendered 'identities' may be more than we can handle.

In arguing for the importance of a progressive sexual politics we need to figure out how to increase the potential confidence of all people to pursue the differing comforts, pleasures and perils of the flesh, free from all intimidation and threat, if only to try to help to undermine the perpetual displacement of people's fear, envy or anxiety into rage against others' pursuit of pleasure. This will mean, however, not just highlighting discursive contradiction and subversive strategy in the complex domain of the 'sexual', but paying attention to distinctive anatomical bodies, which are always distinctively vulnerable – in ways which are as much socially as anatomically determined – along the lines of gender, age, illness or disability, as well as trying to understand the diverse legacies of individual psychic histories. Neither our bodily nor our psychic formations are ever either separable from each other, or their particular positioning within a multitude of privileging or oppressive social meanings and relations. Of course every person occupies certain contradictory social orderings and identities (some so much more powerful or threatening than others), with their significance shifting across time and place. As the now much mourned Audre Lorde was able to recall, back in the fifties 'gay-girls' were the only black and white American women who were even talking to each other. Yet the New York Village gay bars provided only a slightly less hostile terrain for black lesbians than the outside world, which demanded every ounce of their strength just to survive. Yet Lorde could also examine the differences which existed even within that spectacularly courageous group she so evocatively described as occupying 'the very house of difference rather than the security of any one particular difference': 'It was hard enough to be Black, to be Black and female, to be Black, female and gay. To be Black, female, gay and out of the closet . . . was considered by many Black lesbians to be suicidal.'[129]

The point is, it is not just a matter of gender, nor just a matter of heterosexual dominance, to which we need to stay attuned when we concede that both psychic and body matters are mapped *only* through the shifting attention (and inattention) they receive and arouse; nor when we hope that they may be re-mapped through new collective interpretations becoming available to us. Nevertheless, the great gift, or terrifying threat, which recent lesbian and gay productions offer dominant heterosexual culture does lie in their specific challenge to gender certainties. Thus male gay pornography/erotica exposes the curves and softness, the moist openings and penile peculiarities, of the eroticized male body – unmarked in phallic discourses:

> Concave, each cheek looks glossy. . . . If he spreads his cheeks – which feel cold, firm and plump – for the kneeling admirer, he reveals an anus that makes one think of a Leica lens. . . . An expensive aperture, but also a closed morning glory bud. . . . And there are the few silky hairs in the crack of his arse, wet now for some reason and plastered down at odd angles as though his fur had been greedily licked in all directions at once. If he spreads his legs . . . his erection may melt and you might see it drooping lazily into view, just beyond his loosely bagged testicles.[130]

Just as gay actions and writing in recent years has given us some of the most haunting images yet expressed of the human capacity to love and nurture the fragile hold on life of a very sick person:

> Now helped through day itself, eased into chairs
> Or else led step by step down the long stairs
> With firm and gentle guidance by his friend,
> Who loves him, through each effort to descend,
> Each wavering, each attempt made to complete
> An arc of movement and bring down the feet
> As if with that spare strength he used to enjoy,
> I think of Oedipus, old, led by a boy.[131]

It is on behalf of her political affiliation as a lesbian sex radical that Joan Nestle offers her own extraordinary 'gift to the world', passing on to women (and men) the power of her erotic knowledge. It bursts through the polarized shackles of 'activity/passivity' which ground our impoverished and impoverishing 'heterosexuality', our damaged and damaging 'masculinity/femininity'. Working with the inadequacies of existing categories, Nestle's narratives of lesbian passion still today fall off 'the biologically charted maps' (as she illustrates butch–femme roles did back in the 1950s, when *only* the sexual deviants questioned gender destiny).[132] Her 'pornographic' writing celebrates the place and the fluidity of power as it animates non-coercive sexual encounters. The 'passive' partner in her 'butch–femme' couplings is also actively demanding, educating, orchestrating and receiving pleasure; the 'active' partner, also passively dependent in her need, through her gentleness and her desire to please:

> We both had power in our hands. She could turn from me and leave me with my wetness, my need – a vulnerability and a burden. I could close up, turn away from her caring and her expertise. But neither happened. With extreme tenderness she laid me down.[133]

Nestle rewrites submission as power, power as submission, in sexual embraces which, however brief, are invariably loving and respectful:

> My submission in this room with this woman is my source of strength, of wisdom. It informs all my abilities in the other world, but here I can give it time to breathe its own air, and to break the surface, and show its face.

Nestle's generosity and power as she writes for women, all women – lesbian and straight – on the daily tensions of balancing autonomy and intimacy is, to me, breathtaking. She seeks a new alliance between lesbians and straight women in search of a world where women are in control of their destinies, a world where the force of compassion and of pleasure replaces the force of domination and fear. It is only by reading the tensions and inversions of Nestle's politics of passion and desire that I can begin to flesh out what Butler means when she observes that 'heterosexuality offers normative positions that are intrinsically impossible to embody, and the persistent failure to identify fully and without incoherence with these positions reveals hetero-sexuality itself not only as a compulsory law, but as an inevitable comedy . . . a constant parody of itself.'[134]

The question is whether heterosexuals can recognize themselves as part of both a compulsory system *and* an intrinsic comedy. For until they can, the comedy hides only tragedy – for everyone – with the most difficult and painful roles reserved, still, for women and gay men.

6. Rethinking heterosexuality: women with men

> *Desire is what we do not control; goodwill and desire are perhaps, peculiarly and sadly, twins that sit incompatibly in the domestic nest.*
>
> Naomi Segal[1]

> *Heterosexuality cannot be free until we stop thinking in terms of 'opposites' that are 'drawn' to one another.*
>
> Mariana Valverde[2]

> *Ultimately . . . a great deal depends . . . on the fostering of our ability to arrive at understandings of sexuality that will accept a certain irreducibility in it to the terms and relations of gender.*
>
> Eve Sedgwick[3]

Heterosexual feminists have been on a bumpy ride over the last twenty-five years. Women who wanted to think and rethink, rather than presume and preserve, what it means to be heterosexual have come up against one obstacle after another. This is hardly surprising since Western culture remains so deeply ambivalent about both sexuality and women. But Western feminism has proved itself deeply divided over the question of 'straight' women. The problem we face is how to overcome the division.

The first impediment is, of course, men: both as they are and as they are figured in the dominant notions of 'masculinity' which mould acceptable male behaviour. 'Masculinity' in Western culture leans, at least in part, upon the sexual pursuit of women affirmed in a type of sexist braggadocio which betrays both a fear of real intimacy and a horror of any signs of 'weakness' or 'effeminacy'. 'ONCE I LIVED IN CAPITALS/ MY LIFE EXTREMELY PHALLIC/ but now i'm sadly lowercase/ with the occasional *italic*,'[4] Roger McGough mourns. Feeling weak or unimportant, however, fuels more than the poetic regret, or egotistical self-obsession, needed to shore up the flagging presumptions of manhood. As often, it motivates rage and violence, principally aimed at women, and especially their sexuality – 'requiring women's blood for life/ a woman's breast to lay its nightmare on';[5] although the anxiety of having always to proffer the proofs of 'masculinity', even when the word confers little status or authority, is something men themselves have sometimes rebelled against, with still limited success.[6]

The next stumbling block for women's dreams of autonomy and heterosexual pleasure came with feminist impatience to find women's own 'authentic' bodily experiences in the face of men's demeaning images of them. Searching for a desire of their own – free from entanglement with male-centred myths and meanings – led some heterosexual feminists to abandon, and many others to say no more about (and certainly to write no more about), their longings for physical and emotional intimacy with men. An abiding predicament lay coiled within the resilient phallocentric discourses of sex, desire and subjectivity, whatever the new possibilities and encouragement for women to rethink and refashion our sexual encounters with men. The mocking accompaniment of many women's search for sexual empowerment was the ever-expanding sexual marketplace, and the media fashions and fixations targeting sexual fears and longing.

The final impasse for female sex-radicals was, and remains, the inescapable contrariness of sexual passion.

Some level of confusion and contention is inevitable if straight women are ever to wade their way through sexual contradictions. To expect otherwise is to refuse the complexity of this critical but treacherous topic. Yet it has been a powerful strand of feminism itself which has done most over the last decade to oversimplify the issue of heterosexuality and tie it, ineluctably, to women's subordination.

Heterosexual defensiveness: a crisis of confidence

'I am not now and never have been a "heterosexual",' the North American feminist psychologist Sandra Bem declares, despite having lived monogamously and happily with the man she loves for twenty-six years.[7] 'I have often wished that I could love women erotically, but I can't,' her fellow feminist American philosopher Sandra Bartky tells us. She appeals to her feminist readers to 'invent a therapeutic technique for releasing the heterosexual woman . . . from the prisonhouse of necessity into the free space of choice.'[8] A happy heterosexual is hard to find, Celia Kitzinger and Sue Wilkinson gleefully conclude, surveying the comments sent to them by feminists sufficiently foolhardy to reply to their one-sided questions about their experiences as 'heterosexual' feminists.[9]

Kitzinger and Wilkinson ignore the comments from women which do not fit the conclusions they are seeking: conclusions in line with their lesbian-separatist analysis of heterosexuality as the root of women's oppression, and therefore incompatible with feminist struggle. It is with pleasure, rather than distress, that they inform their readers of the guilt they have managed to elicit as one of the main sentiments from their selected sample of victims when describing their (hetero)sexual fantasies and desires. (As though guilt, shame, and self-doubt were not the most depressingly familiar sentiments women have learned to connect with their sexuality.) Their own condescending and self-righteous reaction to women's sexual doubts and anxieties is to treat them as altogether appropriate: 'The qualifier "heterosexual" is, at best, an embarassing adjunct to "feminist"; at worst, it seems a contradiction in terms.'[10]

An irritated heterosexual feminist might conclude that although their book declares its intention of opening up spaces for feminist theorizing and exploration of heterosexuality, it is in fact dedicated, one more time, to closing them down. But we would need to admit that we can find similar reflections coming from totally opposed feminist stables. Eve Sedgwick, a highly theoretical, Foucauldian-influenced scholar with only impatience for separatist feminist polemic – although very closely identified with the predicament of gay men – has added (in her uniquely convoluted way) to a now all too familiar chorus from heterosexual women:

> I have spent – wasted – a long time gazing in renewed
> stupefaction at the stupidity and psychic expense of my
> failure, during that time [my adolescence], to make
> the obvious swerve that would have connected my
> homosexual desire and identification with my need and
> love, as a woman, of women. . . . Yet it went and has still
> gone unmade.[11]

Indeed, we can step right outside feminism to survey collections of women's erotic celebrations throughout the ages, and we will still find a remarkable absence of heterosexual celebration: 'Good erotic poems [by women] are rare, and are to be found more frequently amongst lesbian poets and poems from ancient parts of Japan and China than from contemporary Western heterosexuals.'[12]

Here the chronicler, British poet Wendy Mulford, expresses only bemusement, rather than satisfaction, at this state of affairs. Women rarely brag in their tales of love, unless – like Gertrude Stein – they have never been heterosexual. Similarly, Jean Wyatt tells us, sorrowfully: 'In my own search for an enabling heterosexual femininity, I found the fiction field so bare of examples that I had to turn to life for a better plot – to Elliot's "How I came to Write Fiction".'[13] So if we turn to the actual lives of women, what explains the silence – a silence so seemingly strange in recent decades in which surveys report a remarkable increase in the similarity between women and men's sexual behaviour and attitudes?[14]

We can begin by asking whether bodies and their vulnerabilities, bodies and their meanings, really do place the pursuit of heterosexual freedom at odds with women's liberation. Certainly, sex has something to do with bodies, and in Western thinking, bodies have been central to the construction of our identities. More specifically, however, feminists and their supporters have emphasized that female socialization, unlike male socialization, has been synonymous with 'the sexualization of the body and its parts'.[15] Men's dominance over women has been maintained through their control over and definitions of the female body and its functions, selecting out the 'female reproductive cycle' as the essence of 'femaleness', forever shackling women to the 'demands' of their uterus and ovaries. Thomas Laqueur, among others, has graphically illustrated how shifting biological interpretations of the bodies of women, especially since the late nineteenth century, came to serve as the prestigious 'gold standard' for social discourses resisting the political, economic or social claims of women for equality: 'wherever boundaries were threatened arguments for fundamental sexual differences were shoved into the breach.'[16]

Body matters: cultural inscriptions

Western science has defined not only sexual difference but the purpose and function of sexuality, primarily, in terms of reproductive biology: stressing the role of the penis and testes in male fertilization, and of the breast, ovaries, uterus and vagina in pregnancy and lactation. The reality, however, which twentieth-century sexology could not dismiss, is that while *some* biological narrative may provide a reproductive purpose for men's sexual pleasure in terms of the penis, no parallel narrative can centre women's sexual pleasure in pregnancy and lactation. The human clitoris, physiological site of female orgasm and without reproductive purpose, undermines all attempts to link sexual pleasure to reproductive outcome.[17] And it was Freud, of course, often against the grain of his own teleological thinking, who first suggested that human sexuality in adulthood is built out of its foundations in the autoeroticism and polymorphous perversities of childhood. Here bodily pleasures bear no relation to reproductive ends or acts; nor, significantly, to the supposed gender polarity of adult heterosexuality along lines of activity/passivity. Exactly which areas of the body surface would be eroticized, and with what fixity or fluidity of focus, his case studies suggested, would depend upon the psychic meanings they acquired in young children's interactions with the world around them. Indeed, Freud found the model for adult sexuality in infantile thumb-sucking, propped upon the biological mechanisms for feeding.

It is not so hard to establish that a scientific paradigm picturing the female body as functioning passively in the service of reproductive demands is primarily ideological. It is even easier to expose the ideological nature of the biological paradigm of male sexuality as active and initiating. The knowledge that human females do not have estrous cycles like other primates (with their highly visible genital changes and 'sexual signalling' behaviour during fertile periods) is presented to us in the most familiar biological texts, like Donald Symons's *The Evolution of Human Sexuality*, through accounts of the 'year-round receptivity' of female sexuality, which is said to possess the passive feature of being 'continuously copulable'. Meanwhile human male sexuality is portrayed as perpetually ready to copulate: 'women inspire male sexual desire simply by existing.'[18] Proudly, if naively, Symonds draws our attention to the connection between his biological description of men's ever-ready sexual desire (accompanying women's ever-available sexual condition) and men's pornographic fantasies of 'basic male wishes' as 'easy, anonymous, impersonal, unencumbered sex with an endless succession of lustful, beautiful, orgasmic women.'[19] Quite. His description belongs to the world of male *fantasy*. Corporeal reality is different. Outside the fabulations and fantasmagoria of 'scientific' or pornographic texts the hominid penis is anything but permanently erect, anything but endlessly ready for unencumbered sex, anything but triggered by the nearest passing female – even when she happens to be his wife, mistress or lover, and eager for sex.

With chilling if humorous detail, Emily Martin illustrates how this same imagery of passive 'femininity' and active 'masculinity' is attributed even to the human ovum (or 'egg') and sperm. The ovum is variously depicted in contemporary medical texts as 'floating', 'drifting', 'transported' or 'swept along' the fallopian tube, and contrasted with the 'masculinity' of the 'streamlined', 'strong' sperm: 'lashing their tails' as they make their 'perilous journey' through the 'hostile environment' of the vagina, to 'penetrate', 'assault' or (as one illustration in *Science News* would have us envisage the physiological process) 'ferociously attack the egg' with jack-hammer, pickaxe and sledgehammer. These stereotyped images persist, Martin comments, even as new research suggests the extreme fragility of the sperm, which swim 'blindly' in circles and mill around, unless 'captured' and 'held fast' by the adhesive molecules on the surface of the egg.[20]

There is no doubt that respected biological discourses have traditionally been used to prop up, while themselves feeding upon, a multitude of overlapping discourses and narratives from literature and pornography (although less uniformly in the latter). Tales of the all-powerful, ever-ready, male sex drive, located in the activities of the male sex organ – the penis (or sperm!) – function all too well to console and titillate (if also to intimidate) men, as well as to tease and to silence women. Exemplifying such discourses, Gay Talese reports from his journalistic survey of North American sexual mores in the 1970s on the male sexual member:

> Sensitive but resilient, equally available during the day or night with a minimum of coaxing, it has performed purposefully if not always skilfully for an eternity of centuries, endlessly searching, sensing, expanding, probing, penetrating, throbbing, wilting, and wanting more . . . it is men's most honest organ.[21]

A load of old codswallop, obviously. Its ideological function as mythic male fantasy is seemingly so blatant. Yet it remains entrenched as biological 'truth', however sexist and silly we know it to be from our personal experiences of sex, however familiar we may be with competing biological and clinical narratives of male impotence and sexual dysfunc-tion. It is these myths of penile prowess which we need relentlessly to expose in our rethinking of heterosexuality.

There is a mass of medical and clinical data documenting

men's chronic anxieties in relation to their penile performance. Partly as a result of feminist probing, one text after another in recent years has embarked upon the task of 'deconstructing the phallus': turning the medical and therapeutic gaze upon the penis and its persistent premature ejaculation, impotence, loss of desire; then widening the focus to include venereal disease, testicular cancer and infertility – contemplating all the while the painful remedies men seek for their sexual disorders. But knowledge of suffering and uncertainty in men's sex lives, supposed until recently to be one of men's best kept secrets, is not something which is new. On the contrary, Freud had written in 1908 that to many it was 'scarcely credible how seldom normal potency is to be found in the husband', and Wilhelm Stekel had added in 1927 that the 'percentage of relatively impotent people cannot be placed too high' (himself placing it near 50 per cent and citing premature ejaculation as modern man's most characteristic sexual practice).[22] However, men's routine inability to use the penis as they might wish was to remain a largely private torment, mainly receiving contempt if exposed to medical practitioners. Indeed, Lesley Hall concludes her research on the help and advice men sought and received in Britain on their sexual problems in the first half of this century with the thought: 'Whatever the social potency of men . . . their actual sexual potency is always dubious and open to question.'[23]

The standard biological narrative of active penile prompting and passive vaginal receptivity as the paradigm for human sexual encounter thus serves above all to hide, as well as to create and sustain, the severe anxieties attaching to the penis, while also revealing men's fear of recognizing the existence of women's sexual agency – verbal, behavioural or physiological. As some women artists have recently been keen to affirm, producing art works of the male genitals as changeable, soft, vulnerable and comic, the more we display new bodily images and meanings exposing penile precariousness and mutability, the more we challenge traditional phallic narratives.[24] But there are pitfalls all the way. Seventies feminism was mistaken, according to current feminist rethinking, in its attempt to reclaim women's 'own' bodily experiences in some direct and unmediated way.

Feminists from the late sixties had stressed the distinction between biological 'sex' and socially constructed 'gender', in order to challenge and reject the ubiquitous mythologizing of women's 'nature' and place in the world. They wanted to contrast women's socialization into the constricting roles or performances of submissive femininity they called 'gender', with what their own collectively shared experiences of the body suggested about their biological 'sex': 'We refuse to accept anything as true that we can't confirm by our feelings and experience.'[25] But bodily experiences are themselves socially constructed, not only by the culturally specific ways we have of interpreting them, but by socially variable factors like diet, exercise, training and reactions to ageing, illness and so on. So while aware of the consequences of men's greater social and cultural power in controlling women's behaviour, feminists were – at least at first – less able to problematize the physiological reductionism of the biomedical sciences they wished to transcend. Sharing experiences, as the widely influential *Our Bodies, Ourselves* had promised in the 1970s, 'we rid ourselves of many fears and obstacles and can start to make better use of our untapped energies'.[26] Bodily responses were thus seen as speaking directly to us, rather than through our particular interpretative community. And this supposed access to the body, we know in retrospect, was all the more likely to create a collective prescriptiveness when seeking to bring sexual experiences into speech. Sexual experiences are so tied in with the most keenly felt but peculiarly inexpressible hopes and deprivations, promising either the confirmation of, or threats to, our identites as worthwhile or lovable people, that they can scarcely avoid invoking insecurities and anxieties. This is why, as Carole Vance has written, 'there is a very fine line between talking about sex and setting norms'.[27] And so there was.

When feminist-inspired research, like that of Shere Hite, reported that only 30 per cent of women reach orgasm during penetrative sex, this was quickly transformed, by Hite and by others, into the spurious announcement that most women did not like penetrative sex (against the grain of the complexity of feelings Hite herself uncovered).[28] Before long the coercive message of much feminist sex-advice literature was that wise women, in touch with their 'authentic' needs, would avoid penetrative sex. ('*Hmn . . . do I put it somewhere??*' a feminist cartoon muses, depicting a strong, naked woman, looking dubiously at a penis-shaped vibrator. She moves it around a bit, only to fling it down in horror, repeating in outrage the absurd suggestion, '*In my CUNT?!*')[29] Yet, any feminist preference for clitoral over vaginal, 'active' over 'passive', self-directed over self-shattering, sexual engagement not only ignores the unruliness of desire but reflects, more than transcends, the repudiation of 'femininity' in our misogynist culture.

The repetition of this repudiation is easy to understand: even the most recent feminist encyclopaedia or 'Companion' on sexuality, *The Sexual Imagination* (1993), has no entry under 'vagina', although the history and meaning of the 'clitoris' is boldly covered by its presiding editor as playing 'a disproportionately major role in women's sexual pleasure'.[30] It did not go unchallenged, but when affirmed, the reproductive resonance of vaginal iconography as 'birth canal' always threatened to over-ride or undermine any pleasure-encoding signification. It was the pioneer of post-war Western feminism, Simone de Beauvoir, who affirmed, with reference to the vagina that, 'the feminine sex organ is mysterious even to the woman herself. . . . Woman does not recognise its desires as hers.' Her own description of this 'sex organ', so often 'sullied with body fluids', tells us why:

> woman lies in wait like the carnivorous plant, the bog, in which insects and children are swallowed up. She is absorption, suction, humus, pitch and glue, a passive influx, insinuating and viscous: thus, at least, she vaguely feels herself to be.[31]

There is no vagueness in this description. It is a perfect illustration of the horror of what Kristeva has elaborated in her (currently much over-used) conception of the 'abject' object. Kristeva describes abjection as the process whereby the child takes up its own clearly defined ('clean and proper') body image through detaching itself from – expelling and excluding – the pre-Oedipal space and self-conception associated with its improper and unclean, 'impure', connection with the body of the mother. The mother's body, having been everything to the child, threatens its engulfment. On this view, entering the symbolic space of language brings with it a horror of (and fearful attraction to) everything without clear boundaries, everything which suggests a non-distinctiveness between inside and outside.[32] Elaborating Kristeva's thoughts, Elizabeth Grosz explains that in her notion of an 'unnamable, pre-oppositional, permeable barrier, the abject requires some mode of control or exclusion to keep it at a safe distance from the symbolic and its orderly proceedings'.[33] However culturally specific this psychoanalytic narrative of the child's entry into the symbolic may be (and Kristeva, with unconvincing but characteristic Lacanian grandiosity, takes it to be universal), it would seem to resonate with the place of vaginal iconography in our culture, and its absence from respectable discourses and contexts. The vagina has served as a condensed symbol of all that is secret, shameful and unspeakable in our culture.

The question which Grosz raises is whether it is discourse itself which confers the horror of 'abjection' onto female bodies, and whether there might thus be other ways of registering, or resignifying, the sexual specificity of female sexual bodies (which may include, but would not reduce to, reference to the mother's body – however conceived). Neither de Beauvoir nor Kristeva address this question. It is indeed a formidable task. That some interference and shift in standard perceptions and meaning are possible, when old images are repeated in contexts where they may be seen in new ways (always involving contention, and fears of recuperation), is evident from the battles which have already been fought around women's film and art works involving female genital anatomy.

When Anne Severson started showing her short silent film, *Near the Big Chakra*, assembling close-up colour photographs of women's 'cunts' or vulvas, in the early 1970s, it incited extraordinarily strong reactions of both pleasure and disgust. Women fought over it, one supporter telling Severson, 'I would kill for your film.' Some women saw the images as powerful, teasing and pleasurable, suggesting energy and activity, 'an active passivity'.[34] For them the intricate delicacy, complexity, varied shapes and different hues making up the 'whole' female genital (vaginal opening, pubic hair, mons, outer-lips, inner lips, clitoris, magnified pores, secretions, occasional Tampax string, and so on), can mock and reverse the 'hole' male discourse has made of it – as sheath for the penis. Cathy Schwichtenberg explains its subversive effect as follows:

> the absence which is not an absence, gazes back at male viewers producing a double-bind of fear and desire which alternatively sucks them in, pushes them out; and asks for more than a penis/phallus closure. These vulvas ask for textural/sexual caresses – a pleasurable foreplay and a questioning of ideas.[35]

They may well ask. Schwichtenberg is right to suggest that these new sexual images of the female body, which some women (and perhaps even men) may find pleasurable, especially in cultural contexts where viewers are already hoping to stir up trouble for traditional meanings, can begin a slow process of resignification. But with other women rejecting Severson's film (and those which would follow it, with similar intent), as disgusting, demeaning and 'pornographic' (one man vomited at a London screening), we have a lot more stirring, and a lot more explaining to do, before female genitals exist securely in language as more than 'manholes'.

Sexual histories: bodily constraints

The place of the body in feminist theory is probably more confusing today than it has ever been. On the one hand, feminists are as eager as ever to rescue the female body from the subordinate and vulnerable place it has occupied in Western discourses, and institutional and interpersonal practices. The material potentialities and vulnerabilities of that body remain central to women's struggles and resistance. On the other hand, with the sex/gender distinction now seen by many as a misleading distinction, and our knowledge of the body primarily a social and political matter, sensual and fleshly reality keeps disappearing into the discourses which contsruct it, the study of which has become an ever more abstract affair. An extraordinary explosion of work on 'the body' has been emerging across Western disciplinary boundaries in recent years, but it is one triggered by the Foucauldian conception of the body as 'the inscribed surface of events, traced by language and dissolved by ideas'.[36] As the feminist philosopher of science, Donna Haraway, expresses this position: 'Bodies are not born; they are made . . . . Their boundaries materialize in social interaction.'[37]

The goal Haraway and others propose is certainly not to ignore the body. It is to explore how it has been coded and made meaningful, and above all, perhaps, how it might be radically recoded or resignified to enhance the sense of women's entitlement to desire and pleasure – on their own diverse terms. But we need to persist with the question: are there, or are there not, prediscursive bodies? Are there constraints which bodies themselves place on the discourses through which they are – or may become – known? Not, it would seem, if we accept a thorough-going social con-structionism. At least, not in any way we could meaningfully or neutrally discuss: 'there is no reference to a pure body which is not *at the same time* a further formation of that body'.[38] Certainly, we can only *know* bodies through discourse, and just as certainly bodily knowledge is invested with all the political and social normativeness of those discourses. Thus, for example, although female bodies often have the capacity for pregnancy and child-bearing, many have not. Some women are infertile, the average thirty-seven (and peak twenty) reproductive years of a woman's life occupies less than half of her life expectancy in Western countries. Most women will spend almost all of their lives not pregnant, not giving birth and not suckling their young.[39] It is, Judith Butler therefore concludes, only the prescriptive discourses and institutions of reproduction that make such attributes the most salient features of female bodies:

> When people ask the question 'Aren't *these* biological differences?' [female pregnability], they're not really asking a question about the materiality of the body. They're actually asking whether or not the social institution of reproduction is the most salient one for thinking about gender. In that sense, there is the discursive enforcement of a norm.[40]

We must always consider both the symbolic and practical frameworks which give meaning to, and perhaps equally significantly, fail to affirm or even register (render 'abject'), particular bodily changes. But I would give more weight than Butler and others have recently allowed to exploring and discussing (with humbling tentativeness) how biological constraints, in different ways at different times in individual biographies, interact with the culturally available, enabling or disabling and potentially changeable, bodily and psychic inscriptions attaching themselves to occurrences which are at one and the same time both the most uniquely personal and the most publicly shared and collective experiences we may have as women in this world today. The biological, psychic and cultural dimensions of bodily experience fuse together, a fact which should be brought home to us by the often reported finding that Japanese people became on average a foot taller in a generation after the Second World War, a process apparently occurring in Taiwan today. (The Japanese 'Butterfly' of Western erotic fantasy – whether woman or boy – will become less available for the Western male!)

If we look at how bodies appear in personal sexual narratives, it is clear that they encode culturally significant, as well

as maturationally specific, understandings of physical organs
and their functioning. For instance, at the close of the 1980s,
Lillian Rubin in the USA set out to discover the impact
of the 'sexual revolution' by conducting long, in-depth
interviews, amassing sexual case histories from 375 people
of diverse ages and backgrounds, while assessing another
600 thirteen-page questionnaire responses from, in the
main, college students. Interestingly, 90 per cent of both
men and women spoke of being 'disappointed' with their
first encounters with genital heterosexuality. But whereas
almost all the men (of whatever age) saw them as an
important 'achievement' on the way to manhood, 'a step in
which they exulted, even if they didn't fully enjoy the
experience itself' no woman talked about first intercourse as
'defining of womanhood'.[41] Women frequently expressed
regrets, which were not of guilt, but of feeling cheated of 'the
romantic fantasy' they had hoped to fulfil.[42] Few women
experienced orgasm, though this was not in itself determining of whether they described their first heterosexual
encounters as 'loving or painful, wonderful or terrible'.

What many women who reflect back upon their sexual
histories recall as symbolizing their entry into 'womanhood'
was the very different, not infrequently frightening, shaming,
or at least foreboding, significance given to their first period
or menstruation: an altogether less affirming 'achievement'
than boys' first heterosexual encounters. A recent British
collection of women reflecting upon the menopause raises
time and again the significance of menstrual stories which, as
Sue O'Sullivan writes, 'revealed so much about how girls
became women, about fear and loathing, about the female
body, about sexuality, about difference'.[43] 'It's not nice for
other people to know, especially not men,' Molly Parkin's
mother warns her daughter when her first period arrives in
the 1940s. Menstruation was 'a source of shame and

embarrassment', a warning that 'worse – much worse – lay ahead', Eva Figes recalls of her 'sex education' at around the same time. 'I did not enjoy having the curse . . . I remember [my mother] sighing heavily in a knowing sort of way, implying I was in for something now which included pain, emotional trauma and MEN,' Phyllida Law writes of post-pubescence in those years.[44]

A generation later, many of the taboos and young women's conflictual feelings remain. One study from the 1970s found that girls were still reporting that periods remained a secretive affair, to be kept from fathers and men generally, rarely even discussed with 'best friends': 'Most seemed to view their [first] period as a kind of illness . . . these girls described themselves as being scared, angry, upset or tearful, although they were unable to account for these feelings.'[45] (The relation between mother and daughter is reported here as the crucial factor in determining with what ease or disquiet the daughter begins menstruating.) Menstruation still serves as most women's sometimes more, sometimes less, troubling initiation into the combination of cultural denial, secrecy and shame marking what it labels 'female functions' as, first of all, issues of health and hygiene, rather than pleasure and fulfilment.[46] Muriel Dimen's rumbustious recollections of her sexual dilemmas of the 1960s are unlikely to have been finally solved over the intervening years: whatever the latest Tampex ads might portray as the sexual allure and athletic skills of the forever young and glamorous menstruating female of today, or the very latest phase of contraceptive technology might promise:

> In high school, when I read *On the Road*, I wanted to be a beatnik and go on the road too, but I could never figure out what I would do when I got my period. . . . The only beatnik I knew who ever dealt with this question was a

woman, Diana diPrima. In her novel, *Memoirs of a
Beatnik*, her heroine describes her first big orgy and
recounts the moment in it when she pulled out her
Tampax and flung it across the room. A grand moment
that. . . . The obligation to worry about the gross mess
became a part of my life from puberty on. A nagging,
seemingly stupid worry became a fact of life. . . . Just
when was I to put in my diaphragm? Once it was in,
would it stay in? And when the time came to take it out,
how, where, and with what would I wash it?[47]

Heterosexual women usually find themselves having to deal
with the possible connections, or lack of them, between their
sexual activity and reproductive matters. For a considerable
part of their lives this involves contraceptive decisions, if
they desire or allow or are forced into coital sex. Sometimes
it will mean mourning the lack of conception, or trying to
facilitate that outcome. Occasionally (over a lifetime) it will
produce the pressing demands resulting from conception
– whether in seeking an abortion, or pursuing the best
options for successful pregnancy and childbirth. But all
these decisions, pressures and demands, involve *at all times*
issues which are as much psychic and cultural (hence
political) matters, as biological ones. Feminists have fought
long and hard for all aspects of reproductive technology to
be used in the interests of increasing women's control over
their own bodies, and their procreative and pleasure-seeking
potential – although their significant successes in different
Western countries remain threatened by the activities of
moral conservatives world-wide, both male and female.

The culturally loaded, conflictual and ambiguous
interaction between women's sexual experiences and our
reproductive cycle continues, as it began, producing diverse
biographical narratives throughout a lifetime. Germaine

Greer, for example, is derisory about both the medical-ization of the menopause, and the persistent ignorance which masquerades as knowledge, expertise and adequacy in the medical care of women. A pioneer spokeswoman for women's sexual liberation in the 1960s, she now welcomes the menopause as a time when 'we' women, who have always devoted ourselves exclusively to servicing husbands, children or employers (oh yes?), can at last be 'released from our leg-irons' and develop our own creativity, spirituality and strength, freed from the 'pain' of relationships.[48] Eva Figes tells us, rather similarly, that menopause brings 'a release from sexual appetite . . . we are no longer driven by our hormones,' adding 'I, for one, find this an immense relief.'[49]

'Hormones', however, have a peculiar way of interacting with mind and body, and neither women nor men are ever ruled by them. Other women, like Ursula Owen, write of 'the odd prospect of happy fucks for the ageing body', or, like Sue O'Sullivan, overcome their fears of vaginal drying with the pleasures of a plastic bottle of lubricant.[50] In line with what we have already seen as the greater avail-ability of celebratory lesbian narratives – from whatever age group – O'Sullivan writes (in the third person) of undiminished, post-menopausal sexual pleasures: 'For her the change was not about accepting a loss of sexual engagement. . . . She felt differently passionate, differently engaged, differently but happily a woman, now that she was free of menstruation.'[51] Not all women, with their silver threads, lose interest in sex, or want to forswear romance, even though the sexism combined with ageism in our culture may lead to greater frustrations for these women – at least, if heterosexual. Whatever hormonal implications exist for declining sexual activity this is greater in men than in women, although one would hardly think so from the linguistic silence surrounding – what shall we call it? – the 'spermdrop', perhaps.

Bodies themselves *are* implicated in the inscriptions they receive, and women's distinctive reproductive cycle and genital anatomy give them particular possibilities and vulnerabilities. But the biological details of reproduction by themselves explain next to nothing about the meaning and significance of those inscriptions. What this means for the ever escalating medicalization of sexuality within sexology, as Leonore Tiefer pointed out in her presidential address to the International Academy of Sex Research in 1993, is that 'qualified sexologists have less and less to say about sexuality in real people's lives'.[52] What it suggests for the rethinking of heterosexuality is that our problems neither begin, nor end, with bodily performances between the sexes, whatever their nature.

Desiring subjects: identification and fantasy

Women consciously pursuing their first sexual encounters with men have mixed impressions of their results. Many begin believing that it is something which should, and therefore does, 'just happen' to them: a situation which leaves them vulnerable to the pressures of young men seeking to prove their 'manhood' through sex with women. For however we play around with images, and nobody does it better than the new queer theorists, active sexuality is still coded as phallic – as 'male'. The lustfully desirous fantasies of my own youth were – as they remain – most easily aroused and fed by the words and images of male homosexual authors. 'I became queer through my readerly identification with a male homosexual author,' lesbian theorist Sue-Ellen Case has written.[53] I don't doubt it. But I became 'straight' through my readerly identification with a male homosexual author or, at least, with the uncompromisingly unconventional passions of the homosexual/bisexual characters he depicted, who distained all forms of hypocrisy for a belief in 'the liberatory possibility of love': in the novels of the black American writer, James Baldwin – *Giovanni's Room* and *Another Country* – which had the added frisson of being banned at the time in my homeland, Australia.[54] The object of gay male desire is, after all, another man, and therefore a particularly suitable object of identification when a young woman's heterosexual fantasies turn to (if they ever strayed from) sex. It enables the comforting doubling of identification, both with the desiring subject and the desired object.

Situating myself in the place of the desiring male longing for the body of another male, homosexual imagery provided the perfect – seemingly the only possible – route into sexual pleasure, into having it both ways, as every straight woman, at least in masturbatory repose, must want and need. Maybe I went just a little further than some women in becoming pregnant by and marrying a previously (and subsequently) unwaveringly homosexual man – just before a more confident gay politics and milieu, and long before queer theory, became available to that huge swathe of Australian manhood desperately in need of it. But given the negatively charged, passively loaded cultural inscriptions of the female body, not to mention the subordinate place of women in cultural narrative and familial or wider social contexts, the attraction of the male homosexual as an identificatory figure for the heterosexual female (like the seemingly universal appeal of the sexually ambiguous, cross-dressed or androgynous cultural icon we looked at in the last chapter) can hardly have been so unusual.

Indeed, I have recently learned that my own sexual excitement consuming Baldwin, and placing his lugubrious photo on my bedroom wall, alongside Dirk Bogarde and other slender/tender males, was shared by many heterosexual women readers at this time. Ironically, in exact parallel to my own thoughts, it is in response to a lesbian feminist – the black American poet Cheryl Clark paying tribute to Baldwin for introducing her to an alternative sexuality – that Cora Kaplan tells us, 'I too was powerfully drawn to Baldwin's interracial, sexually polymorphous fiction.'[55] Kaplan reflects upon Baldwin's somehow hopeful, always erotic depiction of the 'exquisite pain and betrayals' of both heterosexual and homosexual relationships as they crossed class and racial borders. Compared with the sense of hopelessness she recalls, as a woman, reading his white male contemporaries (Norman Mailer, Henry Miller, Saul Bellow, Phillip Roth) – who could only write their celebratory narratives of masculinity through punitively staging women's 'subjection and abjection' – she concludes:

> at least part of what was compelling about Baldwin's work for women readers, whatever their sexual bias, was the lowered threshold he provided for fantasies that were not about the fixing of gender or sexual orientation but about their mobility and fluidity. Women could take up shifting and multiple fantasy positions within his fictional narratives: that possibility, itself wonderfully if terrifyingly liberating, allowed an identification not just with specific characters but with the scenarios of desire themselves.[56]

Like Kaplan, I think that there are a multitude of reasons why the complexities of eroticism and power depicted by Baldwin, who was homosexual and black, as well as male, could construct compelling male identificatory figures for female sexual fantasy. Essentially homoerotic novels, they provided male figures whose investment in the subordination and degradation of women (so poignantly portrayed by the suicidal black jazz musician Rufus in *Another Country*) revealed only weakness and dereliction, rather than the decidedly unerotic, penile-driven proofs of manhood sought by Mailer and his kind. Baldwin believed in the liberatory power of (male homosexual) love to transcend all binaries of gay and straight, male and female, white and black: 'Now Vivaldo, who was accustomed himself to labor, to be the giver of the gift, and enter into his satisfaction by means of the satisfaction of a woman, surrendered to the luxury, the flaming torpor of passivity, and whispered in Eric's ear a muffled, urgent plea.'[57] But even without the Baldwinian complexities, intertwining narratives of class and race with transgressive desire, women have resorted to homoerotic imagery for their own titillation.

Constance Penley illustrates this process at work in what she sees as one of the most radical and intriguing appropriations of mass-produced culture: *Star Trek* fanzines. These are magazines, circulating in the USA from the mid 1970s, in which female fans in their thousands create witty, raunchy stories, poems, erotic drawings, novels and now videos, writing their own erotic fantasies over *Star Trek* characters and narratives. Producing a new female genre of women's romantic, pornographic, utopian science fiction (the 'K/S zine'), these overwhelmingly heterosexual, working-class women writers and consumers enthuse over the explicit sexual and romantic bonds they construct between Captain Kirk and Mr Spock, those two male space travellers from the future. Here, women linger over Spock's soft and succulent cock ('hidden behind a furry mound that becomes tumescent and unfolds like petals from which his emerald green penis unfurls like a stamen') while enjoying, in the archetypal plot twist, Kirk's self-sacrificing realization that he *must* engage in sex with Spock to 'save his life'. Forced by bizarre circumstance, love and loyalty into enjoying sex with each other, the two men (both of whom are coded as heterosexual) acknowledge their mutual love, forming a passionate and heroic lifetime union: 'some forms of love defy, transcend all barriers, all differences or similarities.'[58]

Like many others, Penley draws upon the influential essay on fantasy by Laplanche and Pontalis to show how what she calls 'properly' psychoanalytic approaches can explain the widespread appeal of such fantasy scenarios for women, which encourage multiple and contradictory positionings of female desire, the fantasy providing 'not the object of desire but its setting': 'in the fantasy one can *be* Kirk or Spock (a possible phallic identification) and also still *have* as sexual object either or both of them since, as heterosexuals, they are not *un*available to women.'[59] Penley, in much the same way as Kaplan, displaces our traditional assumptions that women readers or viewers of romance, pornography or whatever, always align themselves with female figures and images – thus reinforcing their probable social and inter-personal positions as subordinate or marginal to men. These traditional assumptions were shared by recent feminist appropriations of 'object relations' psychoanalytic perspectives, like those of Nancy Chodorow or Carol Gilligan, for whom women's fantasy is seen in terms of stable female identifications. Yet even in my least bizarre, most consciously elaborated daydreams, it is never clear even to me whether I am identifying most strongly with the male or the female characters. It is always, at least partially, with both. Like some of Baldwin's heroes, and unlike all too many of the men we know in the present, *Star Trek* males from the future allow – as Penley puns, with apologies – for a 'retooling' of masculinity, one which facilitates the possibilities for both cross-gender identification and desire. Spock, although powerful, controlled and rational, is also the 'feminized' virgin and 'alien'; Kirk, although smaller, sensitive, nurturing, and intuitive, is also the 'masculinized' or 'phallic' leader and sexual initiator. There is a perhaps -similar play with desire and identification in the popular -phenomenon of girls' liking for the many young male singers who are reputed to be gay – like the Pet Shop Boys.

It is all too easy to see why in fantasy women may choose male figures for erotic identification, as well as for objects of desire. At least, this is so if we embrace some of the ideas we have looked at in previous chapters. We can agree with Foucault that in Western thinking from at least the nine-teenth century our public and conscious experience of 'sexuality' has been shaped by various male-centred discursive and institutional practices which give (or deny) meaning to bodily actions and interactions, always mapping them through the active/passive, male/female binaries. These affirm at one and the same time both the meaning of 'gender' and the normality of 'cross' or 'hetero'/sexuality, the pathology of 'same' or 'homo'/sexuality, subordinating women and homosexuals as desiring subjects. But to see why and how easily women may become 'men' in fantasy, we need to follow Freud in his mapping of the unconscious indi-vidual origins of 'sexuality' in the realm of psychical reality.

Here, personal sexual biographies are built up from the unconscious autoerotic fantasies of infancy, expressing a psychic desire for the repetition of the bodily pleasures we have known, directed at the object(s) which aroused or 'implanted' them. This takes us, in however distorted a form, all the way back to the buried pleasures and pains of childhood, to a time when neither we ourselves, nor the objects of our desire, were defined through sexual difference. In Freudian terms, it takes us back to the 'polymorphous perversities' of the pre-Oedipal relations between infant and mother, and to their subsequent gendered fate when overlaid by the child's awareness of the significance of sexual difference, understood in (culturally loaded) fantasies around the fear of, or resentment over, 'castration'. It is only during the complex Oedipal negotiations around sexed identifications that the 'masculine' emerges as powerful and active (phallic), the 'feminine' as subordinate and passive (receptive). The real difficulty, if we try to combine these two perspectives, is not the ease of cross-sex identifications in fantasy, but whether and how we might ever get beyond them. Is it possible, we need to ask, for women to draw upon images of themselves as sexual actors in ways which do not, as Freud suggested, change them into men?

The first point to acknowledge is that, however we look at it, the task of breaking the codes linking active sexuality to hierarchal and phallic polarities of gender won't be a simple matter. Women are continuously held back from affirming active sexual desire, as women, both by language and culture, and by the existing politics of gender. The first trap is to assume, as sexologists and the fashionably (*Cosmopolitan*-led) 'feminine' layer of mass culture does, that we can ignore both the symbolic dimensions of language and the existing power relations between women and men. In these frameworks, women are presented to us as already the active and equal sexual partners of men, and told how to obtain and please their man, as if he were likely to be seeking much the same advice.

Such rhetoric represses the extent of men's sexual violence towards women, and is wilfully blind to the chronic cultural and interpersonal misogyny so frighteningly apparent with the merest scratch on the liberal façade of sexual equality: who's afraid of any signs of women's independence? – of the single working woman? single mother? single sexual female? Most of all, what mainstream sexual liberalism knows, but chooses not to know, is that men's sexual engagement with women is coded first and foremost as an affirmation of healthy 'manhood', making heterosexual practice, so often, so little to do with men pleasing women. This is why men who have any difficulties with penile erection are still seen, by the American Urological Association, for example, to suffer from 'a disease entity'.[60] Once again, mutually satisfying sexual encounters between men and women have little to do with what is seen here as the problem, or the solution: nine times out of ten 'impotency' was 'treated' by these experts on male sexuality with penile implants, or parallel medical interventions to produce erectile results, not with suggestions for alternative erotic pleasures. This is also why, contrary to what we would expect if sexual engagement were seen by men themselves as being about the mutual sharing of pleasure, 'date rape' is neither a meaningless nor even a conceptually peculiar notion. It is rather the depressingly familiar experience most women have tried at some point to prevent – however recent its coinage, and legal contestations.[61]

Women engage in sex with men seeking excitement, pleasure, confirmation of desirability and, perhaps most often, to form or sustain relationships with them; some-times for money, or simply to please. But it is never the sex act itself which publicly confirms healthy 'womanhood'. Culturally, it is more likely to carry messages of vulner-ability or disparagement ('slut of the year'), unless the woman's status is secured by a man's positive contribution to it. No feminist can ignore the symbolism of 'the sex act', nor many men's psychic compulsion, combined with their physical and/or social power, to coerce women into it.

Whatever the dismal visions of sociobiologists, any strictly hormonal component of male sexual arousal can find its release through masturbation far more efficiently than through coercive sex with another – a physiological fact as true for men as for women.

Another reason it is so hard to break the codes linking sexuality to hierarchal polarities of gender is that, outside of sexological discourse, mass cultural production for women is built around the conventions and pleasures of the classic romance narrative. We know the script by heart, with or without the help of Mills and Boon or TV soap. We imbibed it, consciously and unconsciously, from our mother's fantasies and daydreams and our enjoyment of almost any of the narratives of popular fiction or film, where we see ourselves reflected, as women, in the waiting female heroine. Only at the very last moment, after the collapse of enormous obstacles, can we vicariously gain everything we have ever desired: the triumphant bliss of knowing ourselves the infinitely adored object of our always more-forceful, more-thrusting and powerfully assertive (if not reluctantly brutal) male hero – that creature now brought, at last, to his knees, as the book ends, the reel rewinds, by his own helpless love for us. These conventions of magical wish fulfilment, Tania Modelski remarks in her classic analysis of the genre, 'are part of our cultural heritage as women'.[62] Many studies of young women's sexual experiences suggest the disabling aspect of this heritage. Defining sex in terms of love and romance is one of the key reasons, according to recent British investigators, that young women will offer for allowing their male partners to dictate the nature of their sexual practices.[63] It also explains many women's disappointment with sex.

But however powerful these conventions of romance, their effects are received in different ways by different women.

They are filtered through particular personal identifications, within the deeply divided material and social trajectories of class, race, age, sexual orientation and other more specific subcultural belongings. I remember the despondency I would feel in early adulthood in situations where lack of choice forced me to consume the short romances in mass-circulation women's magazines – the limited horizons awaiting their heroines so crushingly visible – long before feminism came to stay with its brash and dismissive scorn for the dangerous myths of romance: 'It starts when you sink into his arms and ends with your arms in his sink.' Narratives of romance, with their forceful familial resonance, play an important role in shaping those identifications and practices through which we are produced as 'feminine', but in their imaginary games with (male) power, they also reveal some of the internal contradictions and ambiguities of these fragilely feminine identifications.

If, for all these reasons, the first point for sex and gender saboteurs is to acknowledge the real constraints of women's limited social power and submissive or compliant cultural legacies, the second point, in contrast, is to acknowledge that the codes linking sexuality to hierarchal polarities of gender, though always present, are never fixed and immutable. On the contrary, they are chronically unstable and actually very easy to subvert and parody – however repeatedly we see them recuperated. Freud observed the fragile ties of sexuality to any fundamental sexual differences of gender. He saw the pain and frustration – in women and men – of trying to hold them in place. But he could not see what to do with his insight except to warn the world: 'Psychology is still so much in the dark in questions of pleasure and unpleasure that the most cautious option is the one most to be recommended.'[64] But his own caution, and that of most of his followers far more so, foreclosed the options of his patients. He steered them towards accepting what he felt they could not change: a developmental narrative of progress towards normative sexual difference and heterosexual maturity, as seen from within the familial framework of patriarchal authority and female subordination, forever captured, he believed, in the child's eye view of the paternal aggression of marital coitus.

After all this time, it is still a rare psychoanalyst who, observing the culturally overdetermined force of that narrative, tries to place it alongside other narratives. Those few, like Adam Phillips, suggest that psychoanalysis is most valuable when most removed from its foolishly conventional knowingness, helping people to discover new things about themselves that they didn't realize they could value: 'there are, and have been, many stories in this culture and in other cultures through which people examine, and do other things to, their lives.' Alternative perceptions, he points out, are hardly more strange than the notion of the unconscious itself, which is 'by definition the saboteur of intelligibility and normative life-stories'.[65]

Along these lines, the French analyst Jean Laplanche points to the ideological basis of the Freudian narrative linking activity and passivity to sexual difference and coitus:

> I think that Freud misses completely the point of activity and passivity. . . . Is penetration more active than receiving the penis? Why? After all it is a very superficial point of view to think the male is active and the female passive in coitus. [Freud] says that every drive, in itself, is active; it is a part of activity which wants to change the world. I would say yes, every drive is active, but it is also the result of passivity, that is, our passivity towards the unconscious representations that push the drive into action. That is my point. As long as you don't have a clear idea of activity and

passivity you get into ideology and say, 'Well, it's too bad women are passive or women are co-active.' Freud was completely taken in by this ideology.[66]

Freud may have missed completely the point, but not a lot of people seem have found it. Certainly not those feminists currently 'theorizing' heterosexuality who inform us that, 'even though many women may enjoy the sensation of a full vagina[!]', we can never escape the passive, subordinating and humiliating meanings of penile penetration through which 'women are "had", "possessed", "taken", "fucked"'.[67] In contrast, Laplanche wants us to see that there is no solid barrier constructing the supposed binary, activity/passivity, without which there is little that is either firmly 'oppositional', or firmly 'hetero', about either sexual difference, or 'the sexual act'. I think, with Laplanche, that feminists have every reason to question and seek to dismantle, rather than remain in thrall to, the meanings which dominant discourse confers upon penile penetration. 'Intimacy', as Naomi Segal writes, 'is surely something to do with penetration without violence, cutting off neither the inside nor the outside.'[68] The very distinction between inside and outside breaks down as loving or desiring fingers, lips, nose or tongue wander over, in and between the flesh of another.

Seeking out possibilities for cultural and familial sabotage, we could add that there is no permanent reason why little girls, identifying with their mothers (and, of course, they may well identify with their father – however queasy it makes him) should not have glimpses of her as an autonomously sexual – as well as a maternal – being, without falling prey to the paralysing terrors inspired by ideas of the 'phallic mother' who must necessarily engulf and destroy her child – of whatever sex. As we have seen

Jessica Benjamin and others argue, it would require the possibility of the child gradually taking in the mother's independence and place in the world – beyond the family – and of identifying as movements of desire bodily activity other than the penile.[69] Women do, of course, have access to metaphors of active sexual desire, especially to eroticized imagery of eating, drinking, kissing, sucking, licking, touching, stroking, rocking, closing around and opening up. But these images are not coded as quintessentially 'sexual', because they are so much more ambiguous in terms of just who or what is active, and who or what is passive, who is giving and who is receiving. They are only likely to be sexualized within a lesbian framework, as in the words of Amy Lowell's poetry:

> I drink your lips,
> I eat the whiteness of your hands and feet.
> My mouth is open,
> As a new jar I am empty and open.[70]

What's sex got to do with it?: subverting the codes of gender

So let us try, however speculatively, to move beyond conventional narratives of sexuality and gender difference, using all the conceptual resources now available to us. These include feminist informed, lesbian- and gay-affirmative, queer-inflected, appropriations of sexological, Freudian and Foucauldian legacies. Sexology told us a story about organs and orgasms, suggesting that as a site of orgasmic pleasure the clitoris is in every way as physiologically endowed with nerve endings, and every day as ready – more ready – for sexual action, as the penis. We should not forget it. But we cannot learn from sexology anything about the source, or the force, of gender ideologies which implant and police a different story. On the contrary, we are simply assured that, with enlightenment, they should just fade away. They don't. There is more to women's emotional life than the most efficient route to orgasm.

The key absence here is the story of desire. All the statistical surveys and self-help books in the world will not themselves excite desire – whatever the real comforts and relaxation of masturbation. Some feminists have tried to produce stories for women to incite a romantic interest in our own bodies, without reference to an/other who desires or responds to us, arguing that 'our greatest love affair is with ourselves'. There is a related vogue for 'celibacy'. But we cannot simply love ourselves. We cannot even treat ourselves to the paradigmatic gesture of love: we cannot kiss ourselves.[71] It is never really 'me, myself, alone', but always thoughts of being desired by, dominated by, or variously handled by others, thoughts of desiring, subordinating or variously using others, that excite us; even during, and perhaps especially in, masturbation. Carol Ann Duffy and others, in their poetry, express more about desire than I can easily capture in prose:

> Under the dark warm waters of sleep
> your hands part me.
> I am dreaming you anyway
>
> You, you. Your breath flares into fervent words
> which explode in my head. Then you ask, push,
> for an answer.
>
> And this is how we sleep. You're in now, hard,
> demanding; so I dream more fiercely, dream
> till it hurts
>
> that this is for real, yes, I feel it.
> When you hear me, you hold on tight, frantic,
> as if we were drowning.[72]

Whether in our dreams (in conscious reverie or in sleep) or in sharing our lives with another (however briefly), it is always some other significant person or persons by whom we are excited, comforted or tormented. It is those special others, real or imaginary, who arouse us with their promise, denial or threat of physical intimacy, pleasure, relationships, or much of the time – at least as I experience it – who incite a fairly constant and chronic desire just to be held close, and to hold, to smell, to taste, to kiss, to stroke and to feel some particular other person deep inside our arms, mouth, cunt . . . . It is always another whom we try to reach when we experience desire, it is their physical contact we want – sometimes, any sort of contact will suffice, perhaps merely an attentive gaze – and by whom we yearn to feel ourselves desired. It is the very greatest of joys, as I experience it, especially when it occurs outside the realm of fantasy, simply to know that we are able to desire, maybe even able to love, some other human adult. (By sexual 'love' I mean that conviction – which may prove mistaken, or fleeting – that we want and need the most intimate, affectionate, physical contact with another person, forever; which is different from, although not therefore more important than, commitments of friendship to nurture and cherish another person, with no necessary connection with desire.)

'Erotic experience', as Muriel Dimen tries to summarize, 'is extraordinary':

> existing somewhere between fantasy and reality, dream and daily life. It knows no shame and no bounds. It effortlessly encompasses pleasure and pain, power and love, mind and culture, conscious and unconscious.[73]

Naomi Segal specifies five elements of pleasure in women's heterosexual desire, which all resonate with what I read, see and feel. Such desire can be characterized by its purposeless playfulness, its recovery of childhood feelings (or whatever consciousness can tolerate of their original polymorphous perversity), its connection with nurturance, its games with power (especially the pleasure of feeling power over the powerful), and its narcissistic sense of completion through access to the body of another: 'The man with whom the woman experiences this range of pleasures is for her sexy.'[74] Except for the games with power – 'power' being culturally symbolized as 'phallic' and 'masculine' – there seems little reason to see the pleasures and risks of desire outlined here as either distinctively 'feminine', or 'heterosexual'. Men, straight and gay, also have very strong psychic investments in the perceived power of their beloved. The female objects of male desire are certainly felt (and often feared) to have enormous 'power' over the desiring male.

Indeed, when John Forrester tells us what men want, he tells a similar story: 'what you desire amounts to finding out whom you have identified yourself with – the history of those you have loved.' There is a twist in the dynamic of power, however, which many have commented upon. Men in search of that elusive thing called 'masculinity' have a stronger, and therefore for many *less playful* need to feel powerful, to reverse the helpless dependency they experience whenever they get what they want: 'to fend off the threat of absorption and being devoured that the image of the mother almost immediately evokes.'[75] What is most frightening for women in contemporary battles to increase women's power and authority is that the proliferating effects of shifting gender relations, as we shall see again in the next chapter, can increase the threat that some men feel from the titillating 'phallic' female, provoking an ongoing and at times grotesque and murderous rage. The evidence of many men's violence towards women certainly tells us that a frightening number of men do use their heterosexual relations to ward off fears of powerlessness through controlling, selfish and violent behaviour towards women.

Yet the brutal extent of some men's sexual violence should not be allowed to block out the reality that, even on its worst estimates, the bulk of women's heterosexual experience does not reduce to violence.[76] Such exclusive emphasis on female victimization is just what has fed many younger women's rejection of feminism.[77] And despite the discursive 'feminization of love', neither sociological surveys, therapeutic observations, world literature, or personal experience, point to any marked gender difference in the capacity for experiencing the risks of desire or uncertainties of love – although women tend to express love or affection more through verbal exchange, men (when they surmount their fears of women) more through practical help and support. Both medical and sociological evidence suggests that men, in general, depend upon intimate relationships when they have them, and suffer when they don't, even more than women, and have fewer resources to cope with their breakdown when they have been long-lasting.[78] In their private lives, as distinct from their public performances, men usually feel similarly intense, irrational and vulnerable in the grip of sexual desire, as Wendy Hollway heard when she talked to men about heterosexual desire: 'Once you've opened yourself, once you've shown the other person that you *need* them, then you've made yourself *incredibly* vulnerable.'[79] 'In the rapture of love', as Kristeva writes, 'the limits of one's own identity vanish, at the same time as the precision of reference and meaning become blurred in love's discourse.'[80] The visible peculiarities of organs and orgasms fade into the background, although a lack of orgasms is frustrating and, if tied to male selfishness, may eventually drown desire.

The picture of desire I have been presenting is one shaped less by the present than by the invisible bodily experiences behind us, their secrets securely hidden even as we strip off every shred of clothing to lie naked beside our lover(s). Sadly, even our lover's knowledge and attentive concern for the anatomical functioning of our bodies cannot guarantee desire, or the continuation of pleasures we have shared, however much we may mutually regret it – as Cheryl Clarke mourns:

> Why can't I want you
> (Or, is it you who don't want me?)
> Are you gone again?
> Or is it me gone?
>
> Is there no rush of feeling
> nor vague chance
> we might meet each other again
> in that formidable place?[81]

Perhaps not. The difficulties, and ease, of sustaining desire are secrets we barely know ourselves, although we can perhaps learn the importance of holding on to nurturing and supportive relationships, and letting go of destructive and damaging ones – with or without desire. This is why we all experience risk in any sexual relations; although women face greater social risks from men's enactments of masculinity, and the privileges still accompanying it.

From the insights of psychoanalysis, we can speculate upon that suitcase full of memories that contains the clues to the past and the future of our sexual desire and, perhaps more importantly, to why it is often so hard simply to desire, and especially to desire exactly who or what we 'should'. To keep on desiring, depth psychology would suggest, we must be able to keep on playing around with those strange erotic bonds investing bodies with seductive power, playing around with, as Ruby Rich put it (writing of men's interest in pornography) 'the shadow world of oedipal and preoedipal desires'.[82] This is one reason there has been such an upsurge of interest in s/m scenarios in much of the feminist writing still daring to be sexy – usually lesbian in focus – which tries to reassure women that we need not feel guilty about the degree of infantilization and strangely perverse, politically incorrect, often sadomasochistic fantasies which turn us on. Good, I don't, anymore. As Amber Hollibaugh reflects, 'it is a bitter irony to me that I was in my mid-thirties before someone explained to me that I was not what I dreamed, that fantasies had a reality of their own and did not necessarily lead anywhere but back to themselves.' Worse, she recalls, she was never so vulnerable as when:

> trying desperately to organize my fantasies correctly . . .
> I sought to forget my desire and act on it at the same
> moment . . . it is always dangerous to refuse the
> knowledge of your own acts and wishes, to create a sexual
> amnesia . . . allowing others the power to name it, be its
> engine or its brake.[83]

However, the lesbian feminist s/m genre, which is best known through the writing and anthologies of Pat Califia in the USA, explores the boundaries between fantasy and real life, pleasure and pain, through rather oddly formalistic and literal notions of mutually agreed rituals for 'acting them out'.[84] Califia's collections have thus proved less titillating for those women (lesbian and straight) who, as I do, prefer the more blurred and ambiguous 'pornography of the emotions' (to borrow Ann Snitow's description of romance fiction),[85] which incites fantasies of sex and submission through the twists and turnabouts of erotic narratives of forbidden desire, hopeless anticipation, helplessness, risk and surrender. 'Nothing so crude as flagellation or bondage', as Elizabeth Wilson writes of lesbian s/m literature, could turn her on, rather 'the refined thrill of psychic pain, the "real thing" of rows, reconciliations, parting, absence'.[86]

In contrast, some of the recently multiplying books on erotica, like Lonnie Barbach's *Pleasures: Women Write Erotica*, or the Kensington Ladies' Erotica Society's *Ladies' Own Erotica*, have eschewed any hint of women as 'victim', to focus instead on foreplay and gentle sex.[87] Designed, as Barbach explains, to make women more 'self-confident' and 'self-satisfied', they have left many cold and dry.[88] But then as Sara Maitland found, asking fifty women to name the most erotic book they had ever read, no two women came up with the same one; although 'the compulsory loss of identity' in the arms of another, she added, seemed to provide the height of female erotic aspiration.[89] Many other texts, by women (and men), confirm this superficially contradictory quest for destruction and safety, for self-shattering experiences consummated in the arms of another who will nurture and protect: combining 'the ache of sensuality, with the ennoblement of love'.[90]

Jessica Benjamin was among the first of many feminists to theorize the psychological satisfactions of scenarios of erotic domination and submission. She analysed the desire present in most forms of sexual eroticism not as an attempt to affirm the self, but an attempt to transcend or escape it, and its gloomy tyranny: 'Erotic masochism or submission expresses the same need for transcendence of self . . . formerly satisfied and expressed by religion.'[91] What we find here, as in Kristeva's *Tales of Love*, is no more than an extension of thoughts originally expressed by Freud on what he saw as the mystery of sexuality, the fact that through sex we seek not simply to rid ourselves of a shattering tension, but to repeat and increase the occasions for experiencing it. Such observations have been elaborated by Leo Bersani in support of his conclusion that sexual excitement is itself primarily a 'tautology for masochism':

> We desire what nearly shatters us, and the shattering experience is, it would seem, *without any specific content* – which may be our only way of saying that the experience cannot be said, that it belongs to the nonlinguistic biology of human life. Psychoanalysis is the unprecedented attempt to psychologize that biology, to coerce it into discourse, to insist that language can be 'touched by', or 'pick up', certain vibrations of being which move us *back from* consciousness of being.[92]

Phallic fictions, female pleasures

What any attempt to track back these barely sayable, infantile origins of sexual excitement or desire intimates is that we should expect little contrast between their initial stirrings in women and in men – at least before, and always underneath, the subsequent (male) fears and (female) resentments which mask earlier erotic attachments, once the full force of sexual (phallic) difference enters psychic awareness. But to understand the Freudian narrative of psychosexual difference, we need to fit it into some type of Foucauldian narrative of historically specific norms through which the body is experienced, and relations of power are maintained. Bodies are given or denied meaning, regulated and regularly demeaned, within institutions and discourses which give value to what is seen as efficiently 'masculine', and actively 'heterosexual'

– attributes treated as more or less synonymous. Children take in these idealizing and diminishing norms, along with the realities of the power relations between, and aspirations and projections of, parents.

Psychoanalytic theory provides us with the fullest account we have of the psychic tensions and difficulties of assuming a sexed identity. But they have ignored and downplayed the cultural and political sources of 'phallic' symbolism, or fixed it in Lacanian absolutism. Either way, by failing to question (let alone seeking to subvert) the cultural production of phallic order and authority as the single means of conferring sexual positions, they are themselves, as Judith Butler argues, 'part of the forming of sexuality, and have become more and more part of that forming'.[93] If we are ever to see how we might dethrone the phallus from its role in conferring anxiety upon men (who can never match up to its transcendental authority), and resentment upon women (who are positioned as lacking, foreclosing female power and men's identification with women), we have first to recognize, but then challenge, the structural basis of phallic law and order.

So how do we struggle against phallic hegemony in defining sex and gender, to affirm more enabling constructions of the female body? Supposedly, it is through sexual activity that we consolidate gender and penile/phallic dominance. As Mailer puts it, celebrating gender polarity, while exposing its dependence upon the heterosexual grid: 'a man can become more male and a woman more female by coming together in the full rigors of the fuck.'[94] But do they? I think the opposite. As soon as we look into this over-worked, heterosexualized normativity, we see what it is working so hard to hide. Sexual relations are perhaps the most fraught and troubling of all social relations precisely because, especially when heterosexual, they so often *threaten* rather than confirm gender polarity. With multiple discourses making sexuality the site of the most diverse and contradictory investments, which cross over the borders between the public and the private, surface and depth, possession and loss, it can draw to itself quite frightening levels of anxiety and tension – past, present and future.

Through sex, trouble looms: 'Now you are strangely vulnerable/ No longer proudly covered', as one woman writes to a male lover from whom she is drifting apart, sorrowfully aware that 'I can no longer/ settle in my own space/ without the pang/ of your desire.'[95] This is one reason men fear homosexual bonding, for its potential threat to their homosocial solidarities – which makes it all the stranger that many feminists fear heterosexual coupling as a threat to women's feminist solidarity. Political alliances and other collective endeavours are as often threatened as consolidated through sexual activity. In particular, however, sex places 'manhood' in jeopardy, with its masculine ideal of autonomous selfhood threatened by the self-abnegation, the self-obliteration, that sexual desire engenders.

In sex, as distinct from in most other social contexts, men who desire women may face their greatest uncertainties, insecurities, dependence and deference towards them. These are tensions which can be poured into apparently increasing levels of misogyny in response to the successfully affirmative actions and images of women which feminism has helped to build. We see this in the escalating levels of reported violence against women.[96] And we see it in the continuing popularity of the Hollywood genre, desiring yet punishing assertively sexual female characters – from Hitchcock's *The Birds* to De Palma's *Dressed to Kill*. Most recently, we find the allure of the independent woman on screen drawing the attention of the psychopathic serial killer. Kathryn Bigelow's film *Blue Steel*, starring Jamie Lee

Curtis as rookie cop pursuing and pursued by a serial killer, while erotically entangled with him, provides both an example of the genre and, in part, an attempt to expose and explore it (as some have said of the earlier films I mentioned). As Cora Kaplan analyses, *Blue Steel* portrays a woman's playful pleasure and career investment in the assertion of 'masculine' power arousing a man's lethal desire for what he sees as the 'phallic' female, the woman with a gun.[97] But while anger is certainly one of the flames fanned by women's increasing assertiveness, it is not the only one. Another is suggested by David Widgery, representing a strand of anti-sexist men influenced by feminism, in response to Norman Mailer's copulatary affirmation of manhood: 'Perhaps we should assert the reverse, that women's liberation allows the possibility of man discovering his own femininity, anality, and the memories of sex before puberty, almost before birth.'[98] And so it could.

How is it, we may wonder, that creatures we first encounter capable of expressing diverse sensual interactions with all manner of people in all manner of ways, end up focussed exclusively on a member of the 'opposite' sex wanting gender specific styles of genital contact? They don't, as often as not. There is nothing natural or inevitable about either the occurrence or the preferred form of heterosexual bonding. In same-sex institutions (and in times and places where homosexual bonds escape censure) people get along, still sexually active, without it. My few short years in boarding school gave me and other young women space for ample erotic encounters, and most of us were in love with older 'girls' much of the time; it was many years before any similar intensity of physical contact developed with 'boys'. But the furthest some men are from feeling affirmed as 'masculine' and 'heterosexual', the more repellingly they feel they must announce it:

Those groans men use
passing a woman on the street
or on steps of the subway

to tell her she is female
and their flesh knows it,

are they a sort of tune,
an ugly enough song, sung
by a bird with a split tongue

but meant for music?[99]

Indeed, it is men's fear of, or distaste for, sex with women, as well known as it is well concealed, that the heterosexual imperative works so hard to hide. Everybody knows – from lovers, wives and prostitutes to sexologists, social researchers and clinicians – that 'passive' and 'masochistic' sexual fantasies and practices, although seen as definitively 'feminine', are at least as frequently the experiences and practices of men. By a ratio of four to one, Nancy Friday informs us, men's fantasies are masochistic.[100] A common feature of men's sexual engagement with prostitutes, Eileen McLeod is told, is their desire to be 'sexually passive': 'I think they must all have it in their minds somewhere they'd like a woman to take advantage of them.[101] Heterosexual sex, Wendy Hollway concludes from her interviews, 'is a primary site of women's power and men's resistance'.[102]

Providing us with a description of heterosexual experience which is at the very least partial, misleading and oppressive to women, normative notions of heterosexuality, filtered through the masculine/feminine, active/passive binaries, are used to encompass and explain homosexual experience. As we saw in the previous chapter, heterosexual imperatives have produced the lasting image of the 'effeminate' and 'passive' male homosexual, the 'masculine' and 'assertive' lesbian. So effective are these constructions that historical research throws up many accounts of men and women (but mainly men), who enjoyed same-sex love and sexual contact but who never saw themselves as homosexual. As John Marshall reports from his own interviews with elderly male homosexuals: 'One man, for example, mentioned the reluctance of any of his partners to act in any way which would be interpreted as "girlish" or "effeminate", since this would render them "queer".'[103] We saw a recent example of the popular investment in such self-deception, with massive audience enthusiasm for Neil Jordan's *The Crying Game*, where the safe 'woman' turns out to be a transvestite man, in contrast with the male-destroying, actual woman.[104]

The idea of the 'active' male homosexual as superior to a 'passive', 'feminized' partner has been widely documented in other times and places. The more pronounced the gender hierarchy in any society, along with the corresponding assumptions of gender polarity, the greater the tendency to distinguish and despise the supposedly 'passive' or 'effeminate' male homosexual partner. Thus in Turkey, Huseyin Tapanic reports, the 'active' inserter in oral or anal sex often sees himself and is seen as 'heterosexual' and 'masculine', indeed as 'hyperheterosexual and hypermasculine', with only the 'passive' insertee typically viewed as 'homosexual' and 'feminine'. Tomás Almager similarly reports far greater stigma attaching to the supposedly passive partner in Mexican and Latin American male homosexual contexts.[105] This strict division of sexual roles, although 'homosexual', thus strengthens ruling heterosexual codes linking gender and sexuality. Being as artificial and forced in homosexual as in straight sex, however, it not surprising to learn, as Alan Sinfield reports from a survey in Mexico, that although most men engaging in homosexual sex present themselves as 'activos', 74 per cent admit privately that they are both insertive and receptive ('active' and 'passive').[106] Sinfield goes on to express his well grounded irritation: 'For lesbians and gay men, the situation is indeed perverse: a model of how heterosexual men and women are supposed to be, which is tendentious, inadequate and oppressive in the first place, is twisted into bizarre contortions in order to purport to describe us.' The problem he fears, ironically, is that the exaggerated macho-shift in Western gay culture is simply reacting against depictions of the 'effeminate' homosexual, but still in collusion with oppressive and heterosexually derived assumptions of 'masculinity': 'But are "real" men the people with whom we want to associate ourselves?'[107] No thanks.

The various debates over the potential subversiveness or recuperability of lesbian and gay 'queering' of heterosexual gender codes were discussed in the previous chapter. Lesbian and gay fantasy and practice has played a crucial role, precisely because of its contentiousness, in feminist debates around the nature of desire and the politics of pleasure. But straight women can offer something in return by helping to overturn those oppressive oppositions tying gender identity to sexuality via heterosexuality; at least, they can once they are no longer guilt-tripped into thinking of 'heterosexuality' as, 'at best, an embarrassing adjunct' to feminism, if not 'a contradiction in terms'. All feminists could, and strategically should, participate in attempting to subvert the meanings of 'heterosexuality', rather than simply trying to abolish or silence its practice. The more familiar and dismissive strategy is not only punitive and unwelcoming – towards women who enjoy straight sex – but misguided, in that it endorses rather than challenges the gendered meanings maintained through normative and oppressive heterosexual discourses and practices. The challenge all feminists face, on top of the need to keep chipping away at men's continuing social power (which gets condensed into 'phallic' symbolism), is to acknowledge that there are *many 'heterosexualities'*.

Sexual experiences and positions are more fluid and tenuous than representation can ever hope to capture, making sexual norms, as Butler suggests, primarily comic – were they not also oppressive. The affirmation of any one sexual position always calls forth the ghosts of that which it supposedly excludes: for me, the ghosts of those boarding school years, and other memories of endless daydreams spent in the arms of some older woman, who would love and tend me because of my heroic sacrifices to gain her love. The more rigid the sexual position a person feels the need to affirm, the greater the extent and the threat of the haunting.[108] Once we look for sexual diversity and fluidity, the fluctuating nature of heterosexual encounters or relation-ships is obvious: some are pleasurable, self-affirming, supportive, reciprocal or empowering; others are compulsive, oppressive, pathological or disabling; most move between the two.

There are, of course, exactly the same potentialities in lesbian and gay sexual relationships with, however, at least two crucial differences. First of all, self-affirming or 'suspected' homosexuals face the daily dangers of life in a homophobic culture so extreme that our tabloids are allowed to orchestrate hate campaigns against them – especially, in these post-AIDS years, against gay men as 'death-driven, death-desiring and death-dealing'. Secondly, while battery and abuse may occur in same-sex relationships, it lacks the institutionalized, social and ideological under-pinning sustaining the exploitation of women by men. But undermining normative and compulsory heterosexuality also means undermining its constructions of its other – 'the homosexual'. These are alliances that can and must be made, as we seek to confound the expectations of straight sex, and slip through the binaries linking sexuality and gender. It is time for more of us to come out: '*How Dare You Assume What It Means to be Straight.*'

There are different heterosexual experiences and different heterosexualities. We need to explore them, both to affirm those which are based on safety, trust and affection (however brief or long-lasting), and which therefore empower women, and also to wonder (because it won't ever be easy) how to strengthen women to handle those which are not. Women can try to maximize their chances of good heterosexual relations through a combination of wariness, new opportunities, playfulness, self-assertion, mutual support and, perhaps above all, luck. Surveys and biographical reports show that women still face more problems around sex than men, especially (though far from exclusively) when they are sexually inexperienced. Liberal discourses and practices by themselves do not dissolve the traditional gendered meanings attaching to sexual experience which encourage coerciveness in men and compliance in women.[109] The ideological struggle must continue. And while both sexes have their fears and anxieties over appearance, desirability and levels of confidence, it is still overwhelmingly women who have experienced or have reason to fear sexual violence and abuse, as well as worries over birth control.[110]

Certain groups of women, such as the young Asian and African Caribbean women interviewed recently in Britain, have been reported as subject to particularly powerful conflicts around sexuality stemming from the strength of the persisting sexual double standards of their ethnic group.[111] Far worse, black and ethnic minority women face the full sexualized perniciousness of white racism, which has always used 'black' or 'coloured' men and women as targets for projecting its own most demeaned private fears and longings.[112] Liberal discourses of sexuality also fail to address or dissolve the traditional racist meanings attaching to sexuality. 'If you're a *black* woman . . . you know how to do *dirty things*!', Baldwin sneers at white men's hypocrisy, and hattie gossett fights back with even richer contempt for white racist sexism:

> you have heard those stories about colored pussy
> so stop pretending you havent
> you have heard how black and latina pussies are
> hot and uncontrollable
> and i know you know the one about the asian
> pussies and how they go from
> side to side instead of up and down
>
> we must have some secret powers!
> this must be why so many people have spent so
> much time vilifying abusing and hating colored
> pussy
> and you know that usually the ones who do all
> this vilifying
> abusing hating and fearing colored pussy are the
> main ones who just cant leave colored pussy
> alone dont you[113]

Yet, accompanying these ongoing battles against the power of sexist and racist imagery and practice to undermine and disable women, we should also pay heed to the fact that when young women today say what they want from sex, it is not so different from what young men say. Both stress the importance of sex with affection, and also emphasize their needs for 'love', 'caring' and 'commitment'.[114] Some women, however, are likely to have more resources than others for pursuing and satisfying those needs and desires. If, as Bourdieu says, 'The main mechanism of domination operates through the unconscious manipulation of the body', we are going to have to keep constructing new sources of women-centred bodily and erotic education, bodily and erotic confidence, through which women feel better able to assert *or* surrender control in situations more likely to prove pleasurable.[115]

In her study of young women's first sexual encounters with men in the USA, Sharon Thompson emphasized their diversity. One group, sadly the larger one, described their sexual initiation in line with traditional heterosexual orthodoxy, displaying little sense of sexual agency. These women, she reports, did not recall masturbating before having sex with men, and sexual intercourse was something that 'just happened' to them without petting, foreplay, desire or contraception. They felt they had little sexual choice, and saw the penis as '"a big thing" that had to go into a "little hole"'. But a second, smaller group of teenage girls presented narratives of considerable sexual pleasure (though rarely involving orgasm, except in sexual encounters with other girls), which linked description of their own sexual desire with romantic encounters with men – holding out for kisses, foreplay, oral sex and passion. Unlike the previous group, these girls had their first heterosexual encounters with some knowledge of sexual pleasure and desire, gained from masturbation, childhood sex play, heavy petting and their mothers' accounts of sex. They had frequently obtained contraception before their first intercourse, and after, if not satisfied: 'They looked for lovers with slower hands, more exploratory tongues, wiser cocks.'[116]

Thompson concludes that for young women to be able to embark on sexual encounters feeling in possession of their sexuality, they need an erotic education – not just talk about and practice in exploring their bodies, but access to more complex narratives of desire: narratives of pleasure and fulfilment that do not reduce to the platitude 'just hold out for "love"'. For this is the old message which sabotages the sense of sexual confidence upon which the pleasure narratives depend, connecting girls' desire for love with the ignorance and guilt which leaves the defining of sex up to boys and men. However, in seeking appropriate narratives of sexual pleasure and fulfilment, it may be hard to specify just what we are looking for. Compared with other pleasurable activities, sexual excitement and its consummation, or the lack of it, is often much too elusive to communicate. When we do find words to describe why certain people – or their actions – serve to please, frustrate, or fail to arouse us, they may make only partial or flimsy connections with what we are feeling, or were hoping to feel. That perhaps, like dreams, remains just beyond words – captured sometimes in the almost genderless words of desire in poetry, as here, in Michelene Wandor's 'Love Poem':

> we are touching
> each other
>
> your skin is warm, follow
> the line of your body, hair and curves,
> shapes mark what sex you are
> but no more than that for the moment
>
> for a time
> (though no one can stop me from
> hoping it will have no end defined
> as such)
>   we locate a contact for which
> there is little imagery   we are
> self-taught in a place where there are
> no witnesses

such reference points as we have lie
outside our shapes, never so oblivious
of 'sex' as when within its active limits
influenced by solidarities we bring with us
to meet each other, we meet
with words, touch, silences, movements
trying to echo as little as possible
those razored blarings which have
destroyed other relationships

sometimes we manage

   we are both explorer and explored, not
concerned to plunder and steal; rather to leave
each encounter with something gained by each
and nothing lost by either –
the meaning, perhaps, of autonomy?[117]

When we try to think or write of sexual desire (in contrast
with the always overemphasized and fixed gender iconography – the 'nuts and bolts' – of dominant talk or images of
'sex'), it is usually through narratives of conflict and
contradiction around giving and receiving, safety and risk,
possession and loss; rarely simply around bodies ('full
vaginas'), whatever their physical entanglements. There are
new narratives of straight sex appearing and many more for
us to collect and elaborate. Here is Wendy Hollway writing
of the empowerment she feels through sex with her partner:

It is surprisingly hard to accept someone's love, no holds
barred, and my increasing openness to that, as I learn to
trust and to risk, is expressed through significations which
are particular to this heterosexual relationship. I want to be
open to him. He wants to be wanted by me, and therefore
welcomed inside me . . . I get pleasure from feeling his

penis inside my vagina because it means feeling him (with all that means about loving, accepting and respecting this particular person) inside me. My sexual desire is fuelled by the joy of being able to be that open and, closely linked, not to have to take responsibility for myself, not to have to maintain that control which in the rest of my life I cannot relinquish. Such feelings cut across my individual boundaries and mitigate my isolation.[118]

Every time women enjoy sex with men, confident in the knowledge that this, just *this*, is what *we* want, and how *we* want it, I would suggest, we are already confounding the cultural and political meanings given to heterosexuality in dominant sexual discourses. There 'sex' is something 'done' by active men to passive women, not something *women do*. It is, after all, only with very particular people that we usually choose to have sex, because of our desire for them. Failing to distinguish when women want to give and receive physical contact with men from being forced into sex (which is indeed 'oppressive, humiliating and destructive'), can foster only guilt and the denial of women's sexual agency. It replaces sexual freedom with the most pernicious form of moral authoritarianism.

Once again, and ironically perhaps, it is fitting that I should give the last word on 'heterosexuality' to that inspirational lesbian feminist, Joan Nestle. Showing just how far we have still to go in finding a new sexual politics for feminism that can include rather than ignore hetero-sexuality, her poignant recollection, 'My Mother Likes to Fuck', roused other lesbians, including Sheila Jeffreys, to picket the office of the London magazine which published it. In it she had dared to protest: 'Don't scream penis at me, but help to change the world so no woman feels shame or fear because she likes to fuck.'[119]

7. Sex in society: social problems, sexual panics

At no other point in one's analytic work does one suffer more from an oppressive feeling that all one's repeated efforts have been in vain . . . than when one is seeking to convince a man that a passive attitude to men does not signify castration and that it is indispensable in many relationships of life.

Sigmund Freud[1]

To resist the integration of personality around the subordination of women or the dichotomy of masculinity/femininity is to court disintegration, gender vertigo. . . . At the same time, it can emerge anywhere in the structure. It is impossible to purge from the gender order.

R.W. Connell[2]

Freud disclosed the displacement of sexuality into culture. . . . But displacement also goes the other way . . . social crisis and conflict are endlessly displaced into sexuality.

Jonathan Dollimore[3]

Sex, however we define it, is not and never has been simply a private affair. Once the province of God and the Church, with non-matrimonial sex threatened by Divine retribution (aided by clerical damnation), it came under the secular, classificatory gaze of sexologists, doctors and psychiatrists over a century ago. But the same reproductive, heterosexual patterns were maintained by the medicalized pathologization of practices which did not culminate in genital contact between a man and a woman. The supposed activity of the man and corresponding passivity of the woman continued to construct oppositional gender attributes and sexual styles. Over the last twenty-five years, however, the authority of this scientific biomedical orthodoxy has been fiercely challenged as intrinsically normative and political. In their inability to thematize existing cultural meanings and coercive practices attaching to sexuality, biomedical discourses have been accused of helping to frame and maintain them.

Everything that I have written in previous chapters on the shifting theoretical understandings of sexuality pushes us in the same direction. Both the diverse inputs from psychoanalysis and the social construction theories of the 1970s, opposed to earlier biological frameworks, point towards one conclusion. It is a conclusion rendered all the more compelling once we consider the human dramas enacted around changing sexual regulations, and the dynamic confrontations staged in the West since the 1960s over all aspects of sexual behaviour. This conclusion asserts the tentative and provisional nature of both gender and sexuality, and of the links currently made between them. Any new agenda for women aiming to increase their social power and sexual autonomy needs to begin from here. The highly contested notions of 'gender' and 'sexuality' are at present conceptually interdependent. They are held together by the cultural imperatives and practices of a heterosexism definitively linking the 'masculine' to sexual activity and dominance, the 'feminine' to sexual passivity and subordination. They are, nevertheless, always poten-tially and frequently actually unstable and separable in any particular case. But here we hit a monstrous problem: the inescapable predicament of modern life is that this is precisely what is so threatening to most of us.

Gender and sexuality provide two of the most basic narratives through which our identities are forged and developed. If there are no certainties here, there are no certainties anywhere. In the West, at least, we live in subjective worlds where the dynamics of gender, tied in with heterosexual imperatives (or our resistance to them), provide the foundations for our sense of self. They constitute whatever certainties we are ever likely to know. If we are to assess the prospects for greater sexual agency and fulfilment for heterosexual women, we will need to consider changes in the broader context and forces out of which our gender and sexual identities are made and remade, always precariously, through conflict, envy and struggle.

Gender uncertainties and sexual crisis

It should come as no surprise that any threat to gender certainties trails in its wake evidence of personal and social panic. While some of us may get our kicks from its transgressive energy, most of us feel decidedly queasy when faced with explicit gender ambiguity (outside the safety of acceptable theatrical performance), inducing in the supposedly dominant sex, in particular, what Bob Connell has called 'gender vertigo' and others 'male hysteria'.[4] More suprisingly, perhaps, given men's continuing control over the levers of power – despite the persistence of feminist agendas – the evidence of panic around the dislocation of gender identities and relations continues to heighten and spread.

The 1990s in Britain, for example, kicked off with the media fanning debate over Neil Lyndon's shallow thoughts on the damage feminism had done to men; swiftly followed by his own book on the topic, and similar arguments from ex-*Punch* editor David Thomas.[5] Also in the early nineties, Robert Bly laid siege to the best-seller lists in the USA for two years with *Iron John*, offering images and suggesting action to 'heal' men's 'damaged' masculinity; while Warren Farrell battled to defend the rights of the 'disposable sex' – men.[6] Lyndon's brief moment of fame came with his declaration that 'something ruinous and evil had happened between men and women in the last 25 years', making men now the disadvantaged sex, held in contempt by those influenced by the 'poisonous orthodoxy' of feminism.[7] Bly similarly argued that 'men are suffering right now – young men especially';[8] as though, once made aware that they belong to a particular sex, rather than represent humanity, men have quickly grasped that it is the wrong one. Bly's 'mythopoetic' men's therapy movement seeks to liberate the Wild Man (the fierce, instinctive, irrational, intuitive, emotional, sexual, hairy essence of man) from its centuries of imprisonment inside each living male, to re-unite the sons with the fathers.

The visibility and at least surface absorption of over two decades of feminist ideas about gender equality has thus created, it would seem, growing gender panic in Western men. Indeed, some cultural commentators suggest that the fortunes of feminism have proved 'one of the most powerful forces reshaping American culture in the seventies and eighties', promising, via its influence on Hollywood, to reshape culture world-wide.[9] Despite so few women moving into positions of political power (well under 10 per cent in both the USA and Britain)[10] and despite only limited economic gains for women overall, evidence of male hysteria abounds. In Hollywood, in particular, men and masculinity often appear under siege, threatened by the shifting gender terrain: 'No longer the old male cock as the privileged sign of patriarchal power . . . but the post-modern penis which becomes an emblematic sign of sickness, disease and waste. Penis burnout, then, for the end of the world.'[11]

In the 1980s we saw some spectacular box-office hits with themes of endangered masculinity. They were ushered in, however, by a remarkable spate of women-in-jeopardy or violence-towards-women films, such as *Don't Answer the Phone*, *He Knows You're Alone*, *The Shining* and (provoking the strongest feminist outrage and substantial picketing of cinemas when it was released in 1980), Brian De Palma's *Dressed to Kill*, in which a mother portrayed as unusually sexually active is murdered by her psychiatrist. Just a few feminists discerned an underlying theme of male anxiety in these films, especially De Palma's, and before long we were seeing the image of men-in-peril addressed more directly. It began with a sudden rush of *film noir* remakes of '40s films, where greedy, seductive women cause men's destruction, as in *Body Heat* (a remake of *Double Indemnity*) and *The Postman Always Rings Twice* (both released in 1981). They were followed by new *films noirs*, like *Black Widow*.

By 1987, described by Susan Faludi as a 'scarlet-letter year' for Hollywood's backlash against women's independence, a new witch/vamp, the single working woman, was stalking Hollywood – more sexually active than ever, and thereby deadlier, for the male objects of her lust.[12] From *Fatal Attraction*, where persistent pressure was put on its script writer, James Deardon, to keep altering his text to demonize the female protagonist and remove blame from the adulterous male, to *Basic Instinct*, where the *femme fatale* actively seduces and then murders her male victims with an ice-pick, the male protagonists are men in danger. (Michael Douglas was the lead actor in both cases.)

Masculinity was threatened on all fronts in some of

the top-grossing films of the 1980s. It was threatened
from within in Scorsese's *Raging Bull* (1980), with Robert
De Niro portraying former boxing champion Jake
LaMotta as trapped by his own inarticulate, aggressive
physicality, even as it destroys him. And it was threatened
from without by new challenges to traditional assumptions
of the authority of white manhood from the demands for
equality of all those it once excluded and subordinated:
women, 'blacks', 'orientals', chicanos, and foreigners
and 'pensioners' of all sorts. The theme of masculinity
under threat finds its apotheosis in Joel Schumacher's
Falling Down (1993), distinctive in the precision of its
placing of the 'Average White Male', middle-aged and
middle-class, as the supposedly unacknowledged, confused
new 'victim', at the end of his tether. 'This is not a bad
guy, but he's had it,' the director explains, indulging his
hero's march of unmotivated murder and mayhem. As an
ex-worker, in the defence industry, and ex-husband, its star
(Michael Douglas, yet again) is driven to the edge by
his wife (who has kicked him out of the family home),
by chicano gangs, by the homeless, by Asian shopkeepers,
and by all those others who have claimed to be the white
man's victims, and are, in fact, the standard Hollywood
scapegoats. Douglas was applauded by men in his
audiences in the USA with each new act of murderous
violence against his 'tormentors'.[13]

There were softer films, of course, where similar
themes were handled with self-mocking humour, as in
Woody Allen's romps, or Steven Soderbergh's popular, *Sex,
Lies and Videotape* (whose hero claims to be impotent in
the presence of a woman). And Hollywood studios were
certainly still celebrating a dominating, phallic and
threatening, masculinity, if only when removed from the
dangers of Woman: safe in the swamps of Vietnam, or a

cockpit in the clear blue skies. Blockbusters from *Rambo* to *Top Gun* (via *Die Hard*) appealed directly to American male chauvinism and war-mongering, while spelling out the ascendent New Right agenda of the Reagan years: a patriotic, patriarchal, free-market fundamentalism, to wipe out the 'humiliation' of the first US military defeat in history, in Vietnam in 1975.

Even the more adventurous independent films of this period were steadily replacing sex (at least, any explicit heterosexual pleasure) by violence. Audiences saw male bodies victimized; bodies that bleed and bleed, like some wound at the centre of masculinity. In these films, men's violence (though accompanied by ubiquitous hate speech against women, 'blacks' and 'queers') is directed primarily towards other men for little love, pleasure or profit. Violence is, seemingly, the only pleasure these films choose to identify with the threatened white male, especially those faced with unemployment, or shrinking social prestige and status. As Amy Taubin writes of what she calls the white 'underclass' portrayed in *Reservoir Dogs*: 'It's what allows them to believe that they're the oppressor and not the oppressed (not female, not black, not homosexual).'[14]

The violence offers the most aggressive resistance possible to anything that smacks of the 'feminine' position, the subordinate position. Except there's a catch. Highlighting the inevitable threat at the centre of any hierarchical binary (which must forever exclude and dominate all that it fails to articulate), many have noticed the sadomasochistic dynamic between these films and their audiences. Is there more than masochistic pleasure for men to gain from Rambo's muscled display of his grunting, passive, patriotic flesh – repeatedly wounded, in pain, humiliated, and tortured with his own knife – or the mutilated, bleeding cop in *Reservoir Dogs*, as his tormentor asks: 'Was that as good for you as it was for me?' Cataloguing a general cinematic shift from the explicit sexuality prominent in films of the sixties and seventies to new levels of dizzy violence, Ruby Rich comments on their ambiguous pleasures: 'Too angry and uptight for the old sexual fix. How much better to sign on to violence and see the rage explode on screen – but comfortingly restrained within the familiarity of genre.'[15] Such films offer covertly much the same emotional triggers as the overt sadomasochistic (homo)eroticism of a film like *Sebastiane* by Derek Jarman, whose death is such a loss. (No wonder the Right is so keen to ban the latter, which threatens to blow the cover of male passivity and narcissistic eroticism!) Traditionally made as 'men's movies', though also enjoyed by many women, we have also begun to see the appearance of mainstream women-with-gun movies, such as *Thelma and Louise*, *Blue Steel*, *Guncrazy* and *Dirty Weekend*. Although predictably accompanied by social controversy and condemnation, the women's violence is never simply random and is thus quite unlike that of the men.

Backlash USA: managing economic dislocation

Off the screen, with the USA again leading the way, the increasing strength of the 'gun lobby' testifies to the more material threat contained in many men's desire for guns.[16] With guns as Western culture's quintessential, if clichéd, phallic symbol, men's growing need for them suggests a threatened and precarious masculinity.[17] With or without their use of guns, the Reagan years in the White House saw a massive increase in men's resort to violence: against both women and themselves. There was a 100 per cent increase in women seeking shelter from men's violence, rising levels of reported rape, a huge majority of women announcing in surveys that they were now more afraid of attack on the streets than ever before, and a 160 per cent increase in sex-related murders – a third of them men killing women who made their bid for independence, immediately upon leaving their husbands and filing for divorce.[18] But what is it, we may wonder, which is inducing such a sense of 'crisis' and hysteria in these angry and aggressive men?

Is it, for example, something born and bred in the USA, although more widely disseminated? Sadly, it is not. British men have found advocates to rail against feminism, forming pressure groups like Families Need Fathers and Dads After Divorce, to campaign for men's rights and against 'man bashing'.[19] And in Britain, men's levels of personal failure and aggression have kept rising after a decade of Thatcherite policies adopting the ruthless economic priorities of monetarism associated with US capitalism, and a dramatic deterioration in the lives of the poorest sectors of society. The 70 per cent increase in male suicides during the 1980s, paralleling unemployment, has occurred alongside corresponding leaps in reported levels of men's violence against women, drug addiction, crime, incarceration and educational failure. Girls at school have moved 10 per cent ahead of boys in overall educational attainment over the decade of the 1980s, although their educational success is not reflected in their subsequent employment status.[20] Nevertheless, it is in the USA that the pattern, causes and outcomes of apparently gender-related troubles and tensions can be seen most clearly. In a media-saturated society with its motor in Washington, a new sex-war agenda has been framed.

Certainly, it is in the USA, above all, that tens of thousands of middle-class white heterosexual men seek out the 'male-healing' of Robert Bly, or Sam Keen, Robert Moore, Douglas Gillette, and their ilk, almost all promoting some populist version of Jungian archetypal imagery to restore the 'deep masculine' and create a new gender balance in society.[21] It is there that 7 February has been declared International Men's Day by the men's rights groups, celebrated in Kansas City in 1994 as a day for campaigning against the legal recognition of 'marital rape', the supposedly many 'false' rape and harassment charges brought against men, and for fathers' rights. Their agenda suggests the origins of these middle-class men's fears in women's growing readiness to abandon marriages with men who make them miserable, once they have some means of economic independence. They may be miserable because of men's violence, rejection, selfishness, dislike of domestic sharing or perhaps, as women most often complained to Shere Hite, simply because of men's emotional illiteracy or 'reluctance to talk about personal thoughts and feelings'.[22] These men, who still have access to many of the cushions reserved for the dominant sex, both at home and work, feel threatened by womens' more confidently proclaimed and publicly endorsed complaints and grievances.

It is also in the USA, in proportionately far greater numbers than in other Western nations, that hundreds of thousands of working-class, black and Latino men die young or are victims of violence and murder, use drugs, face jail, or commit suicide (far exceeding the women of their own backgrounds).[23] Of course, these men are threatened by women's continuously increasing – though relatively underpaid – economic independence through changes in the labour market, and the closely connected increase in their sexual autonomy and confidence, assisted by feminist gains around birth control, abortion, and the lessening social stigma against divorce, and motherhood outside marriage. But their fears must be seen, primarily, in terms of the far deeper social insecurities of joblessness and personal disintegration caused by economic recession and restructuring over the last decade.[24] Such personal powerlessness clashes violently with prevailing conceptions of the power and prerogatives of manhood. Far more than feminism ever could, these are the social forces which threaten the conventional attributes of manhood, of the work-oriented, skilled, ambitious husband and father.

It is fears of personal failure, under conditions of social crisis, which propogandists of the Right have attempted to displace into fears of men's loss and women's gain, naming 'feminism' the enemy of men, and just for good measure, of women too. They have had considerable success. If most women in the USA remain as removed as ever from the centres of economic, political and social power, so too do most men. As unemployment rose, wages shrunk and mortgages soared in the 1980s, it was men who felt most threatened by their loss of power. What better way to mobilize, displace and hide men's own fears than by drumming up a storm against women?[25] Economic crisis is thereby displaced, rearticulated, and 'managed' as gender crisis, often together with the inflaming of race and ethnic hatred via codings of criminal-ization and fecklessness (especially through stigmatizing the black single mother, accused of 'scrounging' off the state and raising delinquent children). In Susan Faludi's exhaustive mapping of the many-sided fight waged by business corporations, political, legal, evangelical and, above all, media establishments throughout the 1980s in defence of existing elites, we can see the force of their targeting of the supposed feminist threat to men's families and jobs.

Setting out, in characteristic conservative style, to undermine the credibility of protest itself, powerful media voices began to turn women's struggle for equality and independence against itself: in organizing against structures of exploitation and oppression, feminists had succeeded only in changing the world into a worse place – for women. The shifting sands of 'sex' provide the ideal medium for conveying conservative messages. Seen as the seat of personhood, and calling up fragmented memories of childhood humiliations and threatening pleasures, talk about 'sex' can absorb any amount of fear and anxiety. Those ideologues around the world who, like Jerry Falwell, found punitive moral meaning in the tragic spread of the AIDS epidemic in the 1980s, using it to promote their Moral Right agenda, were merely adding new levels of callous malevolence to a very familiar old routine – support for the patriarchal, nuclear family.[26] As Maurice Godelier said, 'It is not sexuality which haunts society, but society which haunts the body's sexuality.'[27]

Faludi's meticulously documented research offers us a brilliant exposition of just how this is done. She explores the media's relentless promotion of misleading research and misguided researchers eager for media fame, often from the most respectable Ivy League colleges. Surveying the cultural panorama in the USA throughout the 1980s, she finds conservatism targeting women, saturating them with sexual messages that they are in dire trouble: suffering from 'man-shortage', 'infertility' and 'more miserable than ever'. Feminism was to blame, making women lonely and sad, forcing upon them notions of independence and career success, while depriving them of their only true source of happiness: marriage, motherhood and men's respect and protection. Although the proportion of unwed American women in the mid-1980s was smaller than it had ever been (especially for college educated women), and the majority of those women who were single said that they wanted to remain so, the dubious research promoting the man-shortage myth frightened many women.[28]

Backlash stories also broadcast women's bleak post-divorce situation. In fact, although women are economically disadvantaged following divorce, it is men who most fear, suffer from and try to forestall marital disruption. Twice as many men as women want to tighten US divorce laws, citing the need to 'protect women'![29] The same upending of reality surrounded reports of women's growing infertility. Female infertility has actually declined over the last two decades, although – carefully hidden behind such talk – men's sperm count has strangely been dropping over the last thirty years. Yet the causes, whether environmental toxins, occupational hazards or whatever, are little known because men are excluded from the US government's national fertility surveys.[30]

With Faludi systematically inverting the conservative routines of recent times, showing how they serve to soothe and conceal the fears and problems of men, it comes as no surprise to read her careful and definitive dismissal of women's growing levels of breakdown and depression in the face of widespread promotion of the personal misery of single and career women. In fact, these are precisely the women found to have the highest levels of psychic and sexual satisfaction and confidence: the most frequent correlations of depression in women remain, as they have always been, low social status and marriage.[31] Surveys over the last two decades have been quietly reporting a remarkable decrease in women's susceptibility to mental illness, despite the marked increase in depression, anxiety and suicide among men in their 20s and 30s. Topsy-turvey once again, the reality we find is just what conservative myth attempts both to hide and to subvert: women's increased independence, in so far as they have achieved it, has not brought increased anxiety or misery to women; but it has– or the threat of it has – brought increased anxiety and misery to men.[32]

Faced with such backlash, how did feminists in the USA respond? The few who remained popular with the media were those who shifted their message to fit its motives. Betty Friedan kicked off, accusing her sisters of becoming too career-oriented. By 1989, the meritricious Erica Jong – ever alert to media fashion – was proclaiming in *Ms* magazine that feminists of her generation now 'look longingly at the marriages of our parents and grand-parents'. She published *Any Woman Blues*, she boasts, 'to demonstrate what a deadend the so-called sexual revolution had become, and how desperate so-called free women were in the last few years of our decadent epoch.'[33] Britain was soon importing some of these North American voices, spearheaded by male media mongrels like Andrew Neil, former editor of the *Sunday Times*, to place them alongside our home-grown woman-bashers like David Thomas and Neil Lyndon. We are now regularly subjected to the unstoppable fifties-throwback prattle of Camille Paglia, or the naive musings of a young Katie Roiphe, brought over and promoted for attacking older feminists who whinge and 'cry rape', thereby serving only to frighten themselves and confuse men. Meanwhile the doom-laden theatricality of Andrea Dworkin and Catharine MacKinnon renews and strengthens the one-dimensional drift of backlash alarmism. While Paglia ridicules, they manipulate women's fears of male violence to make their own dangerous alliances with the anti-feminist Right, promising to 'rescue' women from pornography and the rapaciousness they think intrinsic to all men's heterosexual practice. Often quite unintentionally, strands of academic feminism have assisted the conservative retreat from the now unfashionable, 'boring seventies' agenda of the women's movement. They distance themselves from its passionate attack on traditional family life and job discrimination in the name of gender equality, to stress instead women's distinctive sexual, moral, maternal, intellectual and emotional development in the name of exploring the repressed 'feminine' of sexual difference.[34]

One reason for this conservative turn, influencing feminist thinking itself (despite intense internal conflicts), is its fit with the predicament of second-wave feminism, three decades on.[35] While many men genuinely fear the 'success' of feminism as a threat to their marriages and jobs, many women feel there has been little or no success at all. Feminist criticism has indeed put pressure on men to pay more attention to women's sexual interests, and many of our aspirations for gender equality seem to be accepted: even the most mysogynist, conservative voices now declare themselves against violence towards women and often insist, like Neil Lyndon, that they are 'not against women's equality'. Yet there are many women who face much the same conditions of low pay and overwork as they always did. Others are saddled with increasing burdens of poverty and drudgery due to deteriorating wages and welfare for the less well-off. Employed men, on average, still fail to share housework and childcare, giving men in Britain 15 hours more free time each week than women working full-time, for less money.[36]

Conservative rhetoric resonated with some women's sense of defeat after the fragmentation of feminism. Their hopes for real improvements evaporated with the decay in state resources for those most needy people who depend on the care offered by women in the home. There is much more to be said here. But suffice it to say that anti-feminist rhetoric, coded in terms of women's sexual vulnerability and their need for the 'protection' of men, can demoralize hopes for change in women's lot because feminist strategies, alone, have no hope of withstanding broader attacks on the living standards of the most vulnerable sectors of people world-wide. (Women form the bulk of the growing sector of marginalized, unprotected labour pools, and of single parents and elderly people relying on welfare.)

Blaming the victim can appeal to the powerful and the powerless alike. This is just what is happening when the media turns the abused into abusers, ignores the tens of thousands of cases of women raped, battered and abandoned (except when wanting to scare women), and turns the world's attention onto the occasional odd instance where men claim to have been harassed or raped, subject to discrimination, or left alone with the kids. Let's hear it now from Michael Crichton, wired in to the manufactured media topic of the moment (just back from banking the mega-millions he earned exciting the kids with his cunning, fast-breeding female dinosaurs in *Jurassic Park*), fanning sex-war vitriol with his latest *Disclosure*, the 'true tale' of one man's sexual harassment, by a female of the *human* species – his boss. There will be few benefits for women if signs of our sexual autonomy only increase men's insecurities and paranoia, and hence hostility or violence towards us. What can a strong woman do, either individually or collectively?

Beyond the phallus: male passivity

To want more than gender fixity, it appears, is to invite backlash against women, male aggression, and even murder.

We should already know this. Weren't women's killers, like Norman Bates in Hitchcock's *Psycho* (1960), always mother-fixated men, confused about their gender and their sexuality? The serial killer today, as we learn from the 'effeminate' Buffalo Bill in *Silence of the Lambs*, is still a man driven to murder women because of his deep desire to become a woman: to make himself 'a girl suit out of girls'.[37] In the collective fantasy of our culture, gender confusion is deadly, for women.

But gender confusion is also inevitable. Gender fixity is always under threat, its fragility provides no reason for retreat from feminist goals. On the contrary, the single clear finding relating to the causes and continuation of violence against women is that women are most likely to become – and remain – victims of men's violence when they are most powerless. True, such abuse can occur across all social groups, but those women most at risk are those who are poor, unemployed or holding the least prestigious jobs.[38] Historically and globally, as studies of the fate of Chinese brides coming to America or dowry deaths in rural India attest, those women who are most consistently brutalized are precisely those who can offer not a whisper of challenge to the patriarchs supposed to protect them.[39] It is not feminism which is the motor of male insecurities, but the fact that being a male entails no psychological essence of 'masculinity', merely a penis and scrotum – in most cases. What Blind Willy (with his head in the sand and a gun in his hand) is trying to forget, is that there are gentle, caring, celibate, submissive, unassertive, dependent and passive men, just as there are lusty, authoritative, aggressive, insensitive, dominating, independent and assertive women. We all criss-cross these supposedly gendered lines, displaying greater variation within our own sex than between sexes – without becoming psychopaths or serial killers – depending upon individual circumstance and social context.[40] 'Masculinity' is a relative term, maintained only through its difference from and dominance over its subordinate terms, 'femininity' and 'effeminacy'. Hence men's often unconscious fearful and dependent relationship with that which most attracts and terrifies them: women, gays, and other black and ethnic minority males coded as 'beastly' and 'inferior'.

Not all men are equally threatened by fears of 'unmanliness'. Recognizing the fluidity and variability of sexual and gender attributes within oneself and others can have other outcomes: positive identifications, conscious desire, intimacies, solidarities and support with and for subordinated 'others'. And here, at last, is some good news – good for some of us, anyway. Those men and women least threatened by changes in gender relations are the people who survive and flourish. They are the ones who always knew that macho-man, whether a proselytizing Hemingway or a performing *Rambo* (even before blowing his brains out, or public ridicule from his ex-wives) is patently hiding his inner fragility, the 'woman' inside, the 'faggot'.

In recent decades 'he' was always under suspicion, anyway, as either a marginal ethnic (hence his Latino label, with its racist overtones) or a laid-off blue-collar worker, fit only for physical service on his now doomed picket line, not female servicing in the bedroom. A new man – open, gentle, sensitive, unaggressive – when not merely a fictive creation for feminist derision or ad-man exploitation, exists and is reaping the benefits of whatever transformations he has so far managed to make. He can emerge and transform himself most easily within job contexts where women are already present in equal numbers and with expectations pushing them closer towards equal status and conditions with men: generally, in a middle-class, public-sector or servicing milieu. Thus researchers have observed that men who actually desire equality with their female partners, and most want to share things with them, are the ones who seem the most contented. (Their lives, it is true, may already be less stressful, suggesting a mutually reinforcing circularity.) The most distressed and angry men are those who are hostile to women's employment and refuse to change themselves to become more involved in housework and childcare, despite living with 'working wives'.[41]

National surveys on health, happiness and sexual patterns in the USA have been highlighting for some time now that, as they like to put it: 'What most men really need is to develop their "feminine" side and become more focussed on relationships, more emotionally expressive and more comfortable with being dependent.'[42] And some men, they suggest, already have. In their massive survey in the early 1980s, Philip Blumstein and Pepper Schwartz found that heterosexual couples reported being sexually satisfied when both women and men tended to initiate or refuse sex equally as often.[43] Heterosexual couples were also, interestingly, happier with their marriages in the more gender-contesting 1970s, than they had been in the earlier more gender-conforming 1950s, even though they recognized more conflicts in their relationships.[44]

There are men who are able to accept, encourage, share in and benefit from women's growing autonomy. How does it, or should it, affect their heterosexual practices? David Lodge has fictionalized his version of such a man pursuing a consciously egalitarian heterosexual ritual:

Robyn . . . was lying naked, face down on the bed. . . . Charles, who was also naked, knelt astride her legs and poured aromatic oil . . . working [it] in to Robyn's neck

and shoulders with his long, supple, sensitive fingers. . . .
[T]his was their customary way of rounding off Saturday
evening. . . . It began as a real massage, and turned
almost imperceptibly into an erotic one. Robyn and
Charles were into non-penetrative sex these days, not
because of AIDS . . . but for reasons both ideological and
practical. Feminist theory approved, and it solved the
problem of contraception . . . [talking continues, until]
Robyn fell silent. The massage had reached its erotic
stage. Without being prompted she rolled over on to her
back. Charles' practised index finger gently probed and
stroked her most sensitive parts. Quite soon she reached a
very satisfactory climax. Then it was Charles' turn . . .
Robyn's massage technique was more energetic than
Charles' . . . she began to pummel him vigorously . . .
'Ow! Ooch!' he exclaimed pleasurably, as the rather
plump cheeks of his buttocks vibrated under this assault
. . . [there is more whimpering and pimple-squeezing, till
Robyn orders] 'Turn over Charles.'[45]

Other men, too, have followed what they see as feminist
directives, dismissing penetrative sex as inadmissable
between equals, and some go further than 'Charles' in
combatting what they see as their own sexism. Collecting
life histories from men grappling with changes in gender
relations in very different circumstances, the Australian
sociologist Bob Connell and his fellow researchers
interviewed a group of men involved in the radical
environmental movement. These were men who lived and
worked with feminists in contexts which genuinely (rather
than formally) promote practices of gender solidarity
and equality, and who tried to eliminate sexism from their
lives and their relationships.[46] Such men were not only
seeking to change themselves, but adopting strategies of
'renunciation' – giving up career opportunities, holding

back in group situations, and feeling guilty about taking any sexual initiatives. It could have painful consequences.

Some of the men had difficulty establishing any sexual relationships at all: 'Both Nigel Roberts and Barry Ryan were uncomfortable in sexual relationships until they met up with heterosexual feminist women who took the initiative and effectively controlled the relationship.'[47] What sometimes happens next, in my own observation of such relationships, is that the feisty feminist turns on her male partner, calls him a 'dependent leech' and becomes a revolutionary feminist, complaining that her 'passive' ex-partner was deviously trying to 'co-opt' her to patriarchy! What happened next in Connell's case histories was that the men 'who adopt[ed] a principled passivity in relation to women' often found themselves in a tense double-bind, 'pressed on one principle to express emotions and on another to suppress them'.[48] More worryingly, partly because such attempts at passive nonassertiveness are so in tune with men's early 'archaic' infant bonding, they carry the risk of self-annihilation:

> I was really amazed that she liked me, and I guess I was like a bit of a lap dog for a while, and all her achievements were my achievements, and her successes were all mine. I had none myself. I felt that I would shrivel up and blow away once the relationship ended.[49]

And he did.

I can see no reason at all why heterosexual men might not gain their fullest pleasure from sexual contact with women which is primarily passive. Such men may well need to construct a sense of self-worth which does not reduce to their supposed 'masculinity', or dominance over women. But some men will have resources from which to fashion it. Their sense of self may come from all manner of collective belongings, as well as from others' recognition of their professional status, creativity, skills, political activity, emotional support, sensitive responsiveness or, despite the contempt of other men, simply from being an object of desire for men or women. Men who have fewer resources for constructing any sense of worth may try to assert it through the sexual 'conquest' of women, drawing upon conventional definitions of 'masculinity' – always a most precarious route in these times, and hence all the more dangerous for women. What I want to know is why a man's indulging, enjoying, or guiltily adopting sexual passivity should be seen as necessarily pro-women? (Giving a massage, as Lodge's text illustrates, although often delightful for its recipient, has nothing to do with passivity.) Do women desire actual or principled passivity in men? Such a 'principled' sexuality is certainly most peculiar *unless* the request for it is coming from a particular woman, rather than a particular strand of feminism. But this would make it not so much principled as simply responsive to that particular woman's (perhaps sadistic) desires. Many men, we know, like nothing better than a good spanking, although it bores the pants off 'Ms Whiplash'. And as Shere Hite found to her chagrin, only 13 per cent of women claimed that they did not like 'vaginal penetration/intercourse'. Over half said that they preferred it, and many that they 'loved' it.[50]

Some anti-sexist men have tied themselves up in some odd knots in constructing new sexual agendas. Jeff Hearn, who has had the courage to write about his own struggles around heterosexuality, describes his 'movement away from intercourse, as well as real uncertainties and confusions about what to do sexually': 'Current issues include the continuation of a long-term heterosexual

relationship, the virtual rejection of heterosexual intercourse, and the acknowledgement of the importance for
me of celibacy, narcissism, masturbation, gayness and my
positive relationship with gay men.'[51] Why this particular
combination? I know from his writing that Hearn has only
the very best of intentions towards women, and yet the
noisy silence here concerns the wishes of his female
partner. Unless we decide to assume, without being told,
that she too dislikes sexual intercourse, Hearn's sexual
agenda would seem either a principled punitiveness or a
massive self-indulgence. If he thinks it goes without saying
that men want to fuck and women do not, he is buying
into the crux of heterosexual myth-making. Yet if not,
it is hard to see how the embargo on intercourse and the
exploration of celibacy helps empower heterosexual women
to change a reality in which, as he claims, 'the dominant
modes of heterosexuality are so oppressive'.[52]

The dominant modes of heterosexuality are indeed
oppressive to women and sexual minorities. This is due
to many men's sexual coerciveness towards women who
have no sexual interest in them; a practice until recently
culturally encouraged, with its often violent consequences
condoned. It is also due to men's continuing fearfulness
of accepting women's sexual initiatives and desires, whatever form they may take. Fuelling both of these problems
is men's frequent fear of admitting the ambivalences and
contradictions of their own wayward, or perhaps dormant,
sexual longing: in particular, their fear of their own
passivity. This commonly takes the form of projected
hostility, and at times even murderous violence, towards
both women and any men seen as engaging in 'deviant'
or alternative sexual practices. But there is no agenda for
progressive sexual *practice* here, other than a principled
acceptance of diverse, consensual sexual activities. What

do women want? Men cannot assume, yet again, to tell us; with a new twist to their old renunciatory fearfulness and confusions around sex.

What men want, as often as not, is to be sexually passive. What men do not want, by and large, is for women (and certainly other men) to know this. What women need, is for men to accept undefensively their tenderness, weakness, passivity. It is the worst of ways of 'helping' women to pretend that men can only be sadistic aggressors – except when in consciously chosen renunciatory mode. A dangerously self-deluding text which exposes ambivalent motives, while concealing ambivalent desires, is Adam Jukes's *Why Men Hate Women*. That Jukes hates women, I have no doubt.[53] But I question his threatening generalizations, carrying with them repeated intimidatory and disabling warnings to those feminists, like myself, who contest them. Women must, he insists, speaking on behalf of the male sex, accept that the need to be in control 'is an "innate" characteristic of our masculinity'.[54] For Jukes, 'masculinity' is neither reducible to culture, nor to institutional arrangements, but rather has its source in the boy's universal experience of separation from the unified mother-infant dyad. He sees that women may feel insulted by this assertion, admitting: 'It places them in an extremely passive position.'[55]

What Jukes cannot see or admit is that men may want to be 'in an extremely passive position' themselves, that men may be kind, compassionate and 'soft', their bodies open to pleasurable entry or assault through their own penetrable orifices, making them rapeable in much the same way as women are. But perhaps Jukes, haunted by his own ignorance, cannot consciously register male entrances. To bolster his disavowal and banish forever the increasingly visible nuances of male desire, he blasts us with gender cliché, rather like a demented male Paglia: men are 'dominated by the urge to conquer and penetrate women'; 'heterosexual desires [are] to penetrate the female and impregnate her'; 'the erect penis is a rock of stability to which most men turn in times of stress'; 'women become what men want them to become and want what men want them to want'; 'the bottom line is that male abusiveness and violence, our power and control, are not negotiable currency'; 'I believe that women will achieve equality only when men grant it to them', and even if changes were to be made which benefit women, 'it is questionable how many women would take advantage of the opportunities they would provide'; 'I do not believe that men are good for women, or good to them'; 'independent women may be able to retain their independence only by refusing partner-ships with men'.[56] So Jukes swaggers – somewhat unsteadily – on, with only the very best of conscious intentions 'to identify and publicize the plight of women'. He does admit, *en route*, that 'the idea of a society differently ordered is beyond my imagination'.[57] Too right.

Others, delving more productively into the recesses of male desire, probing its tensions and resistances to the primordial truths of 'masculinity', are raising a few new questions. Carol Clover, for example, offers an engrossing account of the gender stories being told and re-told in the horror/slasher movie genre of the 1970s and 80s, which remain so popular with male audiences. These films, she suggests, blow the cover of traditional gender assump-tions, revealing male audiences choosing to identify with the multiple fears and final triumph of the anatomically female character: 'one whose point of view the spectator is unambiguously invited, by the usual set of literary-structural and cinematic conventions, to share.'[58] Although feminists have been enraged by the violence towards women occurring in this genre, the films are fascinating, Clover suggests, because, unnoticed by most of their critics, in their obsessive address to men's deeper desires and anxieties they overwhelmingly offer a space *only* for masochistic, 'feminine'-coded identifications.

Clover leads us through the plot, camera angles and special effects of films like *Texas Chain Saw Massacre*, *Halloween*, and *Slumber Party Massacre* (a film scripted by the feminist Rita Mae Brown), to illustrate her argument that since the 1970s, in ways unheard of before, it is always and only the female character, the 'Final Girl', who outsmarts her tormentors and – increasingly after 1980 – fights back against her attackers. (These cinematic formulas pioneered in the more marginalized horror genre would pass over into mainstream films like *Alien* during the eighties.) Emerging as their own saviours, women become heroes: 'abject terror may still be gendered feminine but . . . triumphant self-rescue, is no longer strictly gendered masculine.'[59] In fact, masculine and feminine are collapsed into one and the same in these films, with the Final Girl, played powerfully by actresses like Jamie Lee Curtis and Sigourney Weaver, carefully coded as 'androgynous' to facilitate male identification. So while it is still mostly women who are variously penetrated, beaten, impregnated and raped, with the emergence of the suffering victim as female hero, Clover concludes: 'However you cut it, the male spectator . . . is masochistically implicated.'[60]

In terms of the attraction they hold for men, it is noteworthy that not only is the one character sufficiently on screen to allow possible identification female, but images of traditional masculinity emerge as frightening, repulsive or ineffectual, being constantly punished in these films: 'the man who insists on taking charge . . . or (above all) who tries to play the hero, is dead meat.'[61] (If Adam

Jukes were to wander into a modern horror film, he would be speedily dispatched to oblivion.) If 'bad' or traditional masculinity is punished in slasher films, a remapping of masculinity can be seen in similar 'low culture' genres, Clover suggests, such as the occult film, where the male protagonists, as in *Poltergeist II* or Cronenberg's *Videodrome*, are made to adopt a softer, more open masculinity. David Cronenberg is quite explicit about what he is up to:

> My instinct tells me that . . . human beings could swap sexual organs, or do without sexual organs as sexual organs per se, for procreation. We're free to develop different kinds of organs that would give pleasure. . . . I'm not talking about transsexual operations. . . . Sheer force of will would allow you to change your physical self. I think that there would be a diminishing of sexual polarity, and there would be a reintegration of human beings in a very different way.[62]

But perhaps the most striking evidence of shifts in gender-related identifications in the recent cinema-making and reception which Clover explores is the emergence of the straightforward 'rape-revenge' horror movie. *I Spit on Your Grave* (1977) was only the first to make a controversial impact, and it is still grossing well in video rentals. Before moving into the mainstream with *The Accused* (1988), these films had already eliminated male heroes, and hammered or knifed home their own message that all rape was not only evil and humiliating (and capable of provoking equal levels of anger and violence from its female victim/heroines), but that society and the law were complicit in allowing men to go unpunished, if not in cheering them on. Apart from its feminist-influenced polemic, Clover suggests that here too the (predominantly) male audience is again 'crossing-over' to identify with the raped and vengeful female protagonist:

> What I am proprosing is that the position of the rape
> victim *in general* knows no sex . . . *all* viewers, male and
> female alike, will take [the victim's] part, and via whatever
> set of psychosexual translations, 'feel' her violation.
> Without that identification, the revenge part of the drama
> can make no sense.[63]

With remorseless repetitiveness the gender messages of the slasher, occult and revenge sub-genres of horror films suggest a sense of resistance to aggressive/phallic masculinity, as they call upon the 'feminine' and 'masochistic' fantasies and identifications of their male as well as their female audience. Clover thus gives us every reason to rethink the truisms of gender, showing why the suggestion that men, as a sex, are motivated solely by sadistic aggression is simply a new way of affirming what it pretends to deplore.

This takes us back to ideas we have encountered before in this book, such as many men's phobic rejection of homosexuality, yet obsessive engagement with it. Homosexual men are, in the words of Ellis Hanson, comprehensively feared (and envied?) as: 'sexually exotic, alien, unnatural, oral, anal, compulsive, violent, protean . . . mobile, infectious, suicidal, and a threat to wife, children, home and phallus.'[64] These lurid fears have been reinforced, but not generated, by the appearance of the virus responsible for AIDS. As Leo Bersani argues, 'straight' men are both terrified of, yet passionately attracted to, powerlessness and loss of control. In Bersani's view, phallocentrism is not so much about denying power to women, although it certainly has that corollary, as 'the denial of the *value* of powerlessness in both men and women'.[65]

It is the refusal to recognize that beyond fantasies of power and subordination, fixing and fixed by heterosexualized gender polarities, lies the potential for transcending or obliterating those polarities – in both men and women. Responding to Bly's attempt to heal men's troubled sense of masculinity through further male bonding, Marina Warner comments:

> It seems to me that Bly has framed his cure the wrong way around: the monsters of machismo are created in societies where men and women are already too far separated by sexual fear and loathing, segregated by contempt for the prescribed domestic realm of the female, and above all by exaggerated insistence on aggression as the defining characteristic of heroism and power.[66]

She is not alone in seeing this. It is the wisdom of a strand of feminism, influencing both men and women, which knows that men's damaging and dangerous anxieties over 'manhood' will disappear only with the disappearance of gender hierarchy in society.

There are men who are able to delight consciously in being the objectified target of a woman's or a man's desire, and to move between and across the supposed active/ passive binaries. There are men who can see the penis as a penis, 'drooping shy and unseen', as Walt Whitman wrote in 1855 in his *Leaves of Grass* celebrating the sensual beauty of men's flesh, and causing the anxiously phallocentric D.H. Lawrence to bemoan: 'everything was female in him: even himself.'[67] Men can and do live with a sense of selfhood which is far removed from dominant definitions of the 'masculine' (especially in terms of aggressive sexual agency), and they remain capable of grasping some of the instabilities and complexities of their own identity, without courting disintegration. The idea is not necessarily utopian. It depends on how a man's personal history and, above all, his cultural context, create (or soothe) new tensions with other men and women. Whereas some men, and especially boys, will face merciless policing by their peers for any signs of 'softness', others, usually older men, may occupy spaces where mutuality, equality, openness and intimacy between women and men are genuine goals.[68] But wherever men find themselves at an interpersonal and experiential level, rather than at the performatively rhetorical level, sexual feelings only exist in and through others, 'while the outward face of sexist sex talk is bravado, the inward face is another story'.[69] In actual bodily contact, contrary to the dominant iconographies of sex, the polarities of gender falter and blur.

In sex, bodies meet; and the epiphany of that meeting, the great threat and joy, is precisely that the dichotomies of activity/passivity, subject/object, heterosexual/homosexual which have up until now sustained the charade of their source in the gender ordering of masculinity/feminity are always in danger of collapsing. They all collapse together. For beneath the veil of the phallus is merely a vulnerable penis, which men may or may not gain pleasure from pushing into others; even as they remain vulnerable to the embraces, enclosures and penetrations of others. In sex, beyond phallocentric metaphor, one body actively seeks its passive objectification in and through the desire of another. The heterosexual embrace we seek, simply for its own sake, whatever its form, and whatever our sex, can be as 'queer', or as threatening to the gender order, as its perverse alternatives. Writing of its subversive role within homosexuality, Luce Irigaray suggested, 'once the penis itself becomes merely a means of pleasure, pleasure among men, *the phallus loses its power*.'[70] I agree. However, for the penis in heterosexual encounter to be understood and used as merely a means of pleasure between men and women, that is, for it *finally* to detach itself from the phallus, men must already have lost their power as a sex. But before that final moment, women and men can experience a multitude of moments that could, and should, be used as part of the struggle towards it. The final triumph of the multiple pleasures of the penis over the dry and rigid authority of the phallus requires the success of feminist goals *on all fronts*, with the assertion of women's sexual autonomy but one factor among many. Empowering women sexually, however, has proved somewhat easier than empowering women socially.

Cultural contradictions: female bodies and the power of women

'Madonna let me down', bell hooks, the inspiring black feminist writer announced recently from New York, belatedly joining the chorus of detractors, if not the enraged muck-rakers, who like to accuse this international cultural icon of using her privileged white female body for spectacular self-promotion and profit.[71] 'We long for the return of the feminist Madonna', hooks mourns, describing what was once, for her, a strong, sexy, rebellious image of 'female creativity and power', inspiring millions of particularly young heterosexual women. hooks was criticizing what she, like many others, saw as the loss of 'radical edge' in Madonna's book *Sex*, where the pop star places herself in a variety of classic pornographic scenarios.

Loved or hated, Madonna remains central to contemporary battles around female sexuality, deliberately provoking them. In every video and performance, she flaunts her sexuality, coolly asserting her control, while situating men – and occasionally women – as servants of her volatile needs, desires and pleasures. But does Madonna's aura of rebellious independence, power and chameleon fluidity, help empower her female fans to resist traditional discourses of femininity, as her scholarly admirers suggest?[72] Or does Madonna, as some of her critics conclude (those who do not merely castigate her as a man-eating monster or perverted whore) merely reinforce dominant capitalist mythology of the individual route to success and power, from which many women, young and old, will be forever excluded?[73] Does Madonna, as many of her fans see it, use black, ethnic minority, gay and lesbian actors in her videos in such a way as to help fight the stigma, exclusion and disadvantage usually attaching to these socially subordinated groups?[74] Or does she, as hooks now suggests, only exploit the traditional sexualization of subordinated groups, while asserting the centrality of her white, imperialist mantle? Before we can be clear about the answer to these questions, we need to consider again the significance and limitations of popular cultural shifts, and individualized subversive strategies for empowering women and other subordinate groups.

While some men have been reacting to shifts in traditional gender patterns with cautious approval, and others with violence, women have by and large pursued a steadier course. Most have been influenced, however indirectly, by the combination of feminism and expanding prospects for financial independence through changes in the job market. Since the 1960s, younger women have been increasingly addressed in mainstream culture as individuals with their own needs for personal pleasure and fulfilment and not just as potential homemakers caring for others. From its very first issue in 1965 *Cosmopolitan* kicked off with the assumption that women were having more sex, and enjoying it. By 1980, as Linda Grant wittily explores, *Cosmo* girl would emerge from all the questionnaires she dutifully completed as a confident, assertive woman, seeking to satisfy her own pleasures through men: 28 per cent of readers now claimed to have had between 2 and 5 (male) lovers, and 25 per cent between 11 and 25.[75] Soon fashion magazines and advice literature of all sorts were offering women sex tips, and urging them to hold out for excitement, pleasure, orgasms and personal fulfilment, not just to wait for marriage. And, it seems, they did.

Researching popular culture in Britain, Angela McRobbie argues that even the magazines for school-age girls showed a remarkable shift by the 1980s. The old romance narratives of girl's comics and magazines found in texts like *Jackie* in the 1970s (situating girls in single-minded, competitive, pursuit of the one and only boyfriend, to last them all their life), were being replaced by brand new modes of 'femininity'. Magazines like *Just Seventeen*, launched in 1980, had commissioned market research which suggested that girls had changed and were no longer so dependent on boys for their sense of identity and well-being.[76] They were now aspiring to an image of femininity which was confident, sexy, ambitious and fun: '*It is brimming with expectation. Its optimism is about opportunity, not romantic dependence.*'[77] This new focus on 'self', replacing the former dependency on boys and romance, McRobbie suggests, is more explicit about sex and safety, while emphasizing the importance of girls simply 'having fun' with friends of both sexes. These magazines also devote space to future job and career prospects for their young readers, alongside their main focus on pop-culture, fashion, beauty, friendships and relationships.

Of course, this new, more respectful and intelligent

address to young women is part of the process of creating new consumers: of music, fashion, beauty products and other commodities. Ever younger girls aspire to the slim, 'perfect bodies' of advertising (with more of them suffering from tendencies to anorexia and bulimia), noticing every style-shift of their latest pop icon. But McRobbie writes optimistically of girls in their own specific subcultures actively negotiating their interaction with popular culture. She sees them strengthened by the overall feminist-inflected message of much of the media targeting adolescent girls (sometimes coming from older feminists), which typically endorses ideas of gender-equality and female autonomy, while adopting a playful, almost mocking rather than subservient attitude to boys, alongside useful information on contraception and safer sex. Other British commentators on girls' popular culture, like Janice Winship and Charlotte Brunson, agree.[78]

Winship analyses what she describes as new erotic codes of female pleasure in many of the girls' magazines which emerged in the eighties. The 'street-wise' fashion displays of *Etcetera*, *Mizz* or *Undercoat*, while inevitably drawing upon traditional codes of femininity, also partially subverted them – with wit, humour and a confident knowingness:

> It is young women who flash their bodies, and with their gaze and pose coolly confident, they express less the customary passive sexuality of women than an assertive strength. Their sexuality is constructed around a difference with 'the masculine' – cropped hair and firm body, clumpy boots and dark mac – and 'the feminine' – shiny lips and lacy camisole. Maybe it isn't a sexuality which wholly breaks from the oppressive codes of women as sexual commodities but neither does it straightforwardly reproduce them.[79]

These magazines show much more awareness of what young women get up to, and what they are – or may be – up against, than would ever have been found before. Unemployment, poverty and the threat of violence are all discussed, alongside articles on women's self-defence and how to make the streets safer for women. Girls feel themselves to be men's equals, yet know men could be awful trouble. Not surprisingly, the conventions of this teenage culture enshrine notions of individual choice, self-display and self-improvement. They are all consumer-oriented and heterosexual. Yet a type of feminist consciousness about the need for equality is taken for granted, reflecting a reality where, as Winship says of her students: 'These are young women who are much tougher and more together than my generation were at the same age . . . partly because of the changes feminism has made in women's lives.'[80]

But there is another side to this more hopeful view of the confidence and expressiveness of girls and women today. As we have seen with queer readings, what may be seen as an empowering image by one woman, is still read as sexist and disparaging by the next woman (particularly if she is an anti-pornography feminist) or man. Thus Madonna has indeed represented a powerful, sexually assertive 'femininity' disturbing gender and sexual hierarchies, and served 'to counter feminine ideals of dependency and reserve' for many young women, although others may see her videos as reminiscent of 'sex exploitation of women'.[81] The contradiction is so stark, that one study of audience responses found women almost equally split between positive and negative responses: half seeing her as challenging, and the other half as embodying sexist stereotypes of female sexuality.[82]

It is significant that at least 50 per cent of women feel empowered by such sexual imagery, in ways they would have had little opportunity to until recently. But does such empowerment dent men's beliefs that sex is primarily about what they want and do? I suspect that it does. The effects, however, are diverse. Madonna has consistently triggered a heightened male hostility, fear of and hatred towards women from tabloid press and music critics alike: 'She is a slutty, self-obsessed, sometimes cruel, always manipula-tive woman,' one typical male critic lashes out.[83] But this unsettling of men underlines, however unconsciously, the existence of a battle being waged by women in their own interests.

Women need more than images and discursive frame-works with which to enter the battlefield, and the victories of 'semiotic warfare' are rarely secure across shifting contexts and interactions. Studying audience reaction to portrayals of feminine imagery in a Michael Jackson video, Linda Kalof found its meanings interpreted differently by women and by men: where women were more likely to describe the female figure 'as either powerful and in control' or else 'vulnerable and weak', men were more likely to contruct the *same* female image as either 'teasing and hard-to-get' or else 'submissive and indecisive'.[84] Girls' pleasure and identificatory sense of sexiness and entitlement watching the British female pop group Banarama singing 'Love in the First Degree', as half-naked male dancers swirl around them on their hands and knees, is one thing; girls negotiating safe and comfortable encounters with men on their own terms is another.

Negotiating sexual conflicts with men means young women having the strength to reject those who hassle or try to dominate them against their wishes. That is no mean feat. Recent in-depth interviewing of young women in London and Manchester by the feminist Women, Risk and AIDS Project (WRAP) suggests that around a quarter had felt pressurized into having sex with boys, and that only 'a tiny minority', who felt able to discuss their sexual preferences with partners, reported 'very positive experiences'.[85] These researchers reject the static pessimistic scenario outlined by other feminists, like Sue Lees, who describe girls in the mid-1980s as still oppressed by and fearful of boys' sexist labelling of them as 'slag' or 'drag'.[86] But they nevertheless emphasize the vulnerability of young women who have no language or model of positive female sexuality and remain dominated by 'the construction of passive femininity, which effectively silences their own desires'.[87]

Others studying teenage girls in the USA suggest that feminists have disproportionately exaggerated the problematic nature of girls' sexuality, projecting their own frames of reference onto young girls' speech, while ignoring its own nuances of power, pleasure and conflict.[88] WRAP, for example, characteristically provides as an example of 'the silencing of female desire' one girl's comment 'I like enjoyment from . . . them actually doing it and them enjoying themselves.'[89] Voyeuristic desire is thus blithely dismissed as some type of category mistake. In contrast Michelle Fine and Pat Macpherson conclude from their own conversations with young women, in circumstances similar to a small consciousness-raising group, that feminist research, including their own, has remained so committed to ideas of women's victimization that it ignores how firmly young women resist being subordinated – alone and sometimes together. Confessing their own resistance to much that they hear, they stress '*how well young women talk as subjects*, passionate about and relishing in their capacities to move between nexuses of power and powerlessness.'[90]

The adolescents in their small group, especially the two black women, had faced very real violence from men: 'When he pulled a gun on me, I said, "This is over.""[91] But in differing ways they all shared a determination not to be dominated by anyone. The black, working-class women drew upon a sense of active female sexuality and mother-hood which they saw 'embodied' in their mothers: 'My mom wouldn't ever take that.' The one white and one Asian middle-class women drew upon a sense of their own individual achievements and 'career' ambitions. But they all longed to be 'one of the boys', seeking an individualistic 'gender-free' adolescence:

> Delighted to swear, spit, tell off-colour jokes, wear hats and trash other girls, they were critical of individual boys, nasty about most girls, rarely challenging of the sex/gender system, and were ecstatic, for the most part, to be engaged as friends and lovers with young men. But we also heard their feminism in their collective refusal to comply with male demands, their wish for women friends to trust, their expectations for equality and search for respect, their deep ambivalence about being 'independent of a man' and yet in partnership with one, and their strong yearnings to read, write and talk more about women's experience among women.[92]

However, even feminists who carefully avoid projecting their own feminist presuppositions onto girls' experience would all agree that they often have a tough battle holding their own with boys in sexual matters, where male-centred heterosexual discourses remain so dominant. Positive negotiations, especially in early encounters with men, are likely to require not just a personal confidence – boosted perhaps by particular styles or images of 'femininity' – but *all* the resources of self-worth a woman has built up throughout a lifetime of contact with significant others; in particular, for most women, from identifying with their mothers. (Daughters of mothers working in nontraditional professions, for example, have been found to be much more likely to espouse ideals of 'femininity' which value the more conventionally 'masculine' attributes of 'potency, activity and independence', when compared with daughters from the same class backgrounds with mothers who have chosen to remain at home.)[93] Young women's ability to negotiate sexual encounters or relationships with men also requires the growth of a woman's acceptance of her body, and the ability to talk about it in the face of a general cultural silence, embarrassment or shame surrounding much of its regular functioning – even though the silence has been broken in more recent magazines targeting teenage girls. This suggests the importance of woman-centred sex education, around masturbation, desire, sexual encounters, sexual practices and relationships, rather than the introduction to reproductive biology which is usually all that is on offer in schools. Only 6 per cent of young women in the WRAP survey thought that their sex education had been good.[94]

There are dangers in relying upon the consumer values of expanding 'choice' to further women's sexual autonomy and liberation. The marketing rationality of a capitalist culture may at times target and serve the interests of subordinated groups, whether women, gays or ethnic minorities. But the language and culture promoting individual 'choice' and self-fulfilment, which inevitably downplays social constraint and inequality, serves conservative ends more readily than progressive ones. Its strengths are also its weaknesses, disguising the social limits of choice. Even a feminist with such optimism of the intellect as Angela McRobbie takes pains to stress that things go quickly awry for many young women as soon as they find themselves in traps of economic dependency. It is a

situation in which women who either choose or feel forced
into young motherhood increasingly find themselves.

McRobbie studied a small group of working-class
teenage mothers in Birmingham in the 1980s, trying to
survive on totally inadequate state benefits. Unlike some of
the young single mothers reported in other surveys, like the
black mothers looked at by Ann Phoenix or a broader
cross-section interviewed by Sue Sharpe, none of these
Birmingham mothers felt either strong or confident (except
for the short periods when exceptional conditions enabled
them to hold down jobs), and some found it almost
impossible to escape situations of violence and abuse.[95]
Surveying the increasingly stigmatized and disadvantaged
condition of this particular group, financially penalized
and made into scapegoats for wider social failures to
provide for the needs of women with children, it is clear
that feminist legacies which have proved empowering
for some women have been unable to protect or empower
others. Moreover, it was the hopes raised around women's
independence which had encouraged some of these women
to form the female-headed families in the first place.
Such a decision by poorer women, however, usually accompanies an enforced choice to leave violent situations, or to
avoid tying themselves to men who cannot support them
financially or emotionally. It is recession and market
restructuring, not feminism, which has taken the jobs from
the young fathers, producing in many an accompanying
sense of failure, irresponsibility and, at times, violence.

The very same rhetorics of individual choice and self-
fulfilment are used by conservative forces aiming to bury
feminism and promote a new traditionalism around
marriage and the home, as the only secure or happy place
for women to dwell. Women have a choice, they stress,
they can choose between home or career, the happy family

or a successful job. As Margaret Thatcher loved to remind
us, along with her belief that 'the battle for women's rights
has been largely won':[96] 'It makes me angry if any woman
is made to feel guilty because she *chooses* to concentrate
on providing that warmth and welcome for the family
instead of having a job.'[97] Like 'Hope' in the US soap *thirty-
something*, women are free to 'choose' to abandon careers
for cosy motherhood, and to pity the fears and anxieties
of their women friends who have 'chosen' to pursue their
careers or creative talents. The folly of the message never
fazes the messenger. The semiotic playfulness of Madonna
or *Mizz* 'matures' into the symbolic seriousness of the
Real Woman anchoring most TV sitcoms, her sexuality
smothered by the unequal sharing of domestic chores, and
financial dependence on men's higher wage packets. This
new traditionalism, as Elspeth Probyn sums it up, 'hawks
the home as the "natural choice" – which means, of course,
no choice.'[98]

Looking at the changes in women's lives today, it is
easy to keep moving in circles. On the one hand, it seems
right to celebrate more women claiming the right to sexual
pleasure. It can give us a strong sense of increased confidence and control over our lives. From this perspective, we
need to oppose and subvert all traditional discourses
and understandings of bodily pleasure which symbolically
position women as necessarily subordinated in and through
heterosexual encounters or partnerships – whether
coming from traditional sexist rhetoric or dissident radical
feminism. On the other hand, the ongoing reality of men's
greater access to positions of status, economic security and
power, symbolized in phallic imagery, means many women
remain dependent on and controlled by the men in their
lives. The sexual consumerism which helps empower some
women, mocks the compromises or 'choices' which other

women have made as they attempt to placate men from within the currently vulnerable positions which mother-hood and family responsibilities often place them. Cruelly, women may find that the men who are most removed from the status and power masculinity supposedly confers (with little support or protection to offer) can be the ones most ready to try to dominate them through physical aggression and sexual control, if only in their rhetoric.

This can be seen in the exaggerated machismo lyrics, celebrating guns, sex and violence, dominating black hip-hop, 'gangster rap' and dance-hall music since the late eighties in the USA and Jamaica; a violence primarily directed against women and gays. Black scholars like Cornel West, or political leaders like the Jamaican Michael Manley, see in such music the shut-down of black political hopes for changing the world – once fired by Bob Marley and other black musicians combining pop and reggae in jubilant celebration of egalitarianism, anti-racism, anti-imperialism and Ethiopianism in the sixties and seventies.[99] With only the private realm to dominate, West mourns, there is more pressure than ever on black male youth to conform to macho roles and deny their own diversity and gentleness, to produce a shared patri-archal black identity. But as Public Enemy, Brand Nubian, Ice Cube, Ice T., and other young black rappers are well aware, as they posture knowingly with their guns to deliver up a theatricalized nihilism, they are playing to what has been white America's representation of the black man all along, both getting off on it and mocking it.[100] And the language of violence, as black men know and articulate only too well, is the language and values of a white capitalist world, determined to achieve profit, power and pleasure, by whatever means necessary. With such values becoming only ever more pervasive today, women's pursuit of their own autonomy and pleasure is going to require a lot more than the choices opened up to them by market consumerism.

Sexual liberation and feminist politics

'There is feminism and then there's fucking', declares the bulimic and alcoholic ex-feminist literary critic Maryse, in the Canadian film *A Winter Tan* (1987), based on the published letters of Maryse Holder, *Give Sorrow Words*. Maryse tells her audience that she is taking a holiday from feminism to indulge herself and her 'natural sluttishness' with young Mexican men – one of whom eventually murders her. After gloomily absorbing this narrative, I found it hard to decide whether it was Maryse's notion of feminism or her own (and her killer's) predatory view of sex which was the more depressing in this harrowing tale of one woman's neurotic self-destruction. The fact that many feminists would proudly endorse Maryse Holder's dual depiction of feminism as anti-heterosexual pleasure and heterosexual pleasure as anti-woman (a dangerous, if not deadly pursuit), only adds to my sinking spirits. Some of us expect cautionary tales warning women of the price we must pay for sexual pleasure to come from our would-be patriarchal 'protectors', determined to stamp out the rich and hopeful dreams of women's liberation. It is harder to know what to think when the same message comes from our own side. (*A Winter Tan* was produced, written, directed and performed by Jackie Boroughs, a leading feminist figure in Canadian film and theatre for the last twenty-five years.)

One thing is clear, however, at least to me. The way to fight the continuing victimization of women cannot be to abandon notions of sexual liberation, or to make women's pursuit of heterosexual pleasure incompatible with women's happiness. It was not only the generation who came of age in the affluent 1960s who discovered that the fight against sexual hypocrisy and for sexual openness and pleasure could inspire both personal and political enthusiasm for creative and co-operative projects of diverse kinds. Such sexual openness lay at the root of the politicization of women and gay people in the 1970s, suddenly fully aware that pleasure was as much a social and a political as a personal matter; well before they discovered Foucault, and his genealogy of the cultural institutions and discourses dictating the norms and regimes of 'sexuality'. It was seeing and hearing the dominant language and iconography of the joys of sex focussed on the power and activity of straight men, while subordinating and disparaging straight women (as 'chics') and gay men and lesbians (as 'queers'), that inspired the women's and the gay liberation movements into a battle against both sexism and heterosexism.

The ramifications of this battle take us all the way from opposing gender hierachies to challenging the very conception of 'gender' itself. From the extensive debate about the care and treatment of women in relation to fertility control and childbirth, alongside pressure on men to share the full responsibilities of household tasks and parenting, to the subsequent highly successful 'safer sex' strategies pioneered by gay communities against the spread of HIV and AIDS, the struggle for sexual liberation has played a crucial role in changing patterns of life in Western countries. Indeed, it was the repression of any moment or movements of sexual liberation in the former Eastern European 'state socialist' countries that constituted the most significant aspect of the oppression of women there.

Despite greater access to childcare facilities and extensive participation in the workforce, Eastern Europe saw almost no politicization of interpersonal relationships or sexual experience, making sexism, violence against women and exclusive maternal responsibility for childcare and housework as unchallenged as it was ubiquitous.[101]

Even in these days of greater insecurity, it is the rediscovering of the pleasures to be found in our bodies and the joy of bringing pleasure to others (of desiring and feeling desired) which, when things go well, feeds personal optimism and strength: 'Oh, when I was in love with you/ Then I was clean and brave', as Housman wrote of his own homosexual passion, mourning its passing, and the resurrection of that gloomy tyrant – his old self.[102] The idea of sexual liberation, as Bob Connell has recently written, may seem 'good mainly for a horse-laugh, or a nanosecond of nostalgia in the world of the new puritanism', but in fact it 'should come back from the dead; we still need it.'[103] We need it, if only because, while many left and feminist radicals have forsaken their former enthusiasm for sexual liberation, the right have stuck doggedly to their task of opposing it. In these 'post-modern' times, we may not see sexual liberation as the struggle to combat the repression of some sexual essence. But we might usefully see it as the struggle to combat the manipulation of people's fears and anxieties around gender and sexuality in a climate of increasing confusion for men, with its accompanying homophobia and violence against women.

Conservative forces have mobilized consistently for battle against abortion, against homosexuality, against divorce, against sex education, against 'pornography', in short, against any change that would promote women's or gay men's sexual autonomy by transforming the order of gender. They have been particularly active in Britain since the mid-1980s. Clause 28 of the Local Government Act was passed in 1988, making it illegal for local authorities to publish material which might 'promote homosexuality' or for state schools to teach 'the acceptance of homosexuality as a pretended family relationship'. We have heard an appalling crescendo of malevolent attacks from Tory leaders on single mothers, accused of jumping housing queues, raising delinquent children and bearing responsibility for their own impoverishment. At the same time, the Minister of Education, John Patten, threatened teachers that providing contraceptive knowledge to girls under sixteen without parental consent 'could amount to a criminal offence', and removed teaching relating to contraception, abortion, HIV and AIDS from the compulsory science curriculum. (The predictable result is that the British rate of conception among 15–19-year-olds, already one of the highest in Europe, seven times higher than in the Netherlands, where sex education is central to the curriculum, will remain unchanged.)[104] There is also an upsurge of scaremongering around the effects of divorce on children, despite the evidence of the extent of psychological damage, violence and sexual abuse that occurs inside traditional families. The repetitious railing against 'permissiveness' as the source of all our ills accompanies each of these moves.

As feminists, we play into the hands of our enemies if we downplay, rather than seek fully to strengthen, ideas of women's sexual liberation. Nor can we leave the goal of expanding personal liberation to a commodity consumer culture eager to expand its markets, whatever its sometimes 'dissident', playful or progressive moments. Women, like gays and lesbians, still need a political movement and agenda of our own, that continues to make demands on the state while providing its own diverse networks of support and cultural resistance.

Two trends have been highlighted in Western surveys of changing sexual patterns over the last few decades (usually undertaken in the USA): the increasing levels of sexual activity outside marriage, and the lowering of double standards as women's sexual experiences draw closer to men's.[105] Both, quite obviously, reflect a decline in men's control over women's sexuality. As the latest survey of sexual behaviour in Britain has concluded (the survey which Margaret Thatcher tried to prevent by withdrawing its promised funding), quite contrary to traditionalists' dire warnings and secret hopes, sex is far safer and less fraught for women today. The importance of female 'virginity' before marriage has all but disappeared as an issue for most groups of women and men, and younger people are far more likely to have used contraception during their first sexual intercourse: over 80 per cent of women, and over 70 per cent of men, had their first heterosexual intercourse with the man using a condom in 1990 – two to three times higher than in preceding decades. Around 90 per cent of women gave either love, curiosity or 'natural follow on' as the main factor leading to their first intercourse, with the majority of women and men feeling it occurred at about the right time; although one in four women, against one in eight men, thought they had had sex too early. Serial monogamy is now the dominant pattern for both sexes. There seems to be 'a genuine long-term decline in the number of men who visit prostitutes.'[106]

By arguing for women's sexual autonomy, fertility rights and the education and resources necessary for each person to encounter or care for themselves and for others in ways that enhance the possibilities for pleasure, mutuality, responsibility and comfort, feminists today would be continuing to participate in changes which they once helped to set in motion. Sexual pleasure is far too significant in our lives and culture for women not to be seeking to express our agency through it. The task confronting feminists today, as yesterday, is to uncover the social forces which ensure that women's sexual agency is suppressed in contexts of significant gender inequality, and to fight to change them. It is also to uncover and challenge the cultural forces which disparage women and gay men through meanings roping gender to sexuality via conceptions of 'masculinity' as 'activity' and 'dominance' coded into heterosexual coitus, however shaky the symbolism at interpersonal levels. It is these tasks which keep sexuality a social and political issue and 'sexual liberation' a goal for which we have still to struggle. There is cause for genuine optimism, yet so much more to be done.

Despite its supposed location as an individual issue within or at the borders of the private sphere, all the usual sites of political action – struggles over state policy, education, the media – as well as issues of self-definition and collective resistance, are as relevant for mobilizing around sexuality as around anything else. Except in unusual times, it has never been easy fighting for social reform – but rarely harder than now. We have slipped bruisingly down a mighty long political snake in recent times. But there is no way that those wanting to combat the forces undermining women's autonomy can give up on the traditional forms of canvassing, lobbying, fighting and arguing for better and more comprehensive welfare provision at state and local levels. There are, at present, more ladders on the ideological than on the resource-delivery front, some more useful than others. Campaigns like those of Zero Tolerance, publicly exposing and condemning men's use of violence against women, have been launched by several local councils in Glasgow and London. Feminists have also continued to make important interventions and recommendations drawing media and state attention to the absurdly low levels of rape convictions (only 14 per cent of reported rapes result in conviction, on Home Office figures for 1991), with many violent men being acquitted over and over again, and women victims continuing to be subjected to humiliating treatment in court, especially when their attackers were already known to them.[107]

Worryingly, however, there is also some official backing for new anti-pornography legislation to 'protect' us from the 'harm' caused by images of 'sexually explicit subordination'.[108] While strengthening the agenda of moral conservatives, this does nothing to rid us of the ubiquitous non-sexually explicit gender imagery depicting men as dominant and aggressive, women as subordinate and servicing in cultural representation generally (the feminine/effeminate/homosexual remain subordinate identities, in and out of their clothes). Since images are read and responded to differently depending upon their framing, context, and the meanings they carry within the milieu in which they are consumed, sexual minorities and dissidents of all sorts rightly fear it is their representations of sexuality which will be censored by any new legislation, just as they have always been. Certainly 'safer sex' campaigning material and sex education generally, in both Britain and the USA has been grotesquely hampered by accusations of 'pornography'.[109] Most significantly, proposing anti-pornography legislation is a cheap diversion from doing anything useful about violence against women. Those most at risk from sexual brutality – overwhelmingly women who feel trapped in relationships with men, as well as prostitutes and gay men (lesbians are less vulnerable, unless occupying one of the first two categories) – need real solutions. These involve increasing women's financial independence, encouraging rather than stigmatizing or trying to penalize 'single' mothers who have fled violent partnerships, as well as combatting homophobia.

Given the poverty of resistance and imagination coming from mainstream political parties, it is campaigning groups, community networks and subcultural consolidations which are going to be the main focus for reflection and struggles around sexuality and personal life in the short term. Sexual freedoms have, however, proved one of the few issues capable of drawing people into progressive collective action in recent years, providing radicals of the Left with the best of reasons for addressing them, even as our opponents mobilize their counter-attack. The Clause 28 legislation, ironically, backfired completely in its goal of reaffirming the sanctity of the family, and silencing its feminist and gay critics. Instead, as many have celebrated, sexual dissidents of every sort, including heterosexuals, took to the streets in their tens of thousands to support 'Stop the Clause' campaigns and marches, and benefits, meetings and publicity stunts occurred throughout the country.[110] With well known media figures like Ian McKellan and Michael Cashman deciding it was time to come out and organize openly for full gay rights, and more gay and lesbian programmes finding their way into mainstream television, debates and struggles around sexuality seemed to have become the most successful area of dissent in the late 1980s.

They will need to remain so. There is no way that sexuality is about to leave the public realm, even without the hypocritical parade of Tory politicians who tell us how to live and how to love, while flouting the rules themselves. However much we may feel we are bored with hearing about sex, it will continue to haunt public life. Its presence was always guaranteed by its function as metaphor for what men most passionately desire, and most desirously fear: the proofs of and threats to 'manhood'. As James Baldwin learned from anguished personal experience, ideas of sexuality are rooted in ideas of masculinity: 'Freaks are called freaks and are treated as they are treated – in the main, abominably – because they are human beings who cause to echo, deep within us, our most profound terrors and desires.' He also knew that it was the same white boys who chased and mocked him most fiercely in the streets in his youth, who frightened him even more if they found him when they were alone; then 'they spoke very gently and wanted me to take them home and make love.'[111] Today, anti-abortion crusaders from the USA come to Britain to teach their auxiliaries here how to attack and terrorize patients and workers at abortion clinics. Men are being encouraged by men's rights groups to take action to prevent women from having abortions or from retaining custody of children. And after all this time, struggle must continue simply to bring basic legal parity for the age of consent in male homosexual encounters.

For those of us who want to see the recognition of women's equality and agency in every sphere of life, [hetero]'sexuality' as confirmation of 'manhood' is an idea we must attack. Its discursive displacement is central to the battle against the hierarchical gender relations which it serves to symbolize. It will only fade away with the passing of that gender order, as we continue to fashion new concepts and practices of gender based upon the mutual recognition of similarities and differences between women and men, rather than upon notions of their opposition. In the meantime, we can continue to insist, with all the passion we can muster, that there is no necessary fit between maleness, activity and desire; any more than there is a fit between femaleness, passivity and sexual responsiveness.

Straight sex, with its tactile, olfactory, oral and visual bodily connections, can be no less 'perverse' than its 'queer' alternatives. Ridiculing hierarchies of sexuality and gender, it too can serve as a body-blow to the old male order of things. There is feminism and there is fucking. As I see it, they can fit together quite as smoothly (or as painfully) as feminism and any other human activity. Straight feminists, like gay men and lesbians, have everything to gain from asserting our non-coercive desire to fuck if, when, how and as we choose.

·····Notes

Preface

1   Celia Kitzinger and Sue Wilkinson, 'Theorizing Heterosexuality: Editorial Introduction' in Wilkinson and Kitzinger eds, *Heterosexuality: A Feminism and Psychology Reader*, London, Sage, 1993, p.12.
2   Susan Ardill and Sue O'Sullivan, 'Sex in the Summer of '88', *Feminist Review*, no. 31, Spring 1989, p.133.
3   John Fletcher, 'Perverse Politics', paper delivered at the Institute of Contemporary Arts, 24 October 1991.

Chapter 1

1   Adrian Mitchell, 'Our Country' in Jeff Nuttall, *Bomb Culture*, London, Paladin, 1970, p.131.
2   Tom McGrath, *International Times*, no. 10, 13 March 1967.
3   Angela Carter, 'Truly, it felt like Year One' in Sara Maitland ed., *Very Heaven*, London, Virago, 1988, p.215.
4   Here, Eric Burden provided the music and lyrics, throwing in his moral philosophy as well, so perfectly in tune with the times: 'My religion just says have a good time without harming anyone else.' Eric Burden, quoted in Richard Hoggart *et al.*, *The Permissive Society: The Guardian Enquiry*, London, Panther, 1969, p.15.
5   Raphael Samuel, 'The Lost World of British Communism', *New Left Review*, Nov./Dec. 1985, pp.8, 12.
6   Robert Hewison, *Too Much*, London, Methuen, 1986, p.6.
7   See Stuart Hall and Tony Jefferson eds, *Resistance through Rituals: Youth Subcultures in Post-war Britain*, London, Hutchinson, 1976.
8   Jane Wibberley, 'Progressive Wardrobes' in Amanda Sebestyen ed., *'68, '78, '88: from Women's Liberation to Feminism*, London, Prism, 1988, p.93.
9   See Lynne Segal, 'Smash the Family? Recalling the Sixties' in Lynne Segal ed., *What is to be done about the Family?*, Harmondsworth, Penguin, 1983, and Segal, *Slow Motion: Changing Masculinities, Changing Men*, London, Virago, 1990, ch. 1.

10   Ronald Fraser, *1968: A Student Generation in Revolt*, London, Chatto & Windus, 1988, p.14.

11   Ibid., p.114.

12   Vernon Bogdanor and Robert Skidelsky eds, *The Age of Affluence, 1951–1964*, London, Macmillan, 1970, p.14.

13   G.K. Galbraith, *The Affluent Society* (1958), Harmondsworth, Penguin, 1969, p.17.

14   Simon Frith, 'Rock and the Politics of Memory' in Sohnya Sayres ed., *The Sixties Without Apologies*, University of Minnesota Press, Minnesota, 1986, p.60.

15   Thom Gunn, quoted in Alan Sinfield, *Postwar Britain*, Oxford, Blackwell, 1989, p.283.

16   Margaret Thatcher, *Daily Mail*, 29 April 1988.

17   Richard Neville, *Play Power*, London, Vintage, 1971, p.98.

18   Sheila Rowbotham, *Woman's Consciousness, Man's World*, Harmondsworth, Penguin, 1973, p.14.

19   Marsha Rowe, 'Masturbation – no Longer a Refuge', *Spare Rib*, no. 21, no date, p.9.

20   Marsha Rowe, 'Up from Down Under' in Maitland ed., op. cit., p.158.

21   In Fraser, op. cit., p.69.

22   See Rose Shapiro, *Contraception: A Practical and Political Guide*, London, Virago, 1987.

23   An interview with 'Jane', 'Unwomanly and Unnatural – Some Thoughts on the Pill' in Maitland ed., op. cit., pp.151–2.

24   Angela Carter, in Maitland, ibid., p.214.

25   Sheila Rowbotham, 'A Muggins Twice Over', *New Statesman and Society*, 10 June 1988, p.26.

26   Mary Quant, in Hoggart *et al.* op. cit., p.22.

27   Ibid., p.22.

28   I am relying here mostly on personal communication, and the many men who have confided what they saw as their own peculiar sexual diffidence as young men in the sixties, many feeling altogether left out of the fun the women seemed to be having.

29   Norman Mailer, *The Prisoner of Sex*, London, Sphere, 1972, p.126.

30   See Stuart Hall, 'Reformism and the Legislation of Consent' in *Permissiveness and Control: The Fate of the Sixties Legislation*, National Deviancy Conference, London, Macmillan, 1980.

31   Ellen Willis, *Beginning to See the Light*, Boston, South End Press, 1981, p.12.

32 Geoffrey Gorer, *Sex and Marriage in England Today*, London, Panther, 1973.

33 Elizabeth Wilson, *Only Halfway to Paradise*, London, Tavistock, 1980, p.110.

34 Roger Scruton, *Thinkers of the New Left*, London, Longman, 1985, pp.1 and 87.

35 Stuart Hall, editorial, *New Left Review*, 1, January/February 1960, p.1.

36 Alan Sillitoe, 'What Comes on Monday', *New Left Review*, 4, July/August 1961, p.59.

37 For example, Raymond Williams, *The Long Revolution*, London, Chatto & Windus, 1961.

38 Raphael Samuel, 'Born-again Socialism', in *Out of Apathy: Voices of the New Left 30 Years On*, ed. Oxford University Socialist Discussion Group, London, Verso, 1989, p.42. A later New Left, which came to dominate *New Left Review* after Stuart Hall resigned, was influenced by Louis Althusser (the philosopher from the French Communist Party) and would reject the earlier humanistic emphasis on self-direction and individual agency for a more abstract structuralist account based on his formulation of the social formation of subjectivity. But this had a limited impact on academic or movement life in the sixties.

39 In Britain R.D. Laing was the guru of anti-psychiatry; see, for example, his, with Aaron Esterton, *Sanity, Madness and the Family*, Harmondsworth, Penguin, 1964.

40 See David Cooper ed., *The Dialectics of Liberation*, Harmondsworth, Penguin, 1968.

41 Ann Popkin, 'The Personal is Political: The Women's Liberation Movement' in Dick Cluster ed., *They Should Have Served That Cup of Coffee: 7 Radicals Remember the 60s*, Boston, South End Press, 1979, p.186.

42 Bernice Reagon talks to Dick Cluster in ibid., p.35.

43 Quoted in Sara Evans, *Personal Politics, the Roots of Women's Liberation in the Civil Rights Movement and the New Left*, New York, Knopf, pp.86–7. Evans, as her title encapsulates, stresses the overwhelming importance of the Civil Rights Movement in the emergence of North American feminism.

44 Herbert Marcuse, *Eros and Civilization* (1955), Boston, Beacon Press, 1966, p.48.

45 Ibid., p.49.

46   Norman O. Brown, *Life Against Death* (1959), London, Sphere Books, 1968, p.277.
47   McGrath, op.cit., p.206.
48   'Where BITS at' in Peter Stansill and David Mairowitz eds, *BAMN: Outlaw Manifestos and Ephemera 1965–70*, Harmondsworth, Penguin, 1971, pp.94–5.
49   Herbert Marcuse, *One-Dimensional Man*, Boston, Beacon Press, 1964, p.1.
50   Paul Breines, 'Notes on Marcuse and the Movement', *Radical America*, vol. 1v, no. 3, 1970, p.30.
51   Ronald Aronson, 'Dear Herbert' in ibid., p.14.
52   R.D. Laing, *The Politics of Experience*, Harmondsworth, Penguin, 1970.
53   Allen Ginsberg, quoted in Nuttall, op. cit., p.192.
54   Aronson, op. cit., p.16.
55   Neville, op. cit., p.275.
56   David Cooper, *The Death of the Family*, Harmondsworth, Penguin, 1971, pp.47–8.
57   Ken Kesey, *One Flew Over the Cuckoo's Nest* (1962), New York, Picador, 1968; Phillip Roth, *Portnoy's Complaint* (1969), Harmondsworth, Penguin, 1970; J.P. Donleavy, *The Ginger Man* (1955), New York, Delacorte Press, 1965; Norman Mailer, op. cit.
58   Kingsley Amis, *Lucky Jim* (1954), Harmondsworth, Penguin, 1977.
59   See Molly Haskell, *From Reverence to Rape*, Harmondsworth, Penguin, 1974.
60   Julie Christie, 'Everybody's Darling', in Maitland ed., op. cit., p.171.
61   Quoted in Nell Dunn, *Talking to Women*, London, MacGibbon & Kee, 1965, p.101.
62   Margaret Drabble, *A Summer Bird-Cage*, Harmondsworth, Penguin, 1963, p.29.
63   Doris Lessing, *The Golden Notebook* (1962), St Albans, Panther, 1972.
64   Fraser, op. cit., p.195.
65   Ibid., p.182.
66   Alix Kates Shulman, *Burning Questions* (1978), London, Fontana, 1980, p.221.
67   Yasmin Alibhai, 'Living by Proxy', in Maitland, op. cit., p.202.
68   Quoted in Neville, op. cit., p.88.

69 Robin Morgan, 'Goodbye to All That', *Underground Press Anthology*, Thomas Forcade ed., New York, ace books, p.127.

70 Germaine Greer, 'A Groupie's Vision', *Oz*, February 1969, reprinted in *The Madwoman's Underclothes: Essays and Occasional Writing 1968–1985*, London, Picador, 1986, p.10.

71 Nigel Fountain, *Underground: The London Alternative Press, 1966–74*, London, Routledge, 1988, pp.121, 125.

72 Ibid.

73 Neville, op. cit., p.90.

74 Germaine Greer, 'The Politics of Female Sexuality', *Oz*, May 1970, reprinted in *The Madwoman's Underclothes*, op. cit., p.40; see also Greer's other essays from the seventies in this collection and her later work, *Sex and Destiny: The Politics of Human Fertility*, London, Picador, 1985, and *The Change: Women, Ageing and the Menopause*, London, Hamish Hamilton, 1991.

75 Sheila Rowbotham, 'Women: the Struggle for Freedom', *Black Dwarf*, 10 January 1969, p.6.

76 Ibid.

77 Marsha Rowe ed., *Spare Rib Reader*, Harmondsworth, Penguin, 1982, p.14.

78 'You don't know what is happening do you, Mr Jones?', *Spare Rib*, no. 8, February 1973, p.30.

79 Eleanor Stephens, 'The moon within your reach: a feminist approach to female orgasm', *Spare Rib*, no. 42, December 1975, p.14.

Chapter 2

1 Angela Hamblin, 'The Suppressed Power of Female Sexuality', *Shrew*, vol. 4, no. 6, December 1972, p.1.

2 Catharine MacKinnon, 'Not a Moral Issue'; in *Feminism Unmodified: Discourses on Life and Law*, London, Harvard University Press, 1987, p.149.

3 June Jordan, 'Where is the Love?' (1978) in *Moving Towards Home: Political Essays*, London, Virago, 1989, p.82.

4 Marge Piercy, 'The Grand Coolee Damn', 1969, in Robin Morgan ed., *Sisterhood is Powerful: An Anthology of Writings from the Women's Liberation Movement*, New York, Vintage, 1970, p.421.

5 German wall slogan, in Ronald Fraser, *1968: A Student Generation in Revolt*, London, Chatto & Windus, 1988, p.13.

6 Rosalyn Fraad Baxandall, 'Feminizing the Sixties', *Socialist Review*, 1, 1991, p.191.

7 Janet Rée, Interviewed in Michelene Wandor ed., *Once a Feminist: Stories of a Generation*, London, Virago, 1990, p.103.

8 Hamblin, op. cit., p.1.

9 Anne Koedt, 'The Myth of the Vaginal Orgasm' in L. Tanner ed., *Voices from Women's Liberation*, New York, Mentor, 1970.

10 The accounts of this conference all come from women interviewed for and quoted in Alice Echols, *Daring to Be Bad: Radical Feminism in America 1967–1975*, Minnesota, University of Minnesota Press, 1989, pp.111, 112, 111.

11 Irene Frick, 'Wot No Orgasm?' *Red Rag*, no. 3, 1973, p.8.

12 Alix Shulman, 'Organs and Orgasms' in V. Gornick and B. Moran eds, *Women in Sexist Society*, New York, Signet, 1971, p.303; Alix Kates Shulman, 'Sex and Power: Sexual Bases of Radical Feminism', *Signs*, vol. 5, no. 4, Summer 1980a, p.601.

13 Frick, op. cit.

14 Shulman, 1980a, op. cit., p.595.

15 Sheila Rowbotham, *The Past is Before Us*, London, Pandora, 1989, p.79.

16 Barbara Seaman, 'The Liberated Orgasm', *Spare Rib*, no. 7, January 1973, p.29.

17 Eleanor Stephens, 'The moon within your reach: a feminist approach to female orgasm', *Spare Rib*, no. 42, December 1975, p.15.

18 Ibid.

19 Lynne Segal, 'Sensual Uncertainty or Why the Clitoris is Not Enough', in S. Cartledge and J. Ryan eds, *Sex and Love: New Thoughts on Old Contradictions*, London, Women's Press, 1983. The anger has been reported to me by intermediaries.

20 Alix Kates Shulman, *Burning Questions* (1978), London, Fontana, 1980, p.346.

21 Eleanor Stephens, 'Making Changes, Making Love', *Spare Rib*, no. 48, July 1976, p.37.

22 Alison Fell, 'in confidence' in Fell *et al.*, *Smile, smile, smile*, London, Sheba, 1980, p.91.

23 Stephens, 1976, op. cit., p.38.

24 Boston Women's Health Book Collective, *Our Bodies, Ourselves: A Health Book by and for Women*, British edition by Angela Phillips and Jill Rakusen, Harmondsworth, Penguin, 1978.

25 Beatrix Campbell, 'Sexuality and Submission', *Red Rag*, no. 5, 1973, p.14.

26 Maria Carroll, 'Changing', *Red Rag*, no. 12, 1977, p.5.

27 Tina Reid, 'Eye to Eye' in Alison Fell ed., *Hard Feelings: Fiction and Poetry from Spare Rib*, London, Women's Press, 1979, pp.60–1.

28 Quoted in Alix Kates Shulman, 1980b, op. cit., p.290.

29 Daphne Davies, 'Falling in Love Again', *Red Rag*, no. 13, 1978, p.14.

30 Anna Davin in Michelene Wandor ed., op. cit.

31 Sue Cooper, 'From 1970' in Amanda Sebestyen ed., *'68, '78, '88: from Women's Liberation to Feminism*, London, Prism, 1988, p.73.

32 Alice Simpson, 'From 1970' in ibid., p.80.

33 Eva Eberhardt, Kerry Hamilton, Sheila McKechnie, 'Amen', *Red Rag*, August 1980, p.10.

34 Shulman, 1980a, op. cit., p.604.

35 Janet Rée in Wandor ed., op. cit., p.103.

36 Julia Kristeva, *Tales of Love*, New York, Columbia University Press, 1987, p.2.

37 Reported in Lillian Faderman, *Odd Girls and Twilight Lovers: A History of Lesbian Life in Twentieth-Century America*, Harmondsworth, Penguin, 1991, p.212.

38 Radicalesbians, 'Woman-identified Woman' in Anne Koedt, Ellen Levine and Anita Rapone eds, *Radical Feminism*, New York, Quadrangle, (1971) 1973.

39 Quoted in Lillian Faderman, op. cit., p.207.

40 Charlotte Bunch, 'Lesbians in Revolt' in *The Furies*, 1, (1), 1972.

41 Sarah Schulman, *The Sophie Horowitz Story*, quoted in Faderman, op. cit., p.188.

42 See Ann Snitow *et al.*, Introduction, *Powers of Desire: The Politics of Sexuality*, New York, New Feminist Library, 1984, p.34.

43 Deirdre English *et al.*, 'Talking Sex: A Conversation on Sexuality and Feminism', *Feminist Review*, no. 11, Summer 1982, p.44.

44 Anja Meulenbelt, *The Shame is Over: A Political Life Story*, London, Women's Press, 1980, p.86.

45 Faderman, op cit., pp.207, 208.

46 Shulman, 1980b, op. cit., pp.271, 273.

47 Adrienne Rich, *The Meaning of Our Love for Women Is What We Have Constantly to Expand*, New York, Out and Out Books, 1977.

326 ···· straight sex

48 Interview reported in Alice Echols, op. cit., p.39.
49 Robin Morgan, 'Lesbianism and Feminism', in *Going Too Far*, New York, Vintage Books, 1978, p.181.
50 Berta Freistadt, 'Lesbian heterosexual dialogue: Women's Liberation 1977', *Spare Rib*, no. 58, May 1977, p.13.
51 Elizabeth Wilson, 'Gayness and Liberalism', *Red Rag*, no. 6, 1974, p.11.
52 See Cate Haste, *Rules of Desire: Sex in Britain: World War I to the Present*, London, Chatto & Windus, 1992, p.241.
53 Jasper Gayford, 'Wife-Battery: A Preliminary Survey of 100 Cases', *British Medical Journal*, 25 January 1975.
54 I have looked at this shift in feminist thinking in more detail elsewhere. See Lynne Segal, *Is the Future Female: Troubled Thoughts on Contemporary Feminism*, London, Virago, 1987, ch.3, and Segal, *Slow Motion: Changing Masculinities, Changing Men*, London, Virago, 1990, ch.9.
55 Susan Brownmiller, *Against Our Will*, London, Women's Press, 1976.
56 Sally Alexander and Sue O'Sullivan, 'Sisterhood under Stress', *Red Rag*, no. 8, 1975, p.19.
57 Susan Griffin, 'Rape: The All-American Crime', *Ramparts*, September 1971.
58 Leeds Revolutionary Feminist Group, 'Political Lesbianism: The Case Against Heterosexuality' in Onlywomen Press ed., *Love Your Enemy? The Debate between Heterosexual Feminism and Political Lesbianism*, London, Onlywomen Press, 1981, p.8.
59 Personal communication on reading a draft of this text.
60 Cherrié Moraga and Gloria Anzaldua, talking to Alison Read in *Spare Rib*, no. 120, July 1982, p.61, about their book, Cherrié Moraga and Gloria Anzaldua eds, *This Bridge Called My Back*, New York, Persephone Press, 1982.
61 Angela Davis, *Women, Race and Class*, New York, Random House, 1981, p.173.
62 Two and a half thousand black men were lynched in the USA between 1925 and 1950. To this day although 50 per cent of men convicted for rape in the Southern states are white, over 90 per cent of men executed for rape are black. No white man has ever been executed for raping a black woman. See Segal, 1990, op.cit., pp.177–9.
63 Toni Cade Bambara, *Gorilla, My Love* (1972), New York,

Random House, 1977; *The Salt Eaters*, New York, Random House, 1980.

64 Toni Morrison, *Sula* (1973), London, Chatto, 1980, *Song of Solomon* (1977), London, Chatto, 1980; Ntozake Shange, *For Colored Girls Who Have Considered Suicide When the Rainbow Is Enuf*, London, Methuen, 1978; Gayl Jones, *Corriegidora*, New York, Random House, 1975; Gloria Naylor, *The Women of Brewster Street* (1982), London, Methuen, 1983; Alice Walker, *Meridian* (1975), London, Women's Press, 1976, *The Color Purple*, London, Women's Press, 1982.

65 Audre Lorde, 'My Words Will Be There' in Mari Evans ed., *Black Women Writers*, London, Pluto, 1983, p.267. These black feminist voices, and others, are looked at in more detail by me in 'Black Feminisn and Black Masculinity' in Segal, 1990, op. cit., pp.195–204.

66 Combahee River Collective, 'Collective Statement' in Barbara Smith ed., *Home Girls: A Black Feminist Anthology*, New York, Kitchen Table/Women of Color Press, 1983.

67 Valerie Amos and Pratibha Parmar, 'Challenging Imperial Feminism', *Feminist Review*, 17, Autumn 1984, pp.12, 16–17.

68 Rhonda Cobham and Merle Collins, *Watchers and Seekers: Creative Writing by Black Women in Britain*, London, Women's Press, 1986, p.30.

69 Michele Wallace, *Black Macho and the Myth of Superwoman*, London, John Calder, 1979, ch.1.

70 Andrea Dworkin, *Pornography: Men Possessing Women*, London, Women's Press, 1981, p.15.

71 Elizabeth Wilson, 'Interview with Andrea Dworkin', *Feminist Review*, no. 11, Summer 1982, p.27.

72 Catharine MacKinnon, 'Pornography, Civil Rights and Speech', in Catherine Itzin ed., *Pornography, Women, Violence and Civil Liberties*, Oxford, Oxford University Press, 1992, p.456.

73 Amber Hollibaugh and Cherrié Moraga, 'What We're Rollin Around in Bed With' in Snitow *et al.*, op. cit., p.405.

74 Carla Freccero, 'Notes of a Post-Sex Wars Theorizer' in Marianne Hirsch and Evelyn Fox Keller eds, *Conflicts in Feminism*, London, Routledge, 1990, p.316.

75 Deidre English, Amber Hollibaugh and Gayle Rubin, 'Talking Sex: A Conversation on Sexuality and Feminism', *Feminist Review*, no. 11, Summer 1982, p.42.

76 Carole S. Vance ed., *Pleasure and Danger: Exploring Female*

Sexuality, London, Routledge & Kegan Paul, 1984, p.5.

77 Quoted in Snitow *et al.*, op. cit., pp.38–9.

78 Carole S. Vance, 'Concept Paper' in Carole S. Vance ed., op. cit., p.446.

79 Carole S. Vance, ibid., p.1.

80 See Lynne Segal and Mary McIntosh eds, *Sex Exposed: Sexuality and the Pornography Debate*, London, Virago, 1992.

81 Mary Loise Ho, 'Patriarchal Ideology and Agony Columns' in *Looking Back: Some Papers from the British Sociological Association 'Gender & Society' Conference*, Department of Sociology, Manchester University, 1984.

82 This pattern is particularly pronounced in the USA, see John D'Emilio and Estelle Freedman eds, *Intimate Matters: A History of Sexuality in America*, New York, Harper & Row, 1985, pp.336–41.

83 Morton Hunt, *Sexual Behavior in the 1970s*, New York, Dell, 1974, pp.192–202.

84 Both Blumstein and Schwartz and *Redbook* quoted in D'Emilio and Freedman, op. cit., p.340.

85 See Cate Haste, op, cit., p.232.

86 Shere Hite, *Women and Love: A Cutural Revolution in Progress*, London, Knopf, 1987, p.5.

87 Ibid., pp.431, 435 and 125.

88 See the various voices in Arlene Stein, *Sisters, Sexperts, Queers: Beyond the Lesbian Nation*, New York, Penguin Books, 1993.

89 Erica Jong, 'AIDS: Is All the Hysteria a Blessing in Disguise?', *Good Housekeeping*, November 1986, p.65.

90 Germaine Greer, *The Change: Women, Ageing and the Menopause*, London, Hamish Hamilton, 1991, p.60.

Chapter 3

1 John Money, 'Commentary: Current status of sex research', *Journal of Psychology and Human Sexuality*, 1, 1988, p.6.

2 Michel Foucault, *The History of Sexuality, Vol 1: An Introduction* (1976), London, Allen Lane, 1979, pp.157–8.

3 Martha Vicinus, 'Sexuality and Power: A Review of Current Work in the History of Sexuality', *Feminist Studies*, 8, no.1, Spring 1982, p.152.

4 B. Ruby Rich, 'Feminism and Sexuality in the 1980s', *Feminist Studies*, 12, no. 3, Fall 1986, pp.538, 555.

5 Carol Morrell talks to Juliet Mitchell, *Spare Rib*, no. 22, 1984, p.6.

6 See, for example, Jonathan Ned Katz, 'The Invention of
Heterosexuality', *Socialist Review*, vol. 20, no. 1, January–February
1990.

7 Foucault, op. cit; Vicinus, op. cit.

8 Paul Abramson, 'Sexual Science: Emerging Discipline or
Oxymoron?' *Journal of Sex Research*, vol. 27, no. 2, 1990,
pp.149–50.

9 Oscar Wilde, 'The Soul of Man Under Socialism' in *Complete
Works of Oscar Wilde*, with introduction by Vivyan Holland,
London, Collins, New Edition, 1966, p.1100.

10 Thomas Laqueur, *Making Sex: Body and Gender from the Greeks
to Freud*, Cambridge, Mass., Harvard University Press, 1990.

11 Thomas Laqueur, 'Orgasm, Generation, and the Politics of
Reproductive Biology', in C. Gallagher and T. Laqueur eds, *The
Making of the Modern Body: Sexuality and Society in the Nineteenth
Century*, Berkeley, University of California Press, 1987, p.2.

12 Laqueur, 1990, op. cit., p.149.

13 Laqueur, 1987, op. cit., p.2.

14 Ibid, p.4, emphasis added.

15 See Mary Jacobus, Evelyn Fox Keller, Sally Shuttleworth eds,
Body/Politics: Women and the Discourses of Science, London,
Routledge, 1990.

16 Mary Poovey, 'Speaking of the Body' in Mary Jacobus *et al.*,
op. cit., p.33.

17 There are now many historical overviews of the pioneers of
sexology; see, for example, Jeffrey Weeks, *Sex, Politics and Society*,
London, Longman, 1981, and *Sexuality and its Discontents*, London,
Routledge & Kegan Paul, 1985; Janice Irvine, *Disorders of Desire:
Sex and Gender in Modern American Sexology*, Philadelphia, Temple
University Press, 1990.

18 Quoted in Laqueur, 1987, op. cit., p.32.

19 Quoted in Weeks, 1981, op. cit. p.146.

20 See Elaine Showalter, *Sexual Anarchy: Gender and Culture at the
Fin de Siècle*, London, Virago, 1990, p.23.

21 Radclyffe Hall, *The Well of Loneliness*, reprinted London,
Virago, 1982, p.187; see Mandy Merck, *Perversions: Deviant
Readings*, London, Virago, 1993, pp.86–92.

22 See Showalter op. cit.; Judith Walkowitz, *City of Dreadful
Delight: Narratives of Sexual Danger in Late-Victorian London*,
London, Virago, 1992.

23 Lesley Hall, 'Forbidden by God, Despised by Men:

Masturbation, Medical Warnings, Moral Panic, and Manhood in Great Britain, 1850–1950', *Journal of History of Sexuality*, vol. 2, no. 3, 1992.

24 Quoted in Margaret Jackson, '"Facts of Life" or the eroticization of women's oppression? Sexology and the social construction of women's oppression' in Pat Caplan ed., *The Cultural Construction of Sexuality*, London, Tavistock, 1987. See also, Weeks, 1981, op. cit., p.147.

25 Walkowitz, op. cit., p.147.

26 Ibid., p.150.

27 See Showalter, op. cit., p.55.

28 Quoted in Paul Ferris, *Sex and the British: A Twentieth Century History*, London, Michael Joseph, 1993, p.43.

29 Quoted in Showalter, op. cit., p.22.

30 Quoted in Sheila Rowbotham, *Women in Movement: Feminism and Social Action*, London, Routledge, 1992, p.156.

31 Paul Ferris, op. cit., pp.54–75.

32 Rebecca West, *Time and Tide* (1926), in Jane Marcus ed., *The Young Rebecca*, London, Virago, 1982, p. 6.

33 Ibid.

34 See Emma Goldman, *Living My Life* (1931), London, Pluto Press, 1987.

35 In Rowbotham, 1993, op. cit., p.156.

36 Linda Gordon and Ellen DuBois, 'Seeking Ecstasy in the Battlefield: Danger and Pleasure in Nineteenth Century Feminist Sexual Thought', *Feminist Review*, no. 13, Spring 1983, p.45.

37 See Sheila Rowbotham, *A New World for Women: Stella Browne – Socialist Feminist*, Pluto Press, 1977.

38 In Rowbotham, 1993, op. cit., p.224.

39 Ibid., p.233.

40 Lawrence Birken, *Consuming Desire: Sexual Science and the Emergence of a Culture of Abundance, 1871–1914*, New York, Cornell University Press, 1988; Steven Seidman, *Romantic Longings: Love in America, 1830–1980*, London, Routledge, 1992.

41 Theodor Van de Velde, *Ideal Marriage: Its Physiology and Technique*, London, Heinemann, 1928, p.232, emphasis in original.

42 See Jackson, in Caplan, op. cit., pp.68–9.

43 In Ferris, op. cit., p.81.

44 In Cate Haste, *Rules of Desire: Sex in Britain: World War I to the Present*, London, Chatto & Windus, 1992, p.157.

45 In Irvine, op. cit., p.64.

46 Alfred Kinsey *et al.*, *Sexual Behavior in the Human Male*, Chicago, Pocket Books, 1949, p.263.

47 Alfred Kinsey *et al.*, *Sexual Behavior in the Human Female*, Chicago, Pocket Books, 1953, p.283.

48 Kinsey *et al.*, 1949, op. cit., p.623.

49 Kinsey *et al.*, 1953, op. cit., p.347.

50 Ibid., p.641.

51 Summary in Edward Brecher, *The Sex Researchers*, London, André Deutsch, 1970, pp.122–7.

52 Paul Robinson, *The Modernization of Sex*, New York, Harper Colophon, 1976, p.91.

53 Kinsey, 1949, op. cit., p.219, 1953, op. cit., p.353.

54 Kinsey, 1953, op. cit., pp.585–7.

55 Irvine, op. cit., p.145.

56 Ibid., p.8.

57 Robinson, op. cit., p.130.

58 Irvine, op. cit., pp.87–8; William Masters and Virginia Johnson, *Human Sexual Response*, Boston, Little Brown, 1966, p.8.

59 Masters and Johnson, ibid., pp.6–7.

60 William Masters and Virginia Johnson, *Human Sexual Inadequacy*, Boston, Little Brown, 1970.

61 Masters and Johnson, 1966, op. cit., p.vi.

62 Ibid.

63 R. Chester and C. Walker, 'Sexual Experience and Attitudes of British Women', in R. Chester and J. Peel eds, *Changing Patterns of Sexual Behaviour*, London, Academic Press, 1980; C.K. Waterman and E.J. Chiauzzi, 'The Role of Orgasm in Male and Female Sexual Enjoyment', *Journal of Sex Research*, vol. 18, no. 2, 1982; J. R. Heiman *et al.*, 'Historical and Current Factors Discriminating Sexually Functional from Sexually Dysfunctional Married Couples', *Journal of Marital and Family Therapy*, vol. 12, 1986, pp.163–74.

64 Masters and Johnson, 1966, op. cit., p.133.

65 Masters and Johnson, 1966, op. cit., p.65.

66 Masters and Johnson, 1970, op. cit., pp.240 and 248–9.

67 Masters and Johnson, 1966, op. cit., pp.34–5, 53–5, 313–14.

68 Masters and Johnson, 1970, op. cit., p.219., emphasis added.

69 Robinson, op. cit., pp.158 and 151–2.

70 Masters and Johnson, 1970, op. cit., p.87.

71 Quoted in Irvine, op. cit., p.142.

72   William Masters and Virginia Johnson, *The Pleasure Bond*, Chicago, Bantam Books, 1975, p.88.
73   Ibid., p.89.
74   Reported in Irvine, op. cit., p.90.
75   Masters and Johnson, 1970, op. cit., p.62.
76   Bernie Zilbergeld and Michael Evans, 'The Inadequacy of Masters and Johnson', *Psychology Today*, August 1980, p.29.
77   Singer, quoted in Irvine, pp.206–7.
78   Leonore Tiefer, 'Commentary on the Status of Sex Research: Feminism, Sexuality and Sexology', *Journal of Psychology and Human Sexuality*, vol. 3, no. 3, 1991, p.5.
79   Ibid., p.7.
80   See, for example, Sheila Jeffreys, *Anti-Climax*, London, Women's Press, 1990; Paula Nicholson, 'Why women refer themselves to sex therapy' in Jane Ussher and Christine Baker eds, *Psychological Perspectives on Sexual Problems: New Directions in Theory and Practice*, London, Routledge, 1993.
81   Martin Weinberg, Rochelle Ganz Swensson and Sue Keifer Hammersmith, 'Sexual Autonomy and the Status of Women: Models of Female Sexuality in U.S. Sex Manuals from 1950–1980', *Social Problems*, vol. 30, no. 3, February 1983, p.318.
82   Quotes from different sex manuals, in ibid., p.318, emphases all in the original texts.
83   Lonnie Barbach, *For Yourself: The Fulfilment of Female Sexuality*, New York, Doubleday, 1975, p.30.
84   Ibid., pp.27 and 77.
85   Ibid., p.30.
86   See Susan Faludi, *Backlash: The Undeclared War Against American Women*, New York, Crown Publishers, 1991, pp.4–5.
87   Dale Spender, 'Preface' in Shere Hite, *Women as Revolutionary Agents of Change: The Hite Reports 1972–1993*, London, Bloomsbury, 1993.
88   Shere Hite, ibid., p.29.
89   Shere Hite, *The Hite Report: A Nationwide Study of Female Sexuality*, New York, Dell, 1976, p.420.
90   Ibid., p.29.
91   Ibid., pp.424–5, 541, 280, 543.
92   Ibid., p.545.
93   Ibid., pp.493, 551.
94   Ibid., pp.275–6.

95 Anja Meulenbelt, *For Ourselves: Our Bodies and Sexuality from Women's Point of View*, London, Sheba, 1981, p.89.

96 Janet Holland *et al.*, 'Power and Desire: The Embodiment of Female Sexuality', *Feminist Review*, no. 46, Spring 1994, p.31.

97 Ibid., p.21.

98 Hite, 1976, op cit., pp.547–8, emphasis added.

99 Hite 1981, in Hite, 1993, op. cit., p.166.

100 Ibid., pp.166–7.

101 Ibid., pp.255 and 612.

102 Hite, 1976, op. cit., pp.530–1.

103 Ibid., pp.419, 270.

104 See Sylvere Lotringer, *Overexposed*, London, Paladin, 1990, pp.138–43.

105 Shere Hite, *Women and Love: A Cultural Revolution in Progress*, New York, Knopf, 1987, pp.5, 7, 215.

106 Ibid., p.219.

107 Ibid., p.654.

108 Ibid., pp.708, 736–65.

109 Richard Sennett, *The Fall of Public Man*, London, Faber and Faber, 1976, p.28; Hite, 1987, op. cit., p.741.

Chapter 4

1 Sigmund Freud, 'Three Essays on the Theory of Sexuality' (1905, n.1, added 1915), in *On Sexuality*, The Pelican Freud Library (PFL), vol. 7, Harmondsworth, Penguin, 1977, p.146.

2 Simone de Beauvoir, *The Second Sex* (1949), Harmondsworth, Penguin, 1972, p.69.

3 Stephen Heath, 'Difference' (1978) in *Screen* ed., *The Sexual Subject: a Screen Reader in Sexuality*, London, Routledge, 1992, p.57.

4 Sigmund Freud, 'Three Essays on the Theory of Sexuality' (1905), op. cit., first sentence added in 1915 edition, p.98.

5 Ibid., pp.99–100.

6 Ibid., p.145.

7 Ibid.

8 Sigmund Freud, 'Instincts and their Vicissitudes' (1915), in *On Metapsychology: The Theory of Psychoanalysis*, PFL, vol. 11, Harmondsworth, Penguin, 1984; Freud, 'The claims of psycho-analysis to scientific interest' (1913), *Standard Edition of the Complete Works* (*SE*), James Strachey ed., London, Hogarth Press, 1955, p.182.

9 Freud, *Three Essays on Sexuality*, op. cit., p.100.

10 Shere Hite, *Women as Revolutionary Agents of Change: The Hite Reports 1972–1993*, London, Bloomsbury, 1993, p.29.

11 Lisa Appignanesi and John Forrester, *Freud's Women*, London, Weidenfeld & Nicolson, 1992, p.426.

12 Freud, 'The Ego and the Id' (1923), PFL, vol. 11, op. cit., p.364.

13 Freud, *Three Essays on Sexuality*, op. cit., p.141.

14 Freud, 'Some Psychical Consequences of the Anatomical Distinction Between the Sexes' (1925), in PFL, vol.7, op. cit., p.333.

15 Freud, 'The Sexual Theories of Children' (1908), PFL, vol. 7, op. cit., pp. 198–201.

16 Freud, 'The Dissolution of the Oedipus Complex' (1924), in PFL, vol. 7, op. cit., p.318.

17 An insightful overview of Freud's writing on the Oedipus Complex, mentioning some of its problems, is provided by John Fletcher, 'Freud and his uses: Psychoanalysis and gay theory' in Simon Shepherd and Mick Wallis eds, *Coming On Strong: Gay Politics and Culture*, London, Unwin Hyman, 1989.

18 Freud, 'On the Universal Tendency of Debasement in the Sphere of Love' (1912), PFL, vol.7, op. cit.

19 An excellent overview of Freud's views on femininity in three key papers between 1923 and 1925 is provided in Appignanesi and Forrester, op. cit., pp.412–29.

20 Freud, 'Some Psychical Consequences . . .', op. cit., p.335.

21 Freud, 'The Dissolution of the Oedipus Complex,' op. cit., p.178.

22 Joan Riviere, 'Womanliness as Masquerade' (1929), in Victor Burgin *et al.* eds, *Formations of Fantasy*, London, Methuen, 1986, p.43.

23 Karen Horney, 'The Flight from Womanhood' (1926), in Jean Strouse ed., *Women and Analysis: Dialogue on Psychoanalytic Views on Femininity*, New York, Dell, 1974, pp.209 and 211.

24 Ibid., pp.206 and 213.

25 See Janet Sayers, *Mothering Psychoanalysis: Helene Deutsch, Karen Horney, Anna Freud and Melanie Klein*, London, Hamish Hamilton, 1991, and Appignanesi and Forrester, op. cit., pp.430–54.

26 Helene Deutsch, *Psychology of Women*, vol. 1, New York, Grove Stratton, 1944, p.240.

27 Helene Deutsch, 'The Psychology of Women in Relation to the

Functions of Reproduction' (1924), in Strouse ed., op. cit., pp.180 and 181.

28 Ibid., p.178.

29 Ibid., p.188.

30 Freud, *New Introductory Lectures in Psychoanalysis* (1933), PFL, vol. 2, op. cit., p.150.

31 Freud, 'Femininity', *SE* vol. 22, London, Hogarth Press, 1964, p.129.

32 John Fletcher, op. cit., p.100.

33 Norman Mailer, *Advertisements for Myself*, London, Putnam, 1959, p.222.

34 Ida, quoted in Maria Torok, 'The Meaning of "Penis Envy" in Women' (1963), in *Differences: The Phallus Issue*, vol. 4, Spring 1992, p.7.

35 Jacques Lacan, *Ecrits: A Selection*, London, Tavistock, 1977, p.61; see also David Macey, *Lacan in Context*, London, Verso, 1988, p.111.

36 Lacan, 'The Meaning of the Phallus' (1958) in Juliet Mitchell and Jacqueline Rose eds, *Feminine Sexuality: Jacques Lacan and the Ecole Freudienne*, London, Macmillan, 1982, p.82.

37 David Macey, 'Phallus: Definitions' in Elizabeth Wright ed., *Feminism and Psychoanalysis: A Critical Dictionary*, Oxford, Blackwell, 1992, p.318.

38 Quoted Lacan, 'The Meaning of the Phallus', op. cit., p.41.

39 In the Saussurean linguistics Lacan appropriates, no signifier has value in and of itself, enabling it to function as privileged over other signifiers. See Macey, op. cit., 1992 p.319.

40 Quoted in Lacan, 'The Meaning of the Phallus', op. cit., p.45.

41 From Lacan, *Encore (1972–3)*, appearing as 'God and the Jouissance of the Women' in Mitchell and Rose eds, op. cit., p.145; see also Bice Benvenuto and Roger Kennedy eds, *The Works of Jacques Lacan: An Introduction*, London, Free Association Press, 1986, p.191.

42 Quoted in Andrew Ross, 'Viennese Waltzes', enclitic, vol. VIII, no. 1–2, Spring/Fall, 1984, p.75.

43 Described by Mandy Merck in 'Difference and its Discontents', *Screen*, vol. 28, no. 1, 1987, p.4.

44 Laura Mulvey, 'Visual Pleasure and Narrative Cinema' (1975) in *Screen* ed., op. cit., p.27.

45 Steve Neale, 'Masculinity as Spectacle', *Screen*, vol. 24, no.6, Winter 1983.

46 Richard Dyer, *Screen*, vol. 23, nos 3–4, September-October 1982.

47 Jacqueline Rose, 'Femininity and its Discontents', *Feminist Review*, no. 14, 1983, p.9.

48 Lemoine-Luccioni, quoted in Heath, op. cit., p.63.

49 Lacan, 'God and the Jouissance of the Women' op. cit., p.144.

50 Quoted in Stephen Heath, 'Male Feminism' in Alice Jardine and Paul Smith eds, *Men in Feminism*, London, Methuen, 1987, p.14.

51 Luce Irigaray, *Speculum of the Other Woman* and *That Sex Which Is Not One*, Ithaca, Cornell University Press, 1985; Hélène Cixous, 'The Laugh of the Medusa', *Signs*, 1, Summer 1976.

52 For example, Elizabeth Cowie, 'Fantasia', *m/f*, no. 9, 1984.

53 For example, Jackie Stacey, 'Desperately Seeking Difference' (1987) in *Screen* ed., op. cit., 1992.

54 Lacan, 'A Love Letter' (1975) in Mitchell and Rose, op. cit., p.151.

55 For an excellent overview of Lacanian positions on the phallus see Kaja Silverman, 'The Lacanian Phallus', *differences: The Phallus Issue*, vol. 4, Spring 1992.

56 Ibid., p.96.

57 Jane Gallop, 'Phallus/Penis: Same Difference' (1981) in Gallop, *Thinking Through the Body*, New York, Columbia University Press, 1988.

58 Charles Bernheimer, 'Penile Reference in Phallic Theory', *Differences: The Phallus Issue*, op. cit., p.116.

59 See Leonore Tiefer, 'In Pursuit of the Perfect Penis: The Medicalization of Male Sexuality', in Michael Kimmel ed., *Changing Men: New Directions in Research of Men and Masculinity*, London, Sage, 1987.

60 Bernheimer, op. cit., p.122.

61 Quoted in *Screen* ed., Introduction, *The Sexual Subiect*, op. cit., pp.8–9.

62 Kaja Silverman, *The Acoustic Mirror: The Female Voice in Psychoanalysis and Cinema*, Bloomington, Indiana University Press, 1988, pp.17–18.

63 Kaja Silverman, *Male Subjectivity at the Margins*, London, Routledge, 1992, p.65.

64 Terry Eagleton, 'It is not quite true that I have a body, and not quite true that I am one either', *London Review of Books*, 27 May 1993, p.8.

65 I discuss this more fully in *Slow Motion: Changing Masculinities, Changing Men*, London, Virago, 1990; see also R.W. Connell, *Gender and Power*, Cambridge, Polity, 1987.

66 Janet Sayers, op. cit., p.3.

67 Melanie Klein, *Love, Guilt and Reparation, and Other Works 1921–1945*, London, Virago, 1989.

68 See Gregorio Kohon ed., *The British School of Psychoanalysis: The Independent Tradition*, London, Free Association Books, 1986.

69 Appignanesi and Forrester, op. cit., p.454.

70 Otto Kernberg, *Internal World and External Reality*, New York, Jason Aronson, 1980, p.293.

71 Michael Balint, 'Perversions and Genitality' (1956) in Balint, *Primary Love and Pscho-Analytic Technique*, London, Tavistock, 1965, p.136.

72 See Balint, ibid., p.141.

73 Betty Friedan, *The Feminine Mystique*, Harmondsworth, Penguin, 1968; Shulamith Firestone (1970), *The Dialectics of Sex*, New York, Paladin, 1971; Kate Millett (1970), *Sexual Politics*, New York, Abacus/Sphere, 1972.

74 Dorothy Dinnerstein, *The Mermaid and the Minotaur: Sexual Arrangements and Human Malaise*, New York, Harper, 1976; Nancy Chodorow, *The Reproduction of Mothering*, Berkeley and Los Angeles, University of California Press, 1978.

75 Chodorow, ibid., pp.47–8.

76 Ibid., p.291.

77 Ibid., p.110.

78 Luise Eichenbaum and Susie Orbach, *What Do Women Want?*, London, Fontana, 1984.

79 Lynne Segal, *Is the Future Female: Troubled Thoughts on Contemporary Feminism*, London, Virago, 1987, pp.134–45.

80 Chodorow, *Feminism and Psychoanalytic Theory*, London, Yale University Press, 1992, p.7.

81 Andrew Samuels, *The Political Psyche*, London, Routledge, 1993, p.274.

82 Chodorow, 1978, op. cit., pp.167–8.

83 Ibid., pp.191–9.

84 Ibid., p.207.

85 Ethel Spector Person, 'Sexuality as the Mainstay of Identity: Psychoanalytic Perspectives', *Signs*, vol. 5, no. 4, 1980, p.619.

86 Ethel Spector Person, 'The Omni-Available Woman and Lesbian Sex', in Gerald Fogel *et al.* eds, *The Psychology of Men:*

New Psychoanalytic Perspectives, New York, Basic Books, 1986.

87 John Munder Ross, 'Beyond the Phallic Illusion: Notes on Man's Heterosexuality', in ibid.

88 Robert Stoller, *Observing the Erotic Imagination*, London, Yale University Press, 1985, p.1.

89 Ethel Spector Person, 1980, op. cit., p.619; Stoller also writes: 'I hear the urgency of most men's stiff cocks and its contrast with most women's greater [physiological] capacity, even when excited, to wait, forego, refuse if they feel it appropriate to the meaning of the moment,' op. cit., p.35.

90 Jessica Benjamin, *The Bonds of Love: Psychoanalysis, Feminism, and the Problem of Domination*, London, Virago, 1990, p.94.

91 Ibid., p.109.

92 Ibid., p.79.

93 Ibid.

94 Freud, *Three Essays on Sexuality*, op. cit., p.73.

95 Thomas Weinberg and G.W. Levi Kamel, *S and M: Studies in Sadomasochism*, New York, Prometheus Books, 1983, p.21.

96 Benjamin, op.cit., pp.130–1.

97 Ibid., p.130.

98 Paper presented at the Institute of Contemporary Arts, London, 18 June 1993.

99 Kenneth Lewes, *The Psychoanalytic Theory of Male Homosexuality*, New York, Simon & Schuster, 1988; Henry Abelove, 'Freud, Male Homosexuality, and the Americans', *Dissent*, Winter 1986.

100 Cited in Chodorow, 'Heterosexuality as a Compromise Formation: Reflections on the Psychoanalytic Theory of Sexual Development', *Psychoanalysis and Contemporary Thought*, vol. 15, no. 3, 1991, p.268.

101 Janine Chasseguet-Smirgel, *Creativity and Perversion* (1984), London, Free Association Books, 1985.

102 Ibid., p.294.

103 Jean Laplanche, *New Foundations of Psychoanalysis*, Oxford, Blackwell, 1989, p.60.

104 Linda Williams, *Hard Core: Power, Pleasure and the 'Frenzy of the Visible'*, London, Pandora, 1990, p.105.

105 Luce Irigaray, *Speculum of the Other Woman*, op. cit., p.26.

106 Luce Irigaray, *This Sex Which Is Not One*, op. cit., p.212.

107 Ibid., pp.24–30.

108 Quoted in Margaret Whitford, 'Irigaray's Body Symbolic', *Hypatia*, vol. 6, no. 3, Fall 1991, p.9.

109 Nancy Friday, *Women on Top: How Real Life Has Changed Women's Sexual Fantasies*, London, Hutchinson, 1991, pp.52, 99, 100.

110 Socarides, quoted in Abelove, op, cit., p.67; Freud, 'An Autobiographical Study, *SE*, vol. 20, London, Hogarth Press, 1964, p.38.

111 Freud, 'Fragment of an Analysis of a Case of Hysteria (Dora)' (1905 [1901]), in *Case Histories I*, PFL, vol. 8, Harmondsworth, Penguin, 1977, p.84.

112 Freud, 'An Autobiographical Study', op. cit., p.38.

113 Fletcher, op. cit., pp.93–4.

114 Freud, 'The Psychogenesis of a Case of Homosexuality in a Woman' (1920), in *Case Histories 2*, PFL, vol. 9, Harmondsworth, Penguin, 1979, p.399.

115 Freud, 'Female Sexuality', (1931) in PFL, vol. 7, op. cit., p.387.

116 Ibid, p.384.

117 Freud, 'The Psychogenesis of a Case of Homosexuality in a Woman', op. cit., p.400, emphasis added.

118 Elizabeth Wilson, *Mirror Writing*, London, Virago, 1982, p.34.

119 Nin Andrews, 'The Dream' in Laurence Goldstein ed., *The Female Body: Figures, Styles, Speculations*, Ann Arbor, University of Michigan Press, 1991, pp.10–11.

120 Thom Gunn, 'The Stealer', *The Man with Night Sweats*, London, Faber and Faber, 1992, pp.42–3.

121 Jean Laplanche and Jean-Bertrand Pontalis, 'Fantasy and the Origins of Sexuality', in V. Burgin *et al.* eds, op. cit., p.26.

122 Quoted in Appignanesi and Forrester, op. cit., p.446.

123 M. Merleau-Ponty, *The Phenomenology of Perception* (1945), London, Routledge, 1989, p.167.

124 Ibid.

125 Simone de Beauvoir, *The Second Sex*, (1949), London, Picador, 1988, pp.16, 17.

126 See, for example, Genevieve Lloyd, *The Man of Reason*, London, Methuen, 1984.

127 Merleau-Ponty, op. cit., p.352.

128 Freud, 'Psychoanalytic Notes on an Autobiographical Account of a Case of Paranoia' (1911), PFL, vol. 9, Harmondsworth, Penguin, 1990, p.166.

129 Wilson, op. cit., p.34.
130 Roland Barthes, *A Lover's Discourse: Fragments* (1977),
Harmondsworth, Penguin, 1990, p.43.
131 Freud, 'On Narcissism: An Introduction', PFL, vol. 11,
Harmondsworth, Penguin, 1991, p.95.
132 Parveen Adams, 'Of Female Bondage' in Teresa Brennan ed.,
Between Feminism and Psychoanalysis, London, Routledge, 1989,
p.264.
133 Ibid., p.262; see Mandy Merck, 'The feminist ethics of
lesbian s/m', in Merck, *Perversions: Deviant Readings*, London,
Virago, 1993, for an insightful commentary on Adams.
134 Freud, *Three Essays on Sexuality*, op. cit., pp.56–7.

Chapter 5

1 Joan Nestle, *A Restricted Country* (1987), London, Sheba,
1988, p.10.
2 Cherry Smyth, *Lesbians Talk Queer Notions*, London, Scarlet
Press, 1992, pp.59–60.
3 Gay and lesbian slogan.
4 As reported in the excellent biography of Foucault by David
Macey, *The Lives of Michel Foucault*, London, Hutchinson, 1993,
p.354.
5 Ibid., p.86–7.
6 Edmund White, *The Beautiful Room is Empty*, New York, Pan,
1988, pp.182–3.
7 Keith Birch, 'A Community of Interests' in Bob Cant and
Susan Hemmings eds, *Radical Records: Thirty Years of Lesbian and
Gay History, 1957–1987*, London, Routledge, 1988, p.51.
8 Gay Liberation Front, *Manifesto*, London, 1971, p.14,
emphasis original.
9 Ibid., p.1.
10 Jeffrey Weeks *et al.*, 'The liberation of affection', in *Radical
Records*, op. cit., p.162.
11 Quoted in John D'Emilio and Estelle Freedman eds, *Intimate
Matters: A History of Sexuality in America*, New York, Harper &
Rowe, 1988, p.322.
12 See ibid., pp.322–5; Dennis Altman, *The Homosexualization of
America*, Boston, Beacon Press, 1982.
13 Ibid., p.167.
14 Quoted in Simon Watney, 'The ideology of GLF' in Gay Left
Collective ed, *Homosexuality, Power and Politics*, London, Allison &
Busby, 1982, p.72.

15 Elizabeth Wilson, *Mirror Writing*, London, Virago, 1982, p.125. See also, Mary McIntosh, 'Queer Theory and the War of the Sexes' in Joseph Bristow and Angelia Wilson eds, *Activating Theory: Lesbian, Gay, Bisexual Politics*, London, Lawrence & Wishart, 1993.

16 Wilson, op. cit., p.130.

17 Richard Neville, *Play Power*, London, Vintage, 1971, p.91, emphasis added.

18 Rita Mae Brown, *Rubyfruit Jungle* (1973), New York, Bantam, 1983; other similar, popular novels read by feminists at that time included Elana Nachman, *Riverfinger Woman*, Plainfield Vt., Daughters Inc, 1974 and June Arnold, *Sister Gin*, Plainfield Vt., Daughters Inc, 1975 as well as Jill Johnston's non fiction, *Lesbian Nation: The Feminist Solution*, New York, Simon & Schuster, 1973.

19 Sue Cartledge and Susan Hemmings, 'How Did We Get This Way?', in Marsha Rowe, ed., *A Spare Rib Reader*, Harmondsworth, Penguin, 1982, p.332.

20 Lynne Harne, 'From 1971: Reinventing the Wheel' in Amanda Sebestyen ed., *'68, '78, '88: From Women's Liberation to Feminism*, London, Prism Press, 1988, p.67.

21 Ibid., p.66 and p.68.

22 Angela Stewart-Park and Jules Cassidy, *We're Here: Conversations with Lesbian Women*, London, Quartet, 1977, p.140.

23 Adrienne Rich, 'Compulsory Heterosexuality and Lesbian Existence', *Signs*, vol. 5, no. 4, Summer 1980, p.653.

24 Ibid., pp.650–1.

25 Onlywomen Press ed., *Love Your Enemy? The Debate between Heterosexual Feminism and Political Lesbianism*, London, Onlywomen Press, 1981.

26 For example, Wendy Clark, 'The Dyke, the Feminist and the Devil', *Feminist Reveiw*, no. 11, Summer 1982.

27 Joan Nestle, op. cit., pp.1, 105–6, 108.

28 *Love Your Enemy*, op. cit., p.5.

29 Lal Coveney, Margaret Jackson, Sheila Jeffreys, Leslie Kay and Pat Mahony, *The Sexuality Papers: Male Sexuality and the Control of Women*, London, Hutchinson, 1984, p.14.

30 Celia Kitzinger, Sue Wilkinson and Rachel Perkins, 'Theorizing Heterosexuality', *Feminism and Psychology*, vol. 2, no. 3, October 1992, p.298. See any issue of the journal *Feminism and Psychology*, from its first issue in February 1991 under the editorship of Sue Wilkinson, for a consistent endorsement of political lesbianism and an attack upon heterosexual feminists and heterosexuality.

31 Celia Kitzinger, *The Social Construction of Lesbianism*, London, Sage, 1987.

32 Lillian Faderman, *Surpassing the Love of Men: Romantic Friendship and Love between Women from the Renaissance to the Present*, London, Junction Books, 1981, p.161.

33 Ibid., p.142. In her latest excellent survey of lesbian life in twentieth-century America, Faderman emphasizes the diversity of lesbian experience and lesbian subcultures: *Odd Girls and Twilight Lovers: A History of Lesbian Life in Twentieth-Century America*, Harmondsworth, Penguin, 1992.

34 Carroll Smith-Rosenberg, 'The Female World of Love and Ritual: Relations Between Women in Nineteenth-Century America', in *Disorderly Conduct: Visions of Gender in Victorian America*, New York, Knopf, 1985, p.61.

35 See Sheila Jeffreys, 'Does It Matter If They Did?' in Lesbian History Group ed., *Not a Passing Phase*, London, Women's Press, 1989 as against, for example, Elizabeth Wilson, 'Forbidden Love', *Feminist Studies*, vol. 10, no. 2, Summer 1984.

36 Martha Vicinus, '"They Wonder to Which Sex I Belong": The Historical Roots of the Modern Lesbian Identity', in Dennis Altman *et al.* eds, *Which Homosexuality? Essays from the International Conference on Lesbian and Gay Studies*, London, Gay Men's Press, 1989.

37 Rich, 1980, op. cit., p.650.

38 See Vicinus, op. cit., p.179.

39 Joan Nestle, op. cit., p.148.

40 Nestle, 'The Fem Question', in Carole S. Vance ed., *Pleasure and Danger: Exploring Female Sexuality*, London, Routledge & Kegan Paul, 1984, p.235.

41 Pat Califia, 'Among Us, Against Us' (1980), in Kate Ellis *et al.* eds, *Caught Looking: Feminism, Pornography and Censorship*, New York, Caught Looking Inc., 1986, p.20; see also, Samois ed., *Coming to Power: Writings and Graphics on Lesbian S/M*, New York, Alyson, 1982.

42 Vicinus, op. cit., p.173; see also Saskia Wieringa, 'An Anthropological Critique of Constructionism: Berdaches and Butches', in Altman *et al.*, 1989, op. cit.

43 Mary McIntosh, 'The Homosexual Role' (1968), in Kenneth Plummer ed., *The Making of the Modern Homosexual*, London, Hutchinson, 1981, p.33.

44 Ibid., p.32.

45 John Gagnon and William Simon, *Sexual Conduct: The Social Sources of Human Sexuality*, Chicago, Aldine, 1973, pp.17, 262.

46 Ibid., p. 26

47 Michel Foucault, *The History of Sexuality, Vol I: An Introduction* (1976), London, Allen Lane, 1979, p.43.

48 Ibid., pp.12, 156.

49 Ibid., pp.105-6.

50 Ibid., p.70.

51 Ibid., p.105.

52 Cited in David Macey, 1993, op. cit., p.364, emphasis added.

53 Foucault, 1979, op. cit., pp.94-5.

54 Any list of some of the more influential texts would include, Jeffrey Weeks, *Sexuality and its Discontents: Meanings, Myths and Modern Sexualities*, London, Routledge and Kegan Paul, 1985; Gayle Rubin, 'Thinking Sex: Notes for a Radical Theory of the Politics of Sexuality' in Carole Vance ed., 1984, op. cit.; Jonathan Dollimore, *Sexual Dissidence: Augustine to Wilde, Freud to Foucault*, Oxford, Oxford University Press, 1991; Judith Butler, *Gender Trouble*, London, Routledge, 1990; Joan W. Scott, 'Deconstructing Equality-Versus-Difference: Or, the Uses of Post-Structuralist Theory For Feminism', *Feminist Studies*, vol. 14, no. 1, Spring 1988.

55 John Rajchman, *Michel Foucault: The Freedom of Philosophy*, New York, Columbia University Press, 1985.

56 Weeks, 1985, op. cit., p.181.

57 Foucault, 1979, op. cit., pp.106–14.

58 John Fletcher, 'Perverse Dynamics', Institute of Contemporary Arts, London, 24 October 1991, p.4, unpublished.

59 R.W. Connell, 'Democracies of Pleasure: Thoughts on the Goals of Radical Sexual Politics', in Linda Nicholson and Steven Seidman eds, *Social Postmodernism*, forthcoming.

60 Weeks, 1985, op. cit., pp.181 and 180.

61 Fletcher, 1991, op. cit., p.4.

62 See R.W.Connell, *Masculinities: Knowledge, Power and Social Change*, Polity Press, forthcoming.

63 Carole S. Vance, 'Social Construction Theory: Problems in the History of Sexuality', in Dennis Altman *et al.* eds, 1989, op. cit., pp.21-2.

64 Liana Borghi, 'Between Essence and Presence: Politics, Self, and Symbols in Contemporary American Lesbian Poetry', in ibid., p.78.

65 Randolph Trumbach, 'Gender and the Homosexual Role in Modern Western Culture: The 18th and 19th Centuries Compared', in ibid., pp.159–61.

66 Quoted in Peter Dews, *Logics of Disintegration: Post-Structuralist Thought and the Claims of Critical Theory*, London, Verso, 1987, p.190.

67 Michel Foucault, 'Introduction' to *Herculine Barbin, Being the Recently Discovered Memoirs of a Nineteenth-Century Hermaphrodite*, Brighton, Harvester, 1980, pp.xiii, vii.

68 Michel Foucault, 'Friendship as a Way of Life', *Foucault Live*, Semiotext(e), 1989, p.204.

69 Edmund White, Foreword, *The Faber Book of Gay Short Fiction*, London, Faber and Faber, 1991.

70 For example, Nancy Harstock, 'Rethinking Modernism: Minority Vs Majority Theories', *Cultural Critique*, vol. 7, 1987, pp.187–206; Barbara Christian, 'The Race to Theory', *Cultural Critique*, vol. 6, 1987, pp.51–63.

71 For example, Nancy Fraser, 'Foucault on Modern Power: Empirical Insights and Normative Confusions', *Praxis International*, vol. 1, October 1988, pp.272–87.

72 Scott, op. cit.; Teresa de Lauretis, 'Eccentric Subjects: Feminist Theory and Historical Consciousness', *Feminist Studies*, vol. 16, no.1, Spring 1990; Jana Sawicki, *Disciplining Foucault: Feminism, Power, and the Body*, London, Routledge, 1991; Diana Fuss, *Essentially Speaking: Feminism, Nature and Difference*, London, Routledge, 1989.

73 Fuss, ibid., p.104.

74 Susan Sontag, 'Notes on "Camp"' (1964) in *A Susan Sontag Reader*, Harmondsworth, Penguin, 1982, pp.116, 107.

75 John Marshall, 'Pansies, perverts and macho men', in Kenneth Plummer ed., op. cit., p.154.

76 Andrew Britton, 'For interpretation – notes against camp', *Gay Left*, vol. 7, 1979, p.12; David Fernbach, *The Spiral Path*, London, Gay Men's Press, 1981, pp.82–3.

77 See Gregg Blachford, 'Male dominance and the gay world', in Plummer ed., op. cit.

78 Butler, 1990, op. cit., p.33.

79 Ibid., p.17; see also Monique Wittig, 'The Straight Mind', *Feminist Issues*, 1, no.1, Summer 1980, where, because their lives defy the heterosexual matrix she sees as constructing gender, Wittig defiantly declares 'Lesbians are not women'.

80   Judith Butler, *Bodies That Matter: On the Discursive Limits of 'Sex'*, London, Routledge, 1993, p.123.
81   Butler, 1990, op. cit., p.31.
82   Ibid., p.137, emphasis in the original.
83   Luce Irigaray, *This Sex Which Is Not One*, Ithaca, Cornell University Press, 1985, p.78.
84   Ibid., p.135.
85   Ibid., p.76.
86   Butler, 1990, p.30; Irigaray, op. cit., p.24.
87   See, for example, Tania Modelski, *Feminism Without Women: Culture and Criticism in a 'Postfeminist' Age*, London, Routledge, 1991.
88   Alan Sinfield, *The Wilde Century: Effeminacy, Oscar Wilde and the Queer Moment*, London, Cassell, 1994, pp.203, 202.
89   Butler, 1990, op. cit., p.31.
90   In Butler, 1993, op. cit., p.231, Butler points out: 'Heterosexuality can augment its hegemony *through* its denaturalization, as when we see denaturalizing parodies that reidealize heterosexual norms *without* calling them into question.' See also 'Gender as Performance? An Interview with Judith Butler', by Peter Osborne and Lynne Segal, *Radical Philosophy*, May 1994.
91   Leo Bersani, 'Is the Rectum a Grave', *October*, no. 43, Winter 1987, pp.207–9.
92   Bersani, ibid., p.209, emphasis in original.
93   Ibid., p.212.
94   Ibid., p.222.
95   Jonathan Dollimore, op. cit., p.28; see also Eve Kosofsky Sedgwick, *Between Men: English Literature and Male Homosocial Desire*, New York, Columbia University Press, 1985; *Epistemology in the Closet*, London, Harvester Wheatsheaf, 1991.
96   J. Laplanche and J.-B. Pontalis, *The Language of Psychoanalysis* (1967), London, Karnac Books, 1988, p.308.
97   Sedgwick, 1985, op. cit., pp.83–96, 184.
98   Ibid., pp.9–11.
99   Ibid., pp.83, 85.
100 Dollimore, op. cit., p.264.
101 Ibid., pp.323, 316.
102 Ibid., p.330.
103 Mikhail Bakhtin, *Rabelais and His World*, Bloomington, Indiana University Press, 1984; see also Mary Russo, 'Female

Grotesques: Carnival and Theory', in *Feminist Studies/Critical Studies*, ed. Teresa de Lauretis, Bloomington, Indiana University Press, 1986; Julia Epstein and Kristina Straub, Introduction, *Body Guards*, London, Routledge, 1992.

104 Marjorie Garber, *Vested Interests: Cross-Dressing and Cultural Anxiety*, London, Routledge, 1992.

105 Colette quoted in ibid., p.160; *Life* magazine quoted in ibid., p.185.

106 Ibid., p.390.

107 See Modelski, op. cit., pp.141–5.

108 Mark Simpson, *Male Impersonators*, London, Cassell, 1994, p.4, emphasis in original.

109 Simon Watney, *Policing Desire: Pornography, Aids and the Media*, London, Comedia, 1987, p.4.

110 Alan Sinfield, 'Beyond Englit' in *Cultural Politics – Queer Readings*, London, Routledge, forthcoming.

111 See Bonnie Spanner, *Gender and Ideology in Science: A Study of Molecular Biology*, Bloomington, Indiana University Press, 1992.

112 Alan Sinfield, forthcoming, op. cit.

113 Elizabeth Wilson, 'Feminist Fundamentalism', *New Statesman and Society*, 2 November 1990.

114 Cherry Smyth, op. cit., pp.59–60.

115 See Julia Creet, 'Daughter of the Movement: The Psycho-dynamics of Lesbian S/M Fantasy', *differences*, vol. 3, no. 2, 1991.

116 See Tessa Boffin and Jean Fraser eds, *Stolen Glances: Lesbians Take Photographs*, London, Pandora, 1991.

117 As described in Sue-Ellen Case, 'Towards a Butch-Femme Aesthetic', *Discourse*, vol. 11, no. 1, 1988–9.

118 Alison Butler, '"She Must Be Seeing Things": An Interview with Sheila McLaughlin', *Screen*, vol. 28, no. 4, Autumn 1987, p.21.

119 Susie Bright, *Susie Sexpert's Lesbian Sex World*, San Francisco, Cleits Press, 1990.

120 Cindy Patton, 'Unmediated Lust', in Boffin and Fraser eds, op. cit., pp.238 and 239.

121 Sue-Ellen Case, op. cit., p.57.

122 Teresa de Lauretis, 'Film and the Visible' in Bad Object-Choice ed., *How Do I Look?: Queer Film and Video*, Seattle, Bay Press, 1991.

123 Roger Scruton, *Sexual Desire*, London, Weidenfeld and Nicolson, 1986, p.308.

124   Statistics for comparative sex frequencies appear in Phillip Blumstein and Pepper Schwartz, *American Couples: Money, Work, Sex*, New York, William Morrow, 1983, p.196; see also Arlene Stein, 'The Year of the Lustful Lesbian' in Arlene Stein ed., *Sisters, Sexperts, Queers: Beyond the Lesbian Nation*, New York, Plume, Penguin Books, 1993, pp.22–7; Lillian Faderman, op. cit., pp. 247–9.

125   See Teresa de Lauretis, 'Sexual Indifference and Lesbian Representation', *Theatre Journal*, 40, 1988, pp.159–69.

126   See Jackie Goldsby, 'What It Means to Be Colored Me', *Out/Look*, no. 9, Summer 1990; 'Queen for 307 Days: Looking B(l)ack at Vanessa Williams and the Sex Wars', in Stein ed., op. cit.; Katie King, 'Audre Lorde's Laquered Layerings: The Lesbian Bar as a Site of Literary Production', *Cultural Studies*, 2, 1988.

127   Alan Sinfield, 'Sexuality and Subcultures in the Wake of Welfare Capitalism', *Radical Philosophy*, no. 66, 1994, p.43.

128   See Lisa Kahaleole Chang Hall, 'Bitches in Solitude: Identity Politics and Lesbian Community' in Stein ed., op. cit., p.228. For the clearest clarification of what she sees as this misreading of her position, see Peter Osborne and Lynne Segal, 'Gender as performance: an interview with Judith Butler', *Radical Philosophy*, no. 67, Summer 1994, forthcoming.

129   Audre Lorde, *Zami: A New Spelling of My Name* (1982), London, Sheba, 1984, pp.225, 224.

130   Edmund White, 'Skinned Alive', in White ed., 1991, op. cit., p.339.

131   Thom Gunn, 'Terminal' in *The Man with Night Sweats*, London, Faber and Faber, 1992, p.65.

132   Nestle, 'Butch-Femme Relationships: Sexual Courage in the 1950s' in Nestle, 1988, op. cit., pp.108, 112.

133   Ibid., 'Esther's Story' p.43.

134   Butler, 1990, op. cit., p.122.

Chapter 6

1   Naomi Segal, 'Why can't a good man be sexy? Why can't a sexy man be good?' in David Porter ed., *Between Men and Feminism*, London, Routledge, 1992, p.35.

2   Mariana Valverde, 'Heterosexuality: Contested Ground', from *Sex, Power and Pleasure*, reprinted in Bonnie Fox ed., *Family Patterns, Gender Relations*, Toronto, Oxford University Press, 1993, p.193.

3   Eve Sedgwick, *Epistemology in the Closet*, London, Harvester Wheatsheaf, 1991, p.16.

4   Roger McGough, 'tailpiece' in *Gig*, London, Jonathan Cape, 1973, p.59.

5   Adrienne Rich, 'Natural Resources', in *The Dream of a Common Language: Poems 1974–1977*, New York, Norton, 1978, p.63.

6   See Lynne Segal, *Slow Motion: Changing Masculinities, Changing Men*, London, Virago, 1990.

7   In Celia Kitzinger *et al.*, *Feminism and Psychology*, vol. 2, no. 3, October 1992, p.436.

8   Sandra Lee Bartky, in ibid., p.427.

9   Celia Kitzinger *et al.*, ibid.

10   Celia Kitzinger and Sue Wilkinson, 'The Precariousness of Heterosexual Feminist Identities', in Mary Kennedy *et al.* eds, *Making Connections: Women's Studies, Women's Movements, Women's Loves*, London, Taylor & Francis, 1993, p.25.

11   Eve Kosofsky Sedgwick, 'A Poem is Being Written' (1987) in *Tendencies*, London, Routledge, 1993, p.209.

12   Wendy Mulford ed., *The Virago Book of Love Poetry*, London, Virago, 1990, p.xiv.

13   Jean Wyatt, *Reconstructing Desire: The Role of the Unconscious in Women's Reading and Writing*, Chapel Hill, University of North Carolina Press, 1990, p.213.

14   Ira Robinson *et al.*, 'Twenty Years of the Sexual Revolution, 1965–1985: An Update', *Journal of Marriage and the Family*, no. 53, February 1991, pp.216–20; John Diepold Jr and Richard Young, 'Empirical Studies of Adolescent Sexual Behavior: A Critical Review', *Adolescence*, vol.14, 1979, pp.45–64; Kaye Wellings *et al.*, *Sexual Behaviour in Britain*, Harmondsworth, Penguin, 1994; Samuel Janus and Cynthia Janus, *The Janus Report*, New York, John Wiley, 1993; Paul Gebhard, 'Sexuality in the Post-Kinsey Era', in Wilt C. Armytage, R. Chester and John Reel eds, *Changing Patterns of Sexual Behavior*, New York, Academic Press, 1980, pp.47–8.

15   See, for example, Frigga Haug ed., *Female Sexualization*, London, Verso, 1987, p.79.

16   Thomas Laqueur, 'Orgasm, Generation, and the Politics of Reproductive Biology', in Catherine Gallagher and Thomas Laqueur eds, *The Making of the Modern Body: Sexuality and Society in the Nineteenth Century*, Berkeley, University of California Press, 1987, p.18.

17 See, for example, Sarah Blaffer Hardy, *The Woman That Never Evolved*, Cambridge, Mass., Harvard University Press, 1981, p.166.
18 Donald Symons, *The Evolution of Human Sexuality*, Oxford, Oxford University Press, 1979, p.284.
19 Ibid., p.177.
20 Emily Martin, 'Body Narratives, Body Boundaries', in Lawrence Grossberg *et al.* eds, *Cultural Studies*, Routledge, 1992, pp.412–13.
21 Gay Talese, quoted in Louise Kaplan, *Female Perversions*, London, Pandora, 1991, p.123.
22 These quotes are taken from Lesley Hall's excellent research into the history of male sexual anxieties and disorders in Lesley A. Hall, *Hidden Anxieties: Male Sexuality, 1900–1950*, Cambridge, Polity, 1991, pp.117–18.
23 Ibid., p.173.
24 See Robin Shaw, 'Open your Eyes for a Big Surprise: Erotic Photos of Men' and 'What She Wants: Clare Bayley talks to Naomi Salaman', both in *Body Politic: Feminism, Masculinity, Cultural Politics*, no. 1, Winter 1992; Jack Butler, 'Before Sexual Difference: Helen Chadwick's "Piss Flowers" ', in Andrew Benjamin ed., *The Body: Journal of Philosophy and the Visual Arts*, London, The Academy Group, 1993.
25 These are the words of a feminist consciousness-raising group, as presented by Alix Kates Shulman, *Burning Questions*, London, Fontana, 1980, p.229.
26 Boston Women's Health Book Collective, *Our Bodies Ourselves: A Health Book By and For Women*, 2nd edn, New York, Simon & Schuster, 1973, pp.11, 13.
27 Carole S. Vance, 'Pleasure and Danger: Towards a Politics of Sexuality' in Carole S. Vance ed., *Pleasure and Danger: Exploring Female Sexuality*, Routledge & Kegan Paul, 1984, p.21.
28 See Chapters 2 and 3.
29 This cartoon appears in Anja Meulenbelt, Johanna's daughter, *For Ourselves: Our Bodies and Sexuality – from Women's Point of View*, London, Sheba, 1981, pp. 100–1.
30 Harriett Gilbert, *The Sexual Imagination: From Acker to Zola*, Harriett Gilbert ed., London, Jonathan Cape, 1993, p.56.
31 Simone de Beauvoir, *The Second Sex* (1949), London, Picador, 1988, pp.406–7.
32 Julia Kristeva, *Powers of Horror: An Essay on Abjection*, New York, Columbia University Press, 1982; see especially pp.3–10, 61–71.

33 Elizabeth Grosz, 'The Body of Signification', in John Fletcher and Andrew Benjamin eds, *Abjection, Melancholia and Love: The Work of Julia Kristeva*, London, Routledge, 1990, p.95.

34 Cathy Schwichtenberg, '*Near The Big Chakra*: Vulvar Conspiracy and Protean Film/Text,' *encritic*, vol. 4, no. 2, Fall 1980, p.81; Anne Severson, 'Don't Get Too Near The Big Chakra' (1974) in Marsha Rowe ed., *Spare Rib Reader*, Harmondsworth, Penguin, 1982.

35 Schwichtenberg, op. cit., p.85.

36 Michel Foucault, *Discipline and Punish: the Birth of the Prison*, London, Allen Lane, 1977.

37 Donna Haraway, 'Biopolitics of Postmodern Bodies' in *Simians, Cybourgs, and Women: The Reinvention of Nature*, London, Free Association Press, 1991, p.208.

38 Judith Butler, *Bodies That Natter: On the Discursive Limits of 'Sex'*, Routledge, London, 1993, p.10, emphasis added.

39 For information on the details of the human female reproductive cycle see Doreen Asso, 'A New Beginning' in Joanna Goldsworthy ed., *A Certain Age: Reflection on the Menopause*, London, Virago, 1993.

40 Lynne Segal and Peter Osborne 'Gender as performance: an interview with Judith Butler', *Radical Philosophy*, no. 67, Summer 1994, p.34.

41 Lillian B. Rubin, *Erotic Wars: What Happened to the Sexual Revolution?*, New York, Harper Collins, 1991, p.43.

42 Ibid., p.57.

43 Sue O'Sullivan, 'Menopause Waltz', in Joanna Goldsworthy ed., op. cit., p.58.

44 Molly Parkin, 'My Menopause' in Goldsworthy, ibid., p.40; Eva Figes, 'Coming to Terms', in ibid., p.136; Phyllida Law, 'Many Thanks' in ibid., p.192.

45 Lynn Whisnant and Leanard Zegans, 'A Study of Attitudes Towards Menarche in White Middle-class American Adolescent Girls' in Elizabeth Howell and Marjorie Bayes eds, *Women and Mental Health*, New York, Basic Books, 1981, pp.318–21.

46 See Shirley Prendergast, 'Girls' Experience of Menstruation in Schools' in L.Holly ed., *Girls and Sexuality Teaching and Learning*, Milton Keynes, Open University Press, 1989.

47 Muriel Dimen, *Surviving Sexual Contradictions*, London, Macmillan, 1986, p.46.

48 Germaine Greer, *The Change: Women, Ageing and the Menopause*, London, Hamish Hamilton, 1991.

49 Figes, in Goldsworthy, op. cit., pp.142–3.

50 Ursula Owen, 'When. the Machinery Stops Working' in Goldsworthy, op. cit., p.88; Sue O'Sullivan, in ibid., p.66.

51 O'Sullivan, in ibid., p.67.

52 Leonore Tiefer, 'Three Crises Facing Sexology', presidential address to the International Academy of Sex Research, June 1993, Asilomar Conference Center, Pacific Grove, California. Reprints, Tiefer, Department of Urology, Montefiore Medical Center, Bronx, New York, 10467.

53 Sue-Ellen Case, 'Tracking the Vampire', *differences*, vol. 3, no. 2, Summer 1991, p.1.

54 James Baldwin, *Giovanni's Room*, London, Michael Joseph, 1957; *Another Country*, London, Michael Joseph, 1963.

55 Cora Kaplan, '"A cavern opened in my mind": The poetics of homosexuality and the politics of masculinity in James Baldwin', forthcoming.

56 Ibid.

57 Baldwin, 1963, op. cit., pp.324–5; for another interesting account of Baldwin's sexual politics, see William Cohen, 'Liberalism, Libido, Liberation: Baldwin's *Another Country*', *Genders*, no.12, Winter 1991.

58 Constance Penley, 'Feminism, Psychoanalysis, and the Study of Popular Culture', in Grossberg *et al.* eds, 1992, op. cit., p.487.

59 Ibid., p.488; Jean Laplanche and Jean-Bertrand Pontalis (1964), 'Fantasy and the Origins of Sexuality', in *Formations of Fantasy*, Victor Burgin *et al.* eds, London, Methuen, 1986, p.26.

60 In Tiefer, op. cit.

61 See, for example, Elizabeth Stanko, *Intimate Intrusions: Women's Experience of Male Violence*, London, Routledge & Kegan Paul, 1985; Pauline Bart and Patricia O'Brien, *Stopping Rape: Successful Survival Strategies*, New York, Pergamon Press, 1985.

62 Tania Modelski, *Loving with a Vengeance: Mass-Produced Fantasies for Women*, London, Methuen, 1984; see also Janice Radway, *Reading the Romance: Women, Patriarchy and Popular Literature*, Chapel Hill, University of North Carolina Press, 1984.

63 Janet Holland *et al.*, 'Pressure, Resistance and Empowerment: Young Women and the Negotiation of Safer Sex', paper delivered at the Fifth Conference on the Social Aspects of AIDS, London, 1991.

64   Freud, 'Three Essays on the Theory of Sexuality', in *On Sexuality*, Pelican Freud Library, vol. 7, Harmondsworth, Penguin, 1977, p.100.

65   Adam Phillips, *On Kissing, Tickling and Being Bored*, London, Faber and Faber, 1993, p.xix.

66   Jean Laplanche, 'The ICA Seminar: New Foundations for Psychoanalysis?', 5 May 1990, in John Fletcher and Martin Stanton eds, *Jean Laplanche: Seduction, Translation, Drives*, London, Institute of Contemporary Arts, 1992, p.80.

67   Celia Kitzinger *et al.*, 'Theorizing Heterosexuality: Editorial Introduction', *Feminism and Psychology*, vol. 2, no. 3, October 1992, p.313.

68   Naomi Segal, op. cit., p.45.

69   Jessica Benjamin, *The Bonds of Love*, London, Virago, 1989.

70   Amy Lowell, 'In Excelsis', *The Complete Poetical Works of Amy Lowell*, Boston, Houghton Mifflin, 1955, p.444.

71   Anja Meulenbelt, op. cit., p.22; Sally Kline, *Women, Celibacy and Passion*, London, André Deutsch, 1993.

72   Carol Ann Duffy, 'Sleeping', *Mean Time*, London, Anvil Press Poetry, 1993, p.35.

73   Muriel Dimen, op. cit., p.16.

74   Naomi Segal, op. cit., pp.38–9.

75   John Forrester, 'What do men want?', in David Porter ed., op. cit., pp.106 and 109.

76   A recent British survey of women in North London found that 9.8 per cent of all women had experienced physical violence from partners or ex-partners in the last 12 months, rising to 11.1 per cent for married mothers, and to 19.2 per cent for the most vulnerable group of women – single mothers living in council housing; from research collected by Jayne Mooney, *The Hidden Figure: Domestic Violence in North London*, Centre for Criminology, Middlesex University, 1993; for fuller discussion and debate around the differing accounts of the incidence and causes of men's violence and sexual abuse, also raising the controversial issue of women's use of violence in relationships, see Richard Gelles and Donileen Loseke eds, *Current Controversies on Family Violence*, London, Sage, 1993.

77   See Katie Roiphe, *The Morning After: Sex, Fear, and Feminism*, London, Hamish Hamilton, 1994.

78   See Francesa Cancian's classic essay on the gendered nature of love, Francesca Cancian, 'Gender Politics: Love and Power in the

Private and Public Spheres' in Alice Rossi *et al.*, eds, *Gender and the Life Course*, New York, Aldine, 1985.
79 Wendy Hollway, 'Heterosexual Sex: Power and Desire for the Other' in Sue Cartledge and Joanna Ryan, eds, *Sex and Love*, London, Women's Press, 1983, p.126.
80 Julia Kristeva, *Tales of Love*, New York, Columbia University Press, 1987, p.2.
81 Cheryl Clarke, 'Prayer', *Experimental Love Poetry*, New York, Firebrand Books, 1993, p.74.
82 Ruby Rich, 'Feminism and Sexuality in the 1980s', *Feminist Studies*, vol. 12, no. 3, Fall 1986, p.541.
83 Amber Hollibaugh, 'Desire for the Future: Radical Hope in Passion and Pleasure', in Vance ed., 1984, op. cit., pp.405, 406.
84 Pat Califia, ed., *Coming to Power*, Boston, Mass., Alyson, 1982.
85 Ann Snitow, 'Mass Market Romance: Pornography for Women is Different' (1980) in Ann Snitow *et al.*, eds, *Powers of Desire: The Politics of Sexuality*, New York, New Feminist Library, 1984, p.255.
86 Elizabeth Wilson, 'Forbidden love', *Feminist Studies*, no. 10, Summer 1984, p.220.
87 Lonnie Barbach, *Pleasures: Women Write Erotica*, London, Futura, 1986; The Kensington Ladies' Erotica Society, *Ladies' Own Erotica*, London, Pocket Books, 1986.
88 Ellen Cantarow, 'Anti-Climaxes', *Women's Review of Books*, vol. 111, no. 8, May 1986, p.13; I would have to add my personal reaction to these collections to that of Cantarow.
89 Sara Maitland, 'Women's Erotica', *Women's Review*, no.13, November 1986, p.11.
90 The words of another of my gay male heroes, Edmund White, lifted from 'Life, love and death', *Guardian 2*, 30 November 1993, p.2.
91 Jessica Benjamin, 'Master and Slave: the Fantasy of Erotic Domination' (1980) in Ann Snitow *et al.* eds, 1986, op. cit., p.296.
92 Leo Bersani, *The Freudian Body: Psychoanalysis and Art*, New York, Columbia University Press, 1986, pp.39–40, emphasis in original.
93 Peter Osborne and Lynne Segal, 'Gender as Performance: An Interview with Judith Butler', *Radical Philosophy* 67, Summer 1994, p.36.
94 Norman Mailer, *Prisoner of Sex*, London, Weidenfeld & Nicolson, 1971, p.171.
95 Sheila Rowbotham, 'Outer Hebrides', in Michelene Wandor

and Michèle Roberts eds, *Cutlasses & Earrings: Feminist Poetry*, London, Playbooks 2, 1977, pp.41–2.

96 For example see, Liz Kelly, *Surviving Sexual Violence*, Cambridge, Polity, 1988, pp.50, 87–8.

97 Jacqueline Rose, 'Paranoia and the Film System', *Screen*, vol. 17, no. 4, Winter 1976–7; Cora Kaplan, 'Dirty Harriet/*Blue Steel*: Femininst Theory Goes to Hollywood, *Discourse*, vol.16, no. 1, Fall 1993.

98 David Widgery, *Preserving Disorder*, London, Pluto Press, 1989, p.107.

99 Denise Levertov, 'The Mutes' in *The Bloodaxe Book of Contemporary Women Poets: Eleven British Writers*, ed. Jeni Couzyn, Newcastle-upon-Tyne, Bloodaxe, 1985, p.82.

100 Nancy Friday, *Men in Love: Men's Sexual Fantasies*, New York, Arrow Books, 1980, p.471.

101 Eileen McLeod, *Women Working: Prostitution Now*, London, Croom Helm, 1982, p.69.

102 Wendy Hollway, 'Women's Power in Heterosexual Sex' in *Women's Studies International Forum*, vol.7, no.1, 1994, p.68.

103 John Marshall, 'Pansies, perverts and macho men' in Kenneth Plummer ed., *The Making of the Modern Homosexual*, London, Hutchinson, 1981, p.149.

104 Mark Simpson, 'A Crying Shame: Transvestism and Misogyny in *The Crying Game*', in Simpson, *Male Impersonators*, London, Cassell, 1994.

105 Huseyin Tapanic, 'Masculinity, Femininity, and Turkish Male Homosexuality', in *Modern Homosexualities: Fragments of Lesbian and Gay Experience*, London, Routledge, 1992, p.48; Tomás Almager, 'Chicano Men: A Cartography of Homosexual Identity and Behavior', *differences*, vol. 3, no. 2, Summer 1991.

106 Alan Sinfield, 'Subcultural Strategies', in *The Wilde Century: Effeminacy, Oscar Wilde and the Queer Moment*, London, Cassell, 1994, p.192.

107 Sinfield, ibid., pp.169–70, 195.

108 See Butler, 1994, op. cit.

109 For useful discussion and interesting qualitative research on this topic, see Susan Kippax, June Crawford, Cathy Waldby, and Pam Benton, 'Women Negotiating Heterosex: Implications for AIDS Prevention', *Women's Studies International Forum*, vol. 13, no. 6, 1990.

110 See, for example, Gail Wyatt *et al.*, 'Kinsey Revisited, Part 1:

Comparisons of the Sexual Socialization and Sexual Behavior of Women Over 33 Years; *Archives of Sexual Behavior*, vol. 17, no.1, 1988; Janet Holland *et al.*, *Pressure, Resistance, Empowerment: Young Women and the Negotiation of Safer Sex*, WRAP Paper 6, London, Tufnell Press, 1991.

111 Janet Holland, *Sexuality and Ethnicity: Variations in Young Women's Sexual Knowledge and Practice*, WRAP Paper 8, London Tufnell Press, 1993.

112 I have written of this at length in 'Devils in Waiting: White Images of Africa' in Segal, 1990, op. cit., pp.169–75.

113 James Baldwin, as quoted in Fern Maya Eckman, *The Furious Passage of James Baldwin*, London, Michael Joseph, 1968, p.32; hattie gossett, 'is it true what they say about colored pussy?' in Vance ed., 1984, op. cit., p.411.

114 See, for example, Michael Moffatt, *Coming of Age in New Jersey: College and American Culture*, New Brunswick, Rutgers University Press, 1989, p.201.

115 Pierre Bourdieu and Terry Eagleton, 'In Conversation: Doxa and Common Life', *New Left Review*, no. 191, 1992, p.115.

116 Sharon Thompson, 'Putting a Big Thing into a Little Hole: Teenage Girls' Acounts of Sexual Initiation', *Journal of Sex Research*, vol. 27, no. 3, 1990, p.253.

117 Michelene Wandor, 'Love Poem', in Michelene Wandor and Michele Roberts eds, 1977, op. cit., pp.53–4.

118 Wendy Hollway, 'Theorizing Heterosexuality: A Response', *Feminist Psychology*, vol. 3, no. 3, London, Sage, 1993, p.415.

119 Joan Nestle, *A Restricted Country*, London, Sheba, 1988, p.10.

Chapter 7

1 Sigmund Freud, 'Analysis Terminable and Interminable', in *The Standard Edition of the Complete Works*, vol. 23 [1937–9], London, Hogarth, 1964, p.252.

2 R.W. Connell, *Masculinities: Knowledge, Power and Social Change*, Cambridge, Polity Press, 1994, forthcoming.

3 Jonathan Dollimore, *Sexual Dissidence: Augustine to Wilde, Freud to Foucault*, Oxford, Oxford University Press, 1991, p.184.

4 Connell, op. cit.; Arthur and Marilouise Kroker eds, *The Hysterical Male: New Feminist Theory*, London, Macmillan, 1990.

5 Neil Lyndon, *No More Sex War: The Failures of Feminism*, London, Sinclair Stevenson, 1992; David Thomas, *Not Guilty: In*

Defence of the Modern Man, London, Weidenfeld and Nicolson,
1993.

6 Robert Bly, *Iron John: A Book About Men*, Reading, Mass.,
Addison-Wesley, 1990; Warren Farrell, *The Myth of Male Power: Why
Men are the Disposable Sex*, New York, Simon & Schuster, 1993.

7 Neil Lyndon, 'Badmouthing', *Sunday Times*, magazine section,
9 December 1990.

8 Bly, op. cit., p.1.

9 Michael Ryan and Douglas Kellner, *Camera Politica: The
Politics and Ideology of Contemporary Hollywood Film*, Bloomington
and Indianapolis, Indiana University Press, 1990, p.136.

10 See Gisela Kaplan, *Contemporary Western European Feminism*,
New York, New York University Press, 1992, pp.41–59.

11 A. and M. Kroker, op. cit., p.171.

12 See Susan Faludi, *Backlash: The Undeclared War Against
American Women*, New York, Crown, 1991, pp.112–23.

13 See Carol Clover, 'White Noise', *Sight and Sound*, vol. 3, no.
5, May 1993, p.8.

14 Amy Taubin, 'The Men's Room', *Sight and Sound*, vol. 2, no.
8, December 1992, p.4.

15 B. Ruby Rich, 'Art House Killers', *Sight and Sound*, vol. 2, no.
8, December 1992, p.6.

16 See Connell, op. cit., p.277.

17 Although Dworkin, comparing the assaultive potential of the
actual fleshy penis to that of the 'atom bomb', would no doubt see
the 'gun' as a mere symbol of the eternal truth of penile power!

18 Faludi, op. cit., pp.xvi–xvii.

19 See Peter Baker, 'Who's afraid of the big bad women?',
Guardian, 24 January 1994, pp.12–13.

20 See Angela Phillips, *The Trouble with Boys: Parenting the Men of
the Future*, London, Pandora, 1993, pp.13–30.

21 Bly, op. cit.; Sam Keen, *Fire in the Belly: On Being a Man*,
New York, Bantam, 1991; Herb Goldberg, *The Inner Male:
Overcoming Roadblocks to Intimacy*, New York, Signet, 1988; Robert
Moore and Douglas Gillette, *King, Warrior, Magician, Lover:
Rediscovering the Archetypes of The Mature Masculine*, San Francisco,
Harper, 1990.

22 Shere Hite, *Women and Love*, London, Viking, 1988, p.5.

23 See, for example, William Julius Wilson, *The Truly
Disadvantaged*, London, Chicago, University of Chicago Press,
1987.

24 Robert Staples, *Black Masculinity: The Black Male's Role in American Society*, San Francisco, Black Scholar Press, 1982; Wilson, op. cit.; see also Segal, *Slow Motion: Changing Masculinities, Changing Men*, London, Virago, 1990, chapters 7, 9 and 10.

25 See R.W. Connell, 'Drumming Up the Wrong Tree', *Tikkum*, vol. 7, no. 1, 1992.

26 See Simon Watney, *Policing Desire, Pornography, Aids and the Media*, London, Methuen, 1987.

27 Maurice Godelier, 'The Origins of Male Domination', *New Left Review*, no. 127, May/June 1981, p.17.

28 Faludi, op. cit., pp.3–19.

29 Ibid., pp.19–27.

30 Ibid., pp.27–35.

31 See, for example, Raymond Cockrane, *The Social Creation of Mental Illness*, London, Longman, 1983.

32 Ronald Kessler and James McRae Jr, 'Trends in the Relationship Between Sex and Psychological Distress: 1957–1976', *American Sociology Review*, no. 46, August 1981; Ronald Kessler and James McRae Jr, 'Trends in Relationships Between Sex and Attempted Suicide', *Journal of Health and Social Behavior*, no. 24, June 1983; Jane Murphy *et. al.*, 'Affective Disorders and Mortality', *Archives of General Psychiatry*, no. 44, May 1987; for the fullest summary of data see Faludi, op. cit., pp.39–41.

33 Quoted in Faludi, op. cit., pp.321 and xi.

34 See Lynne Segal, *Is the Future Female: Troubled Thoughts on Contemporary Feminism*, London, Virago, 1987.

35 See, for example, Ann Snitow, 'Feminism and Motherhood: An American Reading', *Feminist Review*, no. 49, Spring 1992; Judith Stacey, 'Are Feminists Afraid to Leave Home?: The Challenge of Conservative Pro-Family Feminism', in Juliet Mitchell and Ann Oakley eds, *What is Feminism?*, Oxford, Blackwell, 1987.

36 See *Social Trends*, 1994, HMSO, quoted in *Guardian*, 27 January 1994, p.8.

37 See Carol Watts 'The "American Girl" in *Silence of the Lambs*', *Women: A Cultural Review*, vol. 4, no. 1, Spring 1993.

38 Murray Straus *et al.*, *Behind Closed Doors: Violence in the American Family*, New York, Doubleday, 1980; Linda Gordon, *Heroes of their Own Lives: The Politics and History of Family Violence*, London, Virago, 1989; Richard Gelles, 'Through a Sociological Lens: Social Structure and Family Violence' in Gelles and Loseke eds, *Current Contoversies on Family Violence*, London, Sage, 1993.

39   Ko-Lin Chin, 'Out-of-town brides: International marriage and wife abuse among Chinese immigrants', in Richard Gelles ed., 'Family Violence' [Special issue], *Journal of Comparative Family Studies*, forthcoming; Devi Prasad, 'Dowry-related violence: A content analysis of news in selected newspapers', in Gelles ed., forthcoming.

40   See my own study of masculinity, *Slow Motion*, 1990, op. cit.; or that of R.W. Connell, *Gender and Power*, Cambridge, Polity, 1987; R.W. Connell, *Masculinities*, forthcoming, op. cit.

41   Joseph Pleck, 'The Contemporary Man' in Murray Scher *et al.* eds, *Handbook of Counselling and Psychotherapy with Men*, London, Sage, 1987; Kessler and McRae, op. cit.; see also men's accounts of their parenting experiences in Diane Ehrensaft, *Parenting Together: Men and Women Sharing the Parenting of their Children*, New York, Free Press, 1987; Segal, 1990, op. cit., ch. 2.

42   Francesca Cancian, *Love in America: Gender and Self-development*, Cambridge, Cambridge University Press, 1987, p.89.

43   Reported in Gail Wyatt *et al.*, *Sexual Abuse and Consensual Sex*, London, Sage, 1993, p.30; see Philip Blumstein and Pepper Schwartz, *American Couples*, New York, William Morrow, 1983.

44   See Cancian, op. cit., p.107.

45   David Lodge, *Nice Work*, Harmondsworth, Penguin, 1988, pp.154–9.

46   Connell, forthcoming, p.127.

47   Ibid., p.178.

48   Ibid., p.181.

49   Ibid., p.184.

50   Shere Hite, *The Hite Report: A Nation Wide Study of Female Sexuality*, New York, Dell, 1976, pp.422 and 607.

51   Jeff Hearn, 'The personal, the political, the theoretical: the case of men's sexualities and sexual violences', in David Porter ed., *Between Men and Feminism*, London, Routledge, 1992, pp.165 and 167.

52   Ibid., p.167.

53   An impression strongly confirmed on meeting the author who, supposedly seeking my advice, could only intrusively insist upon his own opinions, creating a type of oppressive experience which I nowadays rarely encounter with the men I choose to meet.

54   Adam Jukes, *Why Men Hate Women*, London, Free Association, 1993, p.317.

55   Ibid., p.317.

56 Ibid., pp.78, 83, 83, 313, 317, 321, 319, 317, 322.
57 Ibid., pp.321, 36.
58 Carol Clover, op. cit., p. 61.
59 Ibid., p.60.
60 Ibid., p.142.
61 Ibid., p.65.
62 Quoted in Carol Clover, *Men, Women and Chainsaws: Gender in the Modern Horror Film*, London, BFI, 1992, pp.197–8.
63 Ibid., p.159, emphasis in original.
64 Ellis Hanson, 'Undead' in Diana Fuss ed., *Inside/out: Lesbian Theories, Gay Theories*, London, Routledge, 1991, p.325.
65 Leo Bersani, 'Is the Rectum a Grave', *October*, no. 43, Winter 1987, p.217.
66 Marina Warner, 'Boys Will Be Boys', *The Reith Lectures 1994*, edited version in *Independent*, 3 February 1994, p.18.
67 Quotes from John Bayley, 'Manly Love', *London Review of Books*, 28 January 1993.
68 See Michael Moffatt, *Coming of Age in New Jersey: College and American Culture*, New Brunswick, Rutgers University Press, 1989; Connell, *Masculinities*, forthcoming.
69 Julian Wood, 'Groping Towards Sexism: Boys' Sex Talk' in Angela McRobbie and Mica Nava eds, *Gender and Generation*, London, Macmillan, 1984, p.79.
70 Luce Irigaray, *This Sex Which Is Not One*, Ithaca, New York, Cornell University Press, 1985, pp.192–3 emphasis in original.
71 bell hooks, 'Madonna let me down', *Everywoman*, October 1993, p.16.
72 See John Fiske, *Reading the Popular*, Boston, Mass., Unwin Hyman, 1989; or the majority of articles in Cathy Schwichtenberg ed., *The Madonna Connection: Representational Politics, Subcultural Identities, and Cultural Theory*, Boulder, Westview Press, 1993.
73 See articles by David Tetzlaff, 'Metatextual Girl: Patriarchy, Postmodernism, Power, Money, Madonna', and Susa Bordo, '"Material Girl": The Effacements of Postmodern Culture', both in Schwichtenberg ed., ibid.
74 Thomas Nakayama and Lisa Penaloza, 'Madonna T/Races: Music Videos Through the Prism of Color' in Schwichtenberg ed., ibid.
75 See Linda Grant, *Sexing the Millenium*, London, Harper Collins, 1993, pp.125–6.

76   See Angela McRobbie, 'Shut Up and Dance: Youth Culture and Changing Modes of Femininity', *Cultural Studies*, vol. 7, no. 3, October, 1993.

77   Angela McRobbie, *Feminism and Youth Culture: From Jackie to Just Seventeen*, London, Unwin Hyman, 1991, p.182, italics in original.

78   Janice Winship, 'A Girl Needs to Get Street-Wise: Magazines for the 1980s', *Feminist Review*, no.21, Winter 1985; Charlotte Brunson, 'Pedagogies of the feminine: feminist teaching and women's genres', *Screen*, vol. 32, no. 4, 1991.

79   Winship, ibid., p.25.

80   Ibid., pp.45, 44.

81   Lisa Lewis, *Gender Politics and MTV: Voicing the Difference*, Philadelphia, Temple University Press, 1990, p.123.

82   Quoted in Laurie Schulze *et al.*, '"A Sacred Monster in Her Prime": Audience Construction of Madonna as Low Other', in Schwichtenberg, op. cit., p.30.

83   Quoted in ibid., p.25.

84   Linda Kalof, 'Dilemmas of Femininity: Gender and the Social Construction of Sexual Imagery', *Sociological Ouarterly*, vol. 34, no. 4, 1993, p.655.

85   Janet Holland *et al.*, 'Power and Desire: The Embodiment of Female Sexuality', *Feminist Review*, no. 46, Spring 1994, p.34; see also Janet Holland *et al.*, *Pressured Pleasure: Young Women and the Negotiation of Sexual Boundaries*, WRAP Paper 7, London, Tufnell Press, 1992, p.8.

86   Sue Lees, *Losing Out: Sexuality and Adolescent Girls*, London, Hutchinson, 1986.

87   Holland *et al.*, 1994, op. cit., p.27.

88   Michelle Fine and Pat Macpherson, 'Over Dinner: Feminism and Adolescent Female Bodies', in H. Lorraine Radtke and Henerikus Stam eds, *Power/Gender: Social Relations in Theory and Practice*, London, Sage, 1994, p.221.

89   Holland *et al.*, 1994, op. cit., p.32.

90   Ibid., p.222, emphasis in original.

91   Ibid., p.230.

92   Ibid., pp.241–2.

93   Karen Lee Fingerman, 'Sex and the Working Mother: Adolescent Sexuality, Sex Role Typing and Family Background', *Adolescence*, vol. 24 no. 93, 1989, p.15.

94   Rachel Thomson and Sue Scott, *Learning About Sex: Young*

Women and the Social Construction of Sexual Identity, WRAP Paper 4, London, Tufnell Press, 1991.

95 McRobbie, op. cit., pp.228–34; see also Ann Phoenix, *Young Mothers*, Cambridge, Polity Press, 1991; Sue Sharpe, *Falling For Love: Teenage Mothers Talk*, London, Virago, 1987.

96 Margaret Thatcher, *Women in a Changing World*, Press Office, Downing Street, London, 1982.

97 Margaret Thatcher, interviewed in *Women's Realm*, 6 December 1980, emphasis added.

98 Elspeth Probyn, 'New Traditionalism and Post-feminism – TV does the Home', *Screen*, vol. 31, no. 2, Summer 1990, p.152.

99 See Paul Gilroy, *There Ain't No Black in the Union Jack: The Cultural Politics of Race and Nation*, London, Hutchinson, 1987.

100 These black voices are heard, alongside many others, in Isaac Julian's excellent film documentary *The Darker Side of Black*, which explores the origins and significance of the recent upsurge of sexism and homophobia in black music and dance hall, *Arena*, BBC 2, 12 February 1994.

101 See, for example, Barbara Einhorn, 'Where Have All the Women Gone? Women and the Women's Movement in east central Europe', *Feminist Review*, no. 39, Winter 1991.

102 A.E. Housman, *A Shropshire Lad*, xviii, 'Oh when I was in love with you', London, Harrap, 1940, p.30.

103 R.W. Connell, 'Democracies of Pleasure: Thoughts on the Goals of Radical Sexual Politics' in Linda Nicholson and Steven Seidman, *Social Postmodernism*, forthcoming.

104 Barry Hugill and Judy Jones, 'Cabinet divided over sex education', *Observer*, 20 February 1994, p.3.

105 Samuel Janus and Cynthia Janus, *The Janus Report on Sexual Behavior*, New York, John Wiley, 1993; Ira Robinson *et al.*, 'Twenty Years of the Sexual Revolution, 1965–1985: An Update, *Journal of Marriage and the Family*, vol. 53, 1991; Kaye Wellings *et al.*, *Sexual Behaviour in Britain*, Harmondsworth, Penguin, 1994.

106 All facts and figures are adapted from Kaye Wellings *et al.*, ibid., as reported by the authors in 'Sex and the British', *Independent on Sunday*, 16 January 1994, pp.5–8.

107 For example, Sue Lees and Lynn Ferguson, on *Dispatches*, Channel 4, 16 February 1994; see also Sue Lees and Jeanne Gregory, *Rape and Sexual Assault: A Study of Attrition*, London, Islington Council, Police and Crime Prevention Unit, July 1993.

108 Using the framework of Catharine MacKinnon and Andrea

Dworkin's Minneapolis Ordinance, Catherine Itzin in Britian has been seeking official backing for new anti-pornography legislation to replace the existing Obscene Publications Act. This would allow individuals who believed they had been harmed through pornography to seek compensation from those responsible for producing the 'harmful' images, making use of civil anti-discrimination law in the courts.

109 See Robin Gorna, 'From anti-porn to eroticizing safer sex' and Jane Mills, 'Classroom conundrums: Sex education and censorship', both in Lynne Segal and Mary McIntosh eds, *Sex Exposed: Sexuality and the Pornography Debate*, London, Virago, 1992.

110 Jackie Stacey, 'Promoting normality: Section 28 and the regulation of sexuality' in Sarah Franklin et al. eds, *Off-Centre: Feminism and Cultural Studies*, London, Harper Collins, 1991, pp.310–12.

111 James Baldwin, 'Here Be Dragons' in *The Price of the Ticket: Collected Non-Fiction 1948–85*, London, Michael Joseph, 1985, pp.689 and 684.

·····Index